UNBREAKABLE
HOPE

I0418003

TORI HOPE DENNIS

©2026 by Tori Hope Dennis
All rights reserved. No part of this publication may be reproduced or transmitted in any form or by any means, electronic or mechanical, including photocopying, recording, or any other information storage and retrieval system, without the written permission of the author or publisher. Internet addresses given in this book were accurate at the time it went to press.

The pregnant or birthing women and hospitalized army soldiers described in the book are not real, living, or deceased people. The pregnant or birthing women depicted in homes and birthing facilities are entirely fictional, unless specifically noted. The hospitalized army soldiers are fictional, with exception of SGT Dennis. As a health care provider, the author has an obligation to protect the health care privacy of the actual patients she cared for. Any resemblance to actual persons living or dead is entirely coincidental. Ms. Dennis depicts the events of her life as factual as possible, however she is required to fictionalize various aspects as a nurse and as a midwife.

This book is not a medical or midwifery manual and not a substitute for healthcare.

Printed in the United States of America
Published in Hellertown, PA
Cover design by Christina Gaugler
Library of Congress Control Number 2025925652
ISBN 979-8-89420-082-8
For more information or to place bulk orders, contact the author or the publisher at Jennifer@BrightCommunications.net.

Bright
COMMUNICATIONS

For my husband, Jeff: My heart beats with yours.

For my three precious daughters, Katherine, Kaitlin, and Karaline: You are the joy of my life. You will always be in my heart.

For my grandchildren: May God hold you in the palm of His hand.

Contents

Foreword
by Melissa DeFoor, Ph.D., RN, CLD

Tori Dennis is one of the most incredible women I have ever had the pleasure of knowing. To begin to describe Tori, you need to know a little about her past, which has been shaped by resilience, perseverance, and unbreakable hope. Tori's early life was marked by adversity. Despite her hardships, Tori held on to her dream of becoming a nurse. She could not afford tuition, but she met a military officer who encouraged her to apply for an Army ROTC scholarship. This chance encounter led to Tori securing a full-tuition scholarship with the condition she would serve as an Army Nurse.

Tori honorably served in the military, rising to the rank of Captain. Her time in the military was not without challenges, including a mass casualty event early in her career that left a permanent mark on her. Tori and her husband had a dual-military marriage because both were serving in the Army. Deployments and long separations were simply part of their marriage. A tragic life-altering moment came when her husband suffered a catastrophic injury while on military duty. Tori, caring for their two-month-old baby, faced this crisis with the same strength and unbreakable hope that guided her through so many other previous trials.

Once discharged from the military, Tori became a home-birth midwife, licensed by the state. Her evidenced-based midwifery practice focused on nutritional advice and whole food recommendations while incorporating herbal teas and tinctures into a holistic plan of care.

Tori's knowledge and judicious use of dried herbs, teas, herbal tinctures, essential oils, and healing whole foods is remarkable. Her midwifery practice provided a holistic approach blending herbal knowledge with modern midwifery. The blend of both approaches provided a tailored approach to care.

Tori and I met during the height of her midwifery career. As a labor and birth nurse, I often found myself seeking information to better care for my patients. Working in a healthcare facility, options for natural birth in our area were very limited at the time. Tori and I soon became colleagues, and I often sought out her expertise and gained invaluable insights into natural birthing practices. Together, with other colleagues, we were able to bring a multitude of new options for birthing parents to our facility.

With Tori's guidance, we built the very first HOPE suite in our facility. The concept of this suite was to create a safe, comforting space for naturally laboring patients. This room housed a laboring tub, birthing balls, birthing stool, and fireplace. Tori instilled a passionate drive in me as well as others to help continue to make our facility better.

When we built the new hospital facility, I had Tori in mind while designing certain aspects of the women's care unit. I was determined to not have one but two HOPE suites available to the community. Additionally, inspired by her passion, we were able to implement trials of labor after Cesarean birth, which were previously not supported. Vaginal birth after Cesarean became a reality for our patients.

Through our professional journey, Tori and I quickly became good friends. One day, I confided in her of my struggles with infertility. My husband and I had tried countless years to conceive. Having unexplained infertility with no clear plan of care that would offer a solution to getting pregnant was difficult, to say the least. Tori yet again provided me with that unwavering continued hope. She messaged me randomly one day and said, "I have a deeper understanding about the benefits of sage. Read the attached." Attached was an article link that discussed the fertility benefits of using sage.

I replied, "Thank you for always thinking of me, Tori."

That is who Tori is, a wonderful friend who is always willing to help. She sent this message to me in October of 2017.

I began using sage lotion twice a day after that text message. I conceived my beautiful, baby girl around Thanksgiving of that same year. Just one month of Tori's suggested natural methods succeeded where years of failed pharmacological treatments, injections, ultrasounds, procedures, and intrauterine insemination had not. Tori's guidance gave me the hope I had long prayed for, and now I am blessed with an amazingly beautiful, kind, loving daughter.

Tori has a remarkable passion for uplifting, supporting, and empowering all women, not just during the perinatal period. She continues to inspire others and this book is a true testament on how it is possible to maintain hope through life's most difficult challenges.

Introduction
by Lindsay Crowson, MAT, BSN, RN

The first home birth I attended with Tori was in an Amish house on a sweltering summer day. I had been eagerly anticipating the phone call that would signal not only an impending birth, but also the beginning of my midwifery apprenticeship. As soon as my phone rang, I threw on my shoes and headed out in my Toyota Corolla. It was a beautiful, if muggy, day and my whole body thrummed with nervous excitement. I would soon become familiar with this feeling of anxious anticipation and the fear that my car could never go quite fast enough to a birth.

My anxiety was made worse by the fact that there was construction on my route and my GPS was not at all accommodating of those unmarked country roads. I was so worried I was going to show up late and miss my opportunity to prove that I was reliable. I finally pulled into the driveway of what I hoped was the correct house, no thanks to my GPS. Relief washed over me when I saw Tori's car parked in front of the house. My furious rush to get there had actually served to settle my nerves a bit, as I was in too much of a hurry to overthink things.

Tori and her assistant had just come from another birth but already had things set up for this one. It was very early in this woman's labor though, so I had not missed anything else. I had dressed as instructed by Tori, in a manner that respected the Amish. I was in a long navy skirt, long sleeve black shirt, black tights and plain black shoes. My hair was pulled back in a low ponytail and my face was bare of makeup. I would quickly decide that makeup was pointless in midwifery, Amish birth or not. Laboring women called at all hours of the day and there was little time or reason to be anything other than clean and comfortable.

It was my first time in an Amish house and I would be lying if I said that I felt something other than awkward. I walked in assuming that I would be miserably hot, and it was indeed very warm, but I soon forgot about the heat. Instead, I became wrapped up in the story that is birth. It was clear that this story was in its very early stages and we would likely be there most of the day. As much of an outsider as I felt, Tori seemed just as much at home among the Amish. She spoke with them easily and I could tell that they trusted her. I tried to observe how she interacted with them and take in as much as I could about their way of life.

It was a long day of waiting before the woman began that age-old rhythm signaling birth was nearing. I had seen natural birth in the hospital, where I was a registered nurse, but this was the first home birth I had witnessed. Despite a lengthy labor, the baby was born before the sun set, the only complication being the soaking of Tori's clothes during the birth. The Amish family was kind enough to let her borrow an Amish dress. That was how we found ourselves several hours later at a McDonald's, eating cheeseburgers and laughing at how out of place we looked. I could barely sleep that night for thinking about my day and what the reality of midwifery might look like now that I was really doing it.

I first met Tori when I was a Registered Nurse in the hospital when one of her clients needed a C-section and I was the neonatal nurse for that delivery. I knew that this was not the ideal situation for this woman as she had desired a natural experience. I was several years out from what had been a very unsatisfying, if not mildly traumatic, Cesarean birth of my own and I felt deeply that there was a better way to do things. Yet, I still saw the same things happening over and over in the hospital. Somewhere in the middle of that, I had stumbled upon the midwifery model of care and felt such an affinity for it that I began considering it as a career option. This led me to volunteer for deliveries where the woman desired a natural experience.

I helped this mom initiate breastfeeding as soon as possible and made sure that her husband was able to do skin-to-skin with the baby in recovery. This was not a difficult thing to accomplish, but I am sad to say that it was the first time I'd ever had a father do skin-to-skin in the hospital. He would not be the last, but the truth is, it was still difficult to make small things like that happen in the hospital at that time. It remains a sad truth that natural birth is still hard to accomplish in some hospitals.

I distinctly remember being nervous that I was taking care of one of Tori's clients. She was a "real life" midwife and I wanted to make sure that she knew I understood what that was all about. I had no real idea what it was all about, in all honesty. I would develop a much more nuanced view of things later, including the politics and controversies that come with advocating for midwifery care and its access for women.

What compelled Tori to take a chance and let me become her apprentice, I will never really know. She had no reason to know that I was trustworthy or competent at all in the very beginning, other than word of mouth recommendations from some of my coworkers. It always felt like a bit of a miracle to me. There wasn't a day of my apprenticeship that I didn't feel extremely privileged and grateful that I was witness to the miracle of birth and to Tori's seemingly endless knowledge, even on the days when I was tired. And there were days when I was very, very tired. I was still working 12 hour shifts at the hospital, in addition to being on call for home births and attending as many prenatal and postpartum visits as possible. Still, when my phone would ring in the middle of the night, I rarely had time to think about that. I simply jumped in my car and drove, sipping coffee and singing loud concerts to myself to wake up. I'm sure we had deliveries during the day, but looking back, most of my memories are of waiting for babies to arrive in the stillness of the night.

During my time as Tori's apprentice, I learned many things about her that can't be summed up in one book alone. She has lived a multi-volume kind of life. The more time I spent with Tori, the more I realized she was one of the smartest people I have ever known. Her knowledge of pregnancy and childbirth never ceased to amaze me. As a nurse who had only seen birth inside hospital walls, I was overwhelmed with the differences between those births and what happened at a home birth. In fact, I told Tori that the only similarity between the two was that there was a baby delivered at the end.

Through Tori, I saw an example of a life focused on serving others with dignity and respect. This was not only obvious in the care of her midwifery clients but also in stories she told me of her time in the Army, serving sick and injured soldiers in the midst of dealing with her own personal wounds and those of her husband while raising three daughters. Her innate sense of tenacity and adventure has led her into the lives of so many whose lives are different from hers, including serving pregnant women in India.

When talking about Tori, I have often told my husband, "I can't believe I'm friends with her." I have always felt like I was akin to being friends with a famous person. I have no stories about jumping out of planes and almost dying, assisting women in India, or growing up with such a burning desire to succeed that I would do almost anything to get into college. My life comes off as a bit dull in comparison, but spending time with Tori makes me brave. And that's probably one of the most important things I can say about Tori. These things didn't just happen to her. She went out and did them, on purpose, and well.

Tori holds herself to the highest standard of anyone I know. She is absolutely relentless in her pursuit of making others' lives better. After reading some of the stories in this book, you might think it would be easy to lose hope in a lot of these situations. But if there's anything Tori has taught me, it's that maintaining a sense of hope is crucial to doing whatever work we are called to do. Maintaining hope is not always easy, in fact it is often the harder option. It is much easier to feel hopeless in the face of adversity than it is to continue working towards a better outcome. And yet, Tori has done just that through her faith and her tenacity. In the time I have known her, I have seen her fight to improve the experience of hospital birth, ensure access to midwifery care in our state, and finally, use her passion and extensive knowledge to educate the nurses of tomorrow. It is in this passing on of her knowledge that I think she shows the most hope. Education is nothing if not the hope that a future generation will take the knowledge they are given and use it to make our world a better place. They could have no better example of how to live this than Tori. My own hope is that her stories will inspire you to persevere in whatever you have been called to do with the same expectation that it will indeed improve the lives of others.

PART 1: ARMY NURSE

Lost

I don't think of all the misery but of the beauty that still remains. —Anne Frank

The elevator door opened. I felt detached as I stepped into the confined space. I was fatigued, and my legs hurt after working a long shift on labor and delivery as a nurse. I leaned on the wall while the elevator went down. I hardly heard the bell ding when the elevator doors opened on the ground floor. When I exited the hospital, the humidity of the South engulfed me. As I walked to my SUV in the parking deck, I felt my stomach growl. I realized I hadn't eaten since breakfast. Then I saw Layla standing by her car. She had worked with me throughout the shift.

"Layla?" I asked.

"Hey, Tori," she replied.

"Can I ask you a question? Do you ever get tired of blood and death?"

"Caring for a stillborn is never easy," she said compassionately.

"Yes," I said as I thought of the cold, lifeless baby.

The pregnant woman had noticed the baby had not kicked all day. When she arrived at the hospital, the baby had no heartbeat. When I listened with the monitor, the silence was agonizing. The familiar sound of whoosh, whoosh, whoosh was not there. The subsequent ultrasound showed the heart was not beating. I helped her labor. When the time came to push, I told her it was okay to let go. She delivered the stillborn, and I helped her through her grief. I wrapped the baby and gently carried its body in my arms to the morgue.

"I don't know what's wrong with me today. I feel like death is all around me."

"You need a good night's sleep. Come over to my house on Saturday for breakfast and coffee."

"Thank you, Layla." As Layla hugged me, I choked back tears. She understood without the need for many words.

I drove home with thoughts racing in my head. Death, blood, and the morgue seemed all too familiar. My brain was overwhelmed.

Suddenly, I had a flashback of taking off my bloody combat boots. I remembered the mass casualty and the faces of the soldiers.

I pulled over and cried, overwhelmed with emotion. How did I get to this point in my life? When I finished crying, I thought of my mother. I wished I could call her. I would walk twenty miles just to have one more five-minute phone conversation with her. If only a phone could call heaven.

Chapter 1: Growing Up

Have faith, hope, and charity.—Nancy Ritschard

When I was a child, I loved the outdoors. On warm summer days, I would lie in a neighbor's field, looking at the clouds in the blue sky. I enjoyed gazing at the fluffy clouds for hours, watching the shapes change and imagining that they were animals playing in the open sky. Feeling the warm sunshine on my face brought me joy. The bees buzzed nearby. Robins, blue jays, and cardinals played their own games in the sky. I relaxed, smelling the nearby pine trees and sometimes lying under them, using the pine needles as a soft bed.

I would think about the Amish horse and buggies that I saw on Pennsylvania Route 23 with my grandfather. I dreamed of being a doctor for the Amish, but at six years old, I did not know what the future had in store for me.

Little did I know that as an adult, I would skydive and survive adrenaline-producing mishaps. I would work a mass casualty as a young army nurse. My future husband would serve honorably in the military and suffer a catastrophic injury. I would help the Amish as a midwife, ride in their horse and buggies, and sleep in their homes. Much like how the birds buoyed my emotions as a child, birds would comfort me during my journey battling post-traumatic stress disorder.

But back on that warm summer day, I was happily lying on my back, daydreaming and looking at the clouds.

I heard my mom call me for lunch. I ran to the house and opened the metal screen door that led into the kitchen. A box fan secured in the open window was humming as it blew air through the warm kitchen. I sat in my place at the kitchen table and noticed my mom had cut my sandwich into two triangles. I was excited when I saw my favorite Lebanon bologna and white American cheese sandwiches with spicy brown mustard. My mom loved me, and I knew it. That was a happy day and the idyllic part of my childhood. Because of my mom, our family had faith, hope, and charity.

The Cat

Life is great, as long as you don't weaken—Ellen Hepler

For as long as I could remember, my parents had a contentious marriage. When I was in third grade, they separated. My dad stayed in East End at our ranch-style home with a large backyard. The rest of us moved downtown into a three-story half-double, one of many that lined the streets in a row. It was a run-down, over-100-year-old home, and the neighborhood was mainly poor and rough.

During the winter, we shoveled coal into an old furnace to stay warm. I lived in the only home in our neighborhood that did not have oil heat with an adjustable thermostat.

The windows were old, and the cold air permeated the glass panes. My bedroom was extremely cold because there was not a working furnace vent for my room. I could see my breath as I exhaled during the coldest days of winter, and I would shiver under six blankets until I slowly got warm.

In the spring, the cool night breeze brought in fresh air as I lay under a cotton sheet. I lay in my bed listening to the crickets chirping and owls hooting through the open second story windows. I would gaze at the stars through the window until my eyelids were heavy and I drifted to sleep.

Because our home had no central air-conditioning, we left the windows open in the summertime, using box fans to circulate the air. On the hottest days, my mom turned on the window mounted air-conditioner, which cooled off one room. She tacked up blankets at the doorways to keep that one room cool.

One warm summer day, I was walking on the uneven, cracked sidewalk in front of our half-double house when I saw a dog barking incessantly. A neighbor lady who was outside told me the dog had killed some kittens and chased the cat up the tree.

Two days later, I saw the cat lying on my neighbor's back porch. Curious, I walked over, just in time to see something dark and wet bulging out between the cat's back legs. The cat was lying on her side, and she birthed a kitten right in front of me. Then she birthed another. She licked the two kittens, and they mewed. The kittens snuggled close to her, each found one of her nipples, and nursed.

I was fascinated by the scene before me. Even though I was only ten years old, I astutely realized several facts that shaped my view on birth later in life. First, the cat's fear of the dog had stopped her labor. She held the remaining kittens in until she felt safe. Second, formula was not necessary because nipples supplied warm milk. Most importantly, the mother cat birthed on her side, not on her back. From that moment forward, I was fascinated by birth. Seeing a life born sparked a passion in me. It was joy amid the dismal daily reality of poverty.

Caged In

I have always been athletic, and I spent autumns playing field hockey. One game day, I forgot my mouthguard, which prompted my coach to send me back to the locker room to retrieve it.

I crossed the freshly mowed field in a hurry because I wanted to play in the game. The junior high was a well-built, brick building, without central air. The building was so old that my grandmother had attended school there in the 1930s. I walked down the steps into the lowest level, which was partially underground. The locker room was at the bottom of the stairwell, and I saw the door was locked with a heavy chain. I panicked because I did not know any other way in! As a naïve twelve-year-old girl, getting back to the game was all I could think about, so I ran back up the stairs. That's when I saw several football players coming out another door.

"Is there another way into the locker room?" I yelled to the boys.

"Yes, there is. Go down through here," one boy said with a smirk, waving to another set of stairs.

I walked down those steps, which led me into a locker room—but not the girl's locker room like I expected. When I opened the door, I was mortified. I saw boys changing out of football uniforms. They began hooting and hollering, as surprised to see me as I was to see them.

In the blink of an eye, the football coach crossed the locker room toward me. Then, angrily he grabbed me by the arms, lifted me off the ground, half carried and half dragged me to an isolated area of the locker room, slammed the door, and locked me in. I started crying, banging on the door, and screaming to be let out. I begged for help as the tears streamed down my face. I was horrified that I had been duped into going into the boy's locker room, and I was terrified because I had no idea how long I'd be locked in here. I felt a wave of humiliation and horror overtake me.

Suddenly, the door opened slightly, and I saw a Black boy's face peeking in.

"The boys are changing quickly so you can be let out," he whispered to reassure me.

Suddenly, the large coach appeared beside the boy. He grabbed the boy and slammed the door shut again. Muffled through the closed door, I could hear the coach screaming at the boy. I started crying again, knowing the boy was in trouble because of me.

Then I started screaming again, this time so loudly that a maintenance man heard me. He unlocked a separate door and let me out into a hallway. I hugged the tall, elderly janitor with both my arms and buried my tear-stained face into his gray uniform. At that moment, the coach opened the door. The coach was so angry, his white face was red. He approached us, looking like he was going to make more trouble for me, but the janitor stood his ground. I clung to the janitor.

"There'll be hell to pay for your behavior," the janitor told the coach gruffly, then he walked me out. I felt safe with the janitor, who reminded me of my grandfather—also a maintenance man.

"Go home and tell your parents what happened," the janitor said.

But I never did. I was too scared of the angry coach. I was just a little girl, the coach was a big man, and I believed it was all my fault.

The Fire

We all have hard in life.
We just don't get to pick our hard.

When my mother remarried, she jumped from the frying pan into the fire. There were episodes of domestic violence, and I was subjected to the verbal abuses of my stepfather. He also communicated with sarcasm and inappropriate humor.

My stepfather did not drink alcohol every day, but when he did drink, he came home drunk and screamed obscenities or had a crying jag. I lived life waiting for the other shoe to drop. When he did not appear for supper, I knew he'd come home drunk after the bars closed at 2 in the morning. During the height of his drinking, he would come home two or three times per week drunk and wake the entire house in a rage. However, he would have dry spells and not drink for months.

I often had school the next morning and would find it difficult to focus. I struggled to stay awake. I dreaded the end of the school day. School had a routine. Home was unpredictable.

Sadly, I often had no lunch money. I spent many days in the school library during lunch hour to avoid smelling the food because I was so hungry. A bitterness grew in me when I would think of how my stepfather had money for cigarettes and alcohol, but I was hungry at school.

I was often made fun of by other children. The most memorable teasing was the name calling. My middle name is Hope, and I was called Hope the Dope. I was teased so often that I hated my name. The irony is that years later, a transformation happened. The name I loathed as a child turned into something good and became the name I used. Hope became my source of inspiration. It is what I carried in my heart. But it would take time for this transformation to occur.

The longer I felt bullied and lived in a household with a condescending stepfather, the more my inner rage grew. One day in school, a group of girls started taunting me and calling me names. I asked them to stop. They did not. I told the teacher, who blew me off because she was too busy. The girls kept taunting me, and other kids laughed.

That broke me. I punched one of the girls with all my might. She punched me back, and we fought until the teacher broke it up. I stood before the principal with a bloody nose and was suspended from school. The inner rage from my home life had erupted at school.

Sheep Dog

After that fight, the teasing stopped. I was studious and earned straight As on my report cards. I became a model student.

However, I took matters into my own hands when my younger sister was threatened. I was at school and heard a gang of girls was going to fight her in an alley on the way home from school. I skipped school early and ran home to retrieve a gun from my stepfather's nightstand. The gun was not loaded with bullets, but it would serve as intimidation. I was like a sheep dog in protector mode. I didn't even know what the pending fight was about.

I ran back toward school. Classes had let out, and I saw my sister. She looked scared. She was waiting for me on the sidewalk under the tall oak trees. It would be the two of us against a gang of girls. We walked silently together. As we approached the crowd, I held the gun in my left hand, close to my thigh and pointing toward the ground.

When one girl saw it, she said quietly, "She has a gun."

No one screamed. In fact, the crowd fell silent. Thankfully, several girls knew me and acknowledged me. I said hello back. That simple courtesy seemed to break the tension. The crowd parted and let us walk through, remaining silent as we walked down the alley. My hands were icy cold, and I felt cold sweat on my back under my torn, worn-out T-shirt.

When I returned home, I was shaking. I ran up the stairs and placed the gun in the nightstand in the exact position I had found it. I knew immediately I had done a stupid thing.

Encouraged

Out of the mountain of despair, a stone of HOPE.
—Martin Luther King Jr.

Even amidst a tumultuous upbringing, I studied all the time, earned good grades, and managed to smile while performing cheers as a high school cheerleader. I was driven to succeed. My way out of poverty was a career. Everything hinged on a college scholarship.

Providence provided two stones of hope: Mr. Cressman and Mrs. Johnson. Mr. Cressman was my high school English teacher. He was a White man with thinning brown hair and glasses, who had served in the Army reserves as a Sergeant First Class. He wrote letters of recommendation for my college admission applications and for college scholarships. He encouraged me to shoot for the moon.

Mrs. Johnson was a guidance counselor who supported my effort to win scholastic scholarships. She was a happy Black woman with a beautiful smile, which greeted me with warmth. She cheered me on throughout the entire tedious process of typing applications on my old ribbon electric typewriter. I spent countless evenings typing essays lending support to why I should be chosen. I was living on a prayer.

On the day of the school's awards ceremony, I was seated with other students on the large stage in front of the entire student body. Parents and grandparents were seated in the front rows of the auditorium. My hands were cold and sweaty. This day would decide my future.

I was over the moon as my name repeatedly was announced as a recipient of scholarships. Happy tears were spilling down my smiling face. By the end of the awards ceremony, I had won almost $100,000 in scholarship money, including an Army Reserve Officer's Training Corps scholarship. *That one* had big strings attached. It would pay 100 percent of my college tuition, but I would need to serve in the United States Army for eight years after I graduated from college. But all those scholarships meant that I did it! I was going to college! I had previously been accepted at a prestigious Ivy League University, the University of Pennsylvania, and now I had the money to go.

Karate

The summer before I started college, I spent a lot of time training in the dojo. I had a practical reason to learn how to defend myself. Because I did not have a vehicle or a driver's license, I hitchhiked. Getting into a car with a stranger was not the wisest decision. I used intuition and horse sense when deciding whether or not to open a car door.

At the dojo, I sparred barefoot, wearing the classic white karate gi. When I stepped into the circle, adrenaline coursed through my body. The sparring started, and the goal was to dominate. I fought hard, using back kicks, front kicks, and round house kicks. I would land middle punches at my opponent's solar plexus. I tried my best to block my opponent's punches, allowing me to counterattack. I was so proud when I won a trophy sparring.

Sparring built my resilience and mental toughness, and karate was a positive outlet for me. Karate made me realize I am not powerless. I was no longer a child to be bullied.

At home, I jumped rope in the cellar. I also did push-ups and sit-ups every day, which I knew were part of the Army Physical Fitness Tests. I wanted to do well.

The night before leaving for college, I had open boxes packed with essentials sitting on the floor in the living room. Through the large bay window, I saw my stepfather and a young man fighting on the front porch. Suddenly, their bodies came crashing into the window. Shards of glass scattered across the room and into my open boxes. They continued the fight on the front porch. I was stunned. The police were called for the disturbance. That was not exactly how I envisioned my last night at home.

I spent hours cleaning up glass in the living room and out of the boxes. I cut my fingers and had to bandage them.

The next day, I left home for the University of Pennsylvania. My entire world was about to change. I knew I would face challenges at that prestigious institution, but I was determined to succeed.

When I unpacked the boxes later that day in my dorm room, I cut my fingers on more glass. That was one last reminder of my tumultuous youth. I tossed the glass into the garbage and spit onto it.

You won't beat me, I thought. *I am good enough to be here.*

Chapter 2: College and ROTC

We must embrace the pain and burn it as fuel for our journey. —Kenji Miyazawa

When I was in high school, I had decided to major in nursing. I was in a vocational high school program that arranged clinicals in hospitals and on ambulances. As a student, I took care of many World War II veterans, bathing them and doing basic nursing care. I enjoyed listening to their military stories. The interactions I had with those men cemented what I already knew in my heart: Nursing was my calling. The veterans encouraged me and spoke with admiration and misty eyes about the Army nurses who tended them during the war. I was entering an admirable profession.

In college, I rarely had a break from studying. Nursing school was a challenge. My schedule was overwhelming. I was busy with a rigorous course load, frequent exams, and twice-weekly hospital clinicals. During clinicals, I performed patient care in the hospital for six straight hours.

Because I was attending college on an Army ROTC scholarship, I had an additional, noncredited ROTC class each semester for two hours every Monday evening. My fellow Army cadets and I also had weekly drill practice every Thursday morning. We met several mornings each week for physical training (PT), where we ran, did push-ups and sit-ups, and exercised to keep our bodies in shape to pass the biannual Physical Fitness Test and weigh-ins—both of which we needed to pass to keep our scholarships.

One of the Army ROTC cadre, Sergeant First Class Nord, would run with me through the streets of Philadelphia. He was a muscular Black man with a military haircut. He was an outstanding trainer. At the university's track, he increased my overall running speed through sprint interval training. My endurance was strengthened through long-distance running.

One day I was especially tired because I had just taken an exam. I had crammed all night for the exam, and I really wanted sleep. But I knew I had an obligation to run. SFC Nord met me at the football stadium, and without a word we started our run. In 1990, the streets of Philly were bustling with traffic, bicycles, and pedestrians. The air was alive with sounds of motors, horns, and conversations. SFC Nord and I ran on the sidewalk and deftly crossed streets—often narrowly avoiding getting hit by cars. Sometimes, there were vulgar cat calls and whistles directed at me. We ignored it and kept running.

This day our plan was to run five miles to the Philadelphia Art Museum, then back to the university's football stadium to finish running eight laps around the track. After only a mile in, I was already feeling it. SFC Nord would speak words of encouragement to me just at the right moments. How he knew when to speak was as remarkable as the man himself. He believed in me, and he was determined to make an officer out of me.

I knew reaching the art museum steps, which had been made famous in the movie *Rocky*, would be halfway. I was having to dig deep for inner strength while I ran. I ran as SFC Nord had taught me, breathing in through my nose and slowly exhaling out of my mouth. Step after step, I ran past the many row houses in the Philly neighborhoods. My lungs burned, but I felt mentally relieved when the snarled thoughts in my mind unwound as running put me in the zone.

Mile after mile we ran. Again and again, I had to physically and mentally push myself to go on as all long-distance runners do. Running was a form of mental discipline. I was training to be an Army officer, and perseverance and determination were reinforced. I was not about to quit—though sometimes I might have been tempted to.

Between ROTC and nursing, my schedule was exhausting. I never had enough time for quality sleep. There were many evenings I walked home in the dark from the library. I willed my legs to keep going, even though curling up on the sidewalk and sleeping for thirty minutes seemed strangely appealing. I knew if I just kept trudging forward, eventually, my head would hit the pillow. But not yet. My stomach growled, and my head ached. I needed to eat. I needed to study for tomorrow's exam. Then, maybe I could sleep three hours.

University of Pennsylvania

The University of Pennsylvania, known as UPenn or PENN, is a private Ivy League university. It was founded in 1740 by Benjamin Franklin, and it is one of the most prestigious universities in the world. I spent countless late nights studying in the PENN library with many other students. Among me and my fellow students in the quiet, historic library, I felt an unspoken camaraderie and mutual respect. I knew I was not alone in my determination to succeed.

As I walked the pathways and streets of the university lined by brown and yellow sandstone and granite buildings, I often thought about how many students came before me in the university's 250-year history. The campus and the buildings were full of history. Among those who walked on campus were signers of the Declaration of Independence and the Constitution and Supreme Court Justices, Senators, and Presidents of the United States. When I sat in lectures in the centuries old building, such as College Hall, I wondered what the walls would say if they could talk. Even when I was mentally and physically exhausted, I was encouraged by the history around me. It was as if the ghosts of the past, who had studied and trod there before me, cheered me on.

Another great place to study was in the lounges on the top floors of the three twenty-four-story high rise dorms on the east end of campus. We called them the Rooftop Lounges, and they offered incredible views of the city. The skyline at sunset was breathtaking. When the lights lit up downtown Philly, it was stunning. I loved the view overlooking the city.

When I needed to feel close to God, I would go through the unlocked doors of St. Mary's Episcopal Church, which was located on Locust Walk on campus. I would sit quietly and prayerfully on a pew and look at the beautiful stained-glass windows. The architecture was grand, and in the quietness of the church, I felt God's presence.

Sitting in an old wooden pew, I would face the altar and pray, "God, give me the physical strength I need to stay awake and study. I am so tired. Help me, Lord. Amen."

On campus, having come from a lower-middle-class family, I was intensely aware of the wealth and privilege of so many of my peers. A quick walk or even a glance off campus to the streets of West Philadelphia, however, made it impossible to wallow in self-pity. I was poor in comparison to the elite faculty and students at PENN. However, my life was abundant compared with the streets' homeless men and women, many of whom slept on top of the subway grates to stay warm in the winter. They were a constant reminder of how fortunate I was. Even though I struggled with hunger myself, I would give a hot coffee or my meager lunch sandwich to a destitute person sitting on the cold sidewalk. Somehow that act of charity lessened my hunger.

Fort Lewis

For three years, I had trained hard in ROTC at the University of Pennsylvania. To be commissioned as an officer in the Army, it was mandatory for cadets to attend Advanced Camp between junior and senior years for rigorous military training and evaluation. A failure in training would prevent commissioning and subsequently a loss in college scholarship money.

In June 1991, I arrived at Fort Lewis, Washington, and in-processing began immediately. I was assigned to a platoon and directed to quarter in a World War II barracks. Outside it had old wood siding that was painted white. Inside its large open bay had two long rows of metal bunk beds. I was given white sheets and a woolen Army blanket and ordered to make my bunk.

The latrine had a shower room with multiple showerheads lined up in a row. There were no curtains for privacy. Group showers were a norm.

The toilets had wood walls separating each commode, but there were no doors. There was no privacy. It was an Army barracks, and there was nothing to do but suck it up.

We cadets had to clean the latrine with Pine Sol, and to this day I associate that smell with the Army. We also had to mop the floors, then wax them with a buffer.

At mealtimes, we would stand at parade rest in a single file line at the chow hall waiting to enter, eat quickly without speaking, and stand in formation outside until everyone in our platoon had exited the chow hall.

Every morning, we were up and moving before dawn. Jumping off my top bunk, I hurried into my uniform, tied my boot laces tight, and stood for formation. Standing at attention, saluting, and marching in formation quickly became second nature.

The morning came for the Army Physical Fitness Test. At the PT field, there were multiple stations lined up uniformly in the grass. "Front leaning rest position. Move." That is how the Army tells you to get into the push-up position. The whistle blew, and the two minutes started. For a push-up to count, the participant had to break the plane, which meant that the mid-section of the back had to be flush with the elbows on the downward motion of the push-up. Otherwise, the same number would be repeated over and over, which was disheartening for the person doing the push-up.

Our battle buddies cheered. The examiners counted. The time keeper called out the remaining seconds: Five, four, three, two, one. My score was high. I had maxed the push-ups for the female standard.

Sit-ups were next. I got the maximum score on sit-ups eas-ily. I was about to face the hardest part. My goal was to max the run, but it was going to be difficult. I never scored a perfect 100 points on the run to date.

As we lined up at the starting line, I looked around at all the runners, uniform in a sea of gray cotton T-shirts, gray or black shorts, and numbered pullover vests.

"On your mark, get set, go!" we heard, and the crowd took off in a heap. The runners spaced out, depending on the pace each runner kept. We ran two one-mile laps around the course. I ran as fast as I could. Eventually, my lungs started burning, but I kept going.

At the halfway mark, I was right on pace to max the run, but keeping that pace was pushing me to my limit. As I ran the next half mile, I wanted to vomit.

As I made the turn for the homestretch, I knew the time was tight. I tried to get my legs to sprint, but I had nothing left. I kept running, but I could not run any faster. I heard the time being called out as each runner crossed the finish line. When I crossed, missing my goal time by twenty seconds, I knew I had done my best.

Even though I did not max the run, mine was the third highest female PT score in the entire company. I had done well.

The cool morning air was changing, and I was beginning to feel the heat from the sun. My lungs were still burning, and I was sweating. With the Army Physical Fitness Test concluded, we were bussed to the chow hall for breakfast. Our long train-ing day was just beginning. It's true that the Army does more before breakfast than most people do all day.

Another day at camp, we boarded military buses for water training, wearing full battle dress uniform and boots. At the pool, when it was my turn, I climbed the stairs to the high dive. I walked to the end of the diving board and jumped into the deep end of the pool. I was weighed down by my uniform and boots, but I swam to the side of the pool easily because I was a strong swimmer.

Our next water training was at a river—the one-rope bridge river crossing. One cadet swam across the river and tied a rope to a tree. Everyone else held onto the rope as they walked across the river. The river water was waist deep, and the rope gave us some stability while moving across the river.

Over the several weeks of training, I did many things I had never imagined I'd do. I low-crawled on the muddy ground under barbed wire. I charged forward and stabbed my bayonet into a stuffed burlap bag. I climbed up and over walls on obstacle courses and climbed cargo nets and ropes.

Like most cadets, the camp event I dreaded the most was nuclear, biological, chemical (NBC) training because it concluded with a gas chamber. In the morning, we trained on how to don a gas mask quickly and properly. After completing the training, cadets were led in small groups up to a green canvas field tent. We were instructed to put on our masks, then enter the chamber. Once inside, we had to take off our masks, get a hefty dose of the tear gas that was burning inside, then say our full name to be sure we felt the full effects. The purpose of this military training was to build confidence that the gas masks absolutely work to protect against chemical warfare agents.

Immediately after removing my mask, the tear gas burned my eyes, nasal passages, mouth, and skin. When I was dismissed and ran out into the fresh air, the burn was intense. Snot poured from my nose, and I was spitting from my mouth. Lesson learned.

Every day brought different evaluations. It was mandatory to qualify on the M16A2 rifle, shooting at targets that ranged from 25 to 300 meters away. Also, it was expected that all cadets rappeled off a sixty-four-foot tower.

As I jumped off the back of the Humvee, I looked toward the wooden tower. For a moment I was intimidated. When it was my turn, I stood sixty-four-feet off the ground.

"On rappel," I yelled as I had been instructed.

"On belay," the belayer, who looked very far away, replied.

As I had been taught, I grabbed the rope with my right hand and pulled it taut behind me, which was called my "brake." I stepped over the safety rail and looked over my brake hand shoulder to check for the belay man. With my brake hand in the small of my back, I summoned up all my courage, stepped backward to the edge of the tower, and leaned back to assume an L-shaped position. When commanded to do so, I flexed my knees and jumped vigorously backward. At the same time, I threw my brake hand out at a 45-degree angle, letting the rope slide through my guide hand, which was extended above me. I began the descent down the tower. It was exhilarating. I loved it.

As the days wore on, exhaustion was part of the fabric of each day. I was especially tired when we arrived at the land navigation course. Thankfully it was not raining. Out on the thickly wooded course, I followed the steps that were drilled into our heads. I had four hours to find four points using just a map, protractor to plot the points, and compass. I was alone, except for the trees around me. After several hours, I had completed the course, relieved to be done.

The last water training event was a zipline. First, I had to climb a tall wooden white tower, which gave me plenty of time to realize how high the tower was from the ground. After ascending the tower, I grabbed a bar, slid down a zipline, and dropped into the water below. The water felt refreshing after a long day of training.

One night while on bivouac, I was in my sleeping bag, looking up at the bright stars in the clear night sky. The weather was so mild that it was not necessary to set up shelter halves. I was exhausted and grateful to fall asleep while looking at the beautiful stars and smelling the nearby pine trees. The smell of pine trees reminded me of childhood, lying in the field looking at the clouds. Suddenly, I became homesick. I shook it off. *I'll think of home later*, I thought.

Finally, field training was over. I was leaving to go to phase two of my training the next day. I walked from the barracks to the vending machines, which had been off limits during training. I put in some coins and bought a cold Coca-Cola. That was the best Coke I ever had in my life. Thank God, *that* part of my ROTC training was over.

Washington, D.C.

After the field training was over, I had four weeks of hospital clinicals to complete. Those clinicals were part of the mandatory military training to evaluate if we qualified within the strict standards of the Army Nurse Corps.

I was flown to Washington, D.C., then I took a cab to the billets near Walter Reed Army Medical Center.

I was assigned an Army Nurse Corps officer as my preceptor. She was a tall Black woman with a beautiful smile and sparkling brown eyes. I worked the same full-time schedule as my preceptor. She taught me nursing skills and the duties of an Army nurse. Working with such a kind person was a relief after the grueling field training.

On my off days, I took the metro to see the tourist sites. One evening at twilight, I stood at the fence of the White House, in awe of its beautiful architecture. The lights shining on the white walls gave the building a magnificence and an incredible grandeur.

For me, the most heart-wrenching but inspiring site was the Tomb of the Unknown Soldier at Arlington National Cemetery. This tomb is dedicated to American servicemen who died without their remains being identified. Their remains are "Known but to God."

Viewing the acres of graves of fallen soldiers at Arlington National Cemetery brought tears to my eyes. The sacrifices made to keep America free is a debt that cannot be paid. In a little more than one year, I would see firsthand the cost of freedom when I would wipe the blood of soldiers off my Army boots.

Philadelphia

When I returned to PENN in the fall for my senior year, I was again free to walk the streets of Philly. It was hard for me at PENN because most students came from money and had enjoyed the summer abroad. On weekends, they dined at expensive restaurants and went to comedy clubs, theater events, and art museums. I did not have the money to do any of those things.

At times, I was lonely in Philadelphia during my four years of college because it was hard to relate to the wealthy students. The elite had so much, and I had so little. I often felt out of place and preferred the humble kitchen of my grandparents' home.

I felt more at home in the Philadelphia Italian market, where I'd go to walk around, smelling the good food. I enjoyed listening to the Italian butcher talk to the elderly ladies as their fresh meat orders were being wrapped up in brown paper. I would buy a small amount of fresh sausage to add to my spaghetti sauce. I ate a lot of pasta because it was cheap. I enjoyed the Italian market very much, especially watching the hard-working, friendly people.

Rittenhouse Square was another quaint but vibrant place for me to go relax on the park benches. For me, it was a place of respite and retreat, even though the city kept on moving around me. I would walk a charming cobblestone road named Elfreth's Alley, which was lined with 300-year-old brick houses with window flower boxes and shutters. I loved walking on the old cobblestones, which was in stark contrast to the subway I would ride back to PENN.

The urine stench of the underground subway overwhelmed my nostrils as I walked down the concrete steps to the platform. Near the underground platform, numerous homeless people urinated publicly, loitered, mumbled incoherently, and slept on the concrete. When I exited the subway, I was always relieved.

On occasion, I would go to the wharf and walk on the wooden docks along the river. I found solace at the Schuylkill River that snaked through Philadelphia. If I were to follow the river upstream, it would lead to my hometown. As a youth, I swam in that river. It was comforting to have the river as a thread connecting me to my home. I was often homesick for my family. I felt if I touched the river water, I was touching home.

In my senior fall semester, nursing clinicals resumed. Nursing students rotate through several specialties during our undergraduate training, including medical-surgical, pediatrics, and maternal-child. I was in my labor-and-delivery rotation. When a birth was imminent, the laboring woman was wheeled down the hall to a delivery room where she was moved to the delivery table, which had stirrups for her feet.

I was sick to my stomach watching the typical birthing experience for women. Birthing on one's back with feet in stirrups intuitively seemed barbaric to me. Common sense told me that if I would not lie down with my feet up in stirrups to poop, why would I lie down with my feet up in stirrups to push out a baby? This birthing position is called the Lithotomy position. I knew there had to be a better way to give birth. I saw the women giving birth in the hospital as passive actors—rather than as empowered participants. Why did hospital birth seem so restrictive with only one birthing position?

During my senior year, two friends of mine had delivered their babies at birth centers with midwives, and their birthing experiences were as different as night and day from what I was seeing in the hospital. I absolutely preferred the midwifery model of care.

Empowered Births

I was working at a small, rural hospital as a nurse intern while finishing my degree. One of the physicians in particular empowered women and respected the birth process. He was an older doctor with gray hair who had served as a physician during World War II. After the war, he chose obstetrics as a profession. He seemed to have infinite patience. He spoke with gentleness to the laboring women, and he really made an impression on me.

A woman had arrived at the hospital in labor, but because her baby was in breech presentation (the butt was coming first), she was now scheduled for a C-section. The woman's previous births had been vaginal, and she did not want a surgical birth. However, she grudgingly accepted her situation. In recent years, breech presentations had been deemed too risky for vaginal births. Most new doctors had little to no experience in delivering breech babies. I went into the woman's room to check on her and noticed she was breathing through her contractions while standing and swaying.

Suddenly, the woman squatted at the bedside. She put her forehead on the bed and shifted her weight back and forth on her feet while in a squat. After a moment, she grunted loudly.

"The baby is coming," she said.

I got on my knees and positioned myself to see her perineum. I saw the baby's buttocks pushing out between her labia. I ran out of the door to tell her registered nurse.

"The baby is coming," I said breathlessly.

The nurse was surprised. When we entered the room, the nurse asked the woman to get into the bed. The nurse saw the buttocks emerging. She hollered for another nurse to page the doctor. Two doctors appeared in the room, one a younger doctor and the other the well-respected, nearly retired doctor. He talked the younger doctor through the breech delivery as if he was reading from a textbook. The older doctor was impressive in his knowledge, and he provided a calming force in the room. I watched as the buttocks were born, the legs, the umbilicus with the cord, one shoulder, the second shoulder, and finally the head. The baby was born and cried vigorously.

"I am so glad! I did not want a C-section!" the woman said. "I told you I could do it!"

The breech birth showed me what a woman's body can do. It was beautiful.

Another shift, my favorite older doctor with gray hair told me to don sterile gloves and a gown. He positioned me to do a four-handed delivery with him (when two people deliver a baby together). That was the first time I felt the energy of birth—the force of uterine contractions, and the active maternal efforts—as the baby's head delivered. It was the most intense experience I had ever felt, rendering me full of adrenaline, awe, and joy. For the first time, I felt the power of birth. I was speechless.

In that moment, I knew I wanted to work in this field. But I had made a commitment to the Army. I didn't know what the future would bring, but I knew I loved birth.

Big City Life

During my senior year at the University of Pennsylvania, I lived off campus. A friend owned an old historic house that she and her husband were remodeling. She graciously allowed me to board there. I loved the home very much. I had a room on the third floor and a view of city life below.

One afternoon while I was sitting on the porch stoop, I noticed an Asian female walking past. A tall, lanky man was walking closely behind her. Suddenly, he grabbed her purse and attempted to flee with it. She would not let go. He was fighting her for the purse.

"LEAVE HER ALONE!" I screamed at the top of my voice. In that split second, I felt the sting of injustice, and I was infuriated. Instinctively, I reacted. I leapt up off the porch stoop.

The offender ran off with the purse with me in pursuit. I was yelling, *"STOP HIM"* so loudly that several construction workers started chasing the man as well. I kept running, but he was outpacing me. He had the physique of a basketball player and could run. I stayed in pursuit.

Suddenly, police cars appeared, and the policemen apprehended the robber and returned the purse to the victim. I was still shaking from adrenaline, and it all felt surreal. Only in the city, I thought wryly.

The city crime was troubling, but nothing was more meddlesome than the rats—plump rodents with long tails. In the city, they are the size of small footballs, and they move like lightning. They feast on the garbage put out for the trash collectors. Unfortunately, because there are so many rats, they inevitably find their way indoors.

One morning, my alarm went off, and I grabbed my toiletry bag. It was dark, and I was in a hurry. I lifted the toilet lid and was glad I looked before sitting down. Even though the lid was down, somehow a rat had gotten into the toilet and drowned. I almost screamed, but I contained my reaction so as not to wake the entire house. Not only was I worried I'd be late for ROTC drill, but I had to figure out how to get the rat out of the toilet all while holding my pee. I was afraid I was going to pee my pants and wretch at the same time.

My mind raced, trying to figure out the best course of action. I ran to my bedroom, opened the bedroom window, grabbed the metal tongs I used to flip burgers on my hot plate, and returned to the bathroom. I squeezed the rat between the ends of the tongs with its beady dead eyes staring at me. I wanted to vomit, but I had no time for weakness. The rat dripped water onto the old hardwood floors as I carried it to my bedroom window. I threw it out the third-story window and watched it plop onto the ground. *Good riddance.*

I ran back to the toilet because I could not hold my pee for one more minute. My disgust that a rat had just been in the toilet that I needed to use was overpowered by my overwhelming physical need to urinate. After urinating, I wiped the water from the hardwood floors, then ran out the door. I made it to drill with seconds to spare. While running with the other cadets that early morning, I saw another rat near a metal dumpster. I rolled my eyes and kept running.

Graduation

PENN had two graduations. The first was for the entire graduating class in the football stadium, then my second graduation was with the nursing school. PENN's School of Nursing graduation was intimate and beautiful. Each graduate carried a lit candle, symbolizing Florence Nightingale's nighttime aid to wounded soldiers by candlelight.

I graduated from PENN with a Bachelor's Degree in Nursing, Magna Cum Laude. I was inducted into the Sigma Theta Tau honor society for nurses. Soon, I would take my state nursing boards. When I passed, I would become a Registered Nurse.

My entire family was there that day. My mom brought a cake decorated with a nurse's cap, a graduation cap, and an Army ambulance. My grandfather held his brown wool newsboy cap in his hands. Seeing his beaming face and bright smile made the thousands of hours of studying well worth it. Later that day, I met my father and paternal grandparents at a classy steakhouse on the wharf with exceptional food, ambiance, and service. I was happier than I had been my whole life. It was a grand day.

In the 1990s, when cadets graduated from college and were commissioned second lieutenants, they were granted either a Regular Army or Army Reserve commission. Being selected for a Regular Army commission was highly competitive, and at that time most officers received an Army Reserve commission for active duty.

Commissions were confirmed by the United States Senate. I was humbled and honored the day I was commissioned. I received the coveted Regular Army commission. I presented the sergeant who saluted me with a silver dollar as was military tradition.

I received a hand-written letter in the mail from my old English teacher. He had served in the Army and was giving me advice to heed as a new officer. He wrote:

Congratulations, Ma'am!

Tori, you will be a credit to the military as you have been to yourself and PENN. My thoughts and sincere best wishes are with you.

Just take a moment to reflect on these few words. You've accomplished remarkable things with your life. You are a truly talented and gifted young lady who will be an asset to the Officer's Corps. There will be things that you will see that in no way did ROTC prepare you for. Don't let yourself become discouraged—the vast majority of military personnel are nowhere near your caliber. Shortly you'll learn just how flexible you need to be! Now as a senior enlisted man speaking to a junior officer, Ma'am, don't forget how valuable that working relationship is. Take time to listen—really listen—to your enlisted subordinates, now including me. Don't forget to be good to yourself.

Again, my sincerest congratulations. You are an officer and a lady I do respect, and I have a nice snappy salute for you when we meet—and a big hug, too, Ma'am.

Signed, D.J. Cressman

I teared up when I read his letter. His words and advice meant a lot to me. I hoped I could live up to them. I didn't know it then, but his words ominously foreshadowed how flexible I'd need to be in a few short months when mass casualties filled the halls of the hospital.

Quilt Blocks

When I was a senior at the University of Pennsylvania, I wrote my stepfather a letter, expressing how deeply his words and actions had hurt me growing up. After he received my letter, we talked in person, and he apologized to me. He was open and humble.

When I graduated from the university, he gave me a dozen red roses.

"I'm proud of you," he said, and he meant it.

Before my step-father met my mother, he had served five years in the Army. While on active duty in Germany, he had a traumatic brain injury (TBI) from a motor vehicle accident and wasn't expected to live. But he did. Brain injuries can cause aggression, anger, depression, and irritability. I don't know if his TBI contributed to his alcohol abuse or not. He never received care from the VA and is deceased. I can only wonder if he and those around him would have had better lives if he had received extensive counseling and therapy specific to TBI.

An Amish woman once told me that each chapter of our life is like a quilt block. Some chapters are filled with sadness, trials, and suffering. Other chapters are bursting with joy, happiness, and love. Some chapters are a mixture. Eventually, these quilt blocks make our life's beautiful quilt.

When my stepfather apologized to me, then later told me he was proud of me, I was able to put the past behind me and begin my next quilt block.

Chapter 3: Army Service

After graduation and commissioning, my fellow new Second Lieutenants and I waited for our military orders, which would tell us when and where we were to begin our military service.

While I waited, I worked nights, weekends, and holidays in the neonatal intensive care unit (NICU) at a large hospital. When a premature baby was born, I was handed the baby by the obstetrician in the delivery room. My critical job was to maintain the newborn baby's airway, breathing, and heart rate. Once stabilized, some babies spent months in the unit.

Some of the premature babies did not survive. When a baby died, nurses performed postmortem care. We removed all of the tubes from the baby, then washed the baby and swaddled him or her in blankets. The hardest part for me was taking the baby to the morgue. When I laid a baby to rest in the morgue, I felt devoid of feelings. I had to shut off feelings to lay the baby in its place in the cold morgue and shut the metal door. It was a hard job. While I walked back to the nursery, I felt sad. But as I walked back through the doors, I would once again hear the beeping of machines. There was no time for emotion. It was back to work. The next baby needed me.

One cold winter morning after driving home from a night shift, I was sitting at the breakfast table with my maternal grandparents, who I was living with at the time. I was eating toast and drinking hot tea, when my grandmother handed me a brown manila envelope. I knew before I opened it that it was my military orders. The purpose of ROTC is largely to teach cadets the basics of being an Army Officer. After graduation, the new second lieutenants go to an Officer Basic Course specific to the branch they have been selected for, which in my case was Army Nurse Corps. I was to report to Fort Sam Houston, Texas, for the Nurse Corps Officer Basic Course in six weeks.

It was time to pay back Uncle Sam. The Army had paid my college tuition, and now I was to serve eight years. That was the contract I had signed.

On my last day in Pennsylvania, I got up before the sun rose. I took a walk in the neighbor's farm field. The air was clean and crisp. Even the manure smelled good to me. I was going to miss Pennsylvania.

Standing by my grandfather's favorite old oak tree, I watched the sun come up over the farmer's field. The colors of the sunrise were glorious. When I said goodbye to my grandmother, she had tears on her cheeks. I gave her a hug and choked back my own tears.

"I'll be back, Mommom," I said.

"I heard that once before," she said.

I realized she was struggling with memories of the Second World War.

"Don't make it harder for her, Norma," said my grandfather.

"Keep your chin up, Mommom," I said stoutly.

She laughed because she must have said that to me hundreds of times over the years.

I walked down my grandparents' front steps past the flag pole, where the American flag was waving in the early morning breeze.

Lieutenant

My Nurse Corps Officer Basic Course at Fort Sam Houston was ten weeks long, I spent a lot of time in the gym. I was running the track and getting in the best shape of my life. I thrived in the Army, which valued *meritocracy* and highly skilled soldiers.

When my course was over, I went to my permanent duty assignment at Fort Bragg, North Carolina. When I drove around the large post the first time, I saw soldiers wearing green, maroon, or black berets. Based on their muscular appearance and sharp uniforms, those soldiers made an immediate impression on me. This post was high speed.

When I turned the key and entered my new second-floor condominium, I thought I had died and gone to heaven. It was beautiful, with a balcony overlooking the inground swimming pool and pine trees. I had two large bedrooms, a huge jetted bathtub, a large closet, and even central air-conditioning! It was the first time in my life I had my own beautiful home. I was so happy. I was twenty-three years old and full of hope.

A few months later, on a warm September evening, I went to a cookout with another Army nurse. Her boyfriend, SSG Art Salisbury, introduced me to his friend SGT Jeff Dennis. Jeff and I spent the entire evening together, sitting outside enjoying the stars. We talked about our Army careers and how he wanted to be selected for the United States Army Parachute Team. After spending the evening together, we started dating. I had met my future husband.

Jeff had a sense of humor. He would start each day by telling me a joke, and I would laugh until I cried. Jeff was energetic and hardcore. He was Airborne qualified and jumped static line in an airborne unit. He spent off-duty weekends skydiving and socializing at the drop zone's bar. He loved the Army life.

Special Forces

In 1993, two Black Hawk helicopters went down in Somalia, and two Delta Force soldiers, Master Sergeant Gary Gordon and Sergeant First Class Randy Shughart, were killed defending the second Black Hawk crash site. By the end of the Battle of Mogadishu, eighteen Americans had been killed and eighty-four were wounded.

In the following months, Special Forces Operators occasionally convalesced on my hospital ward. One shift, I was assigned one and was walking to his bedside on the ward to administer some antibiotics. When I pulled back the curtain,

I saw his well-built military buddies standing around his bedside. I saw glass beer bottles in a cooler and in their hands.

The patient swallowed his mouthful of beer, then set the glass bottle on the hospital overbed table. He smiled a lightning-quick grin, flashing white teeth in his tanned skin.

"Hello, ma'am," he said.

His friend started to explain away the beer, but I stopped him. "I see nothing but all-American refreshments."

The soldiers smiled. I hung my patient's antibiotic and closed the curtain around them. Their jobs fell in a special category that allowed ordinary Americans to sleep well at night. If he wanted a beer, he could have it.

The Longest Shift

Yea, though I walk through the valley of the shadow of death, I will fear no evil.—Psalm 23

For my first year as a military nurse, most shifts had been the same. That was about to change.

Spring had come, and the sky was a clear blue. One day, I was on my way to work, listening to music and enjoying the beautiful warm weather. I enjoyed the warmth, light, and smells wafting in through my black Beretta's small rectangular sunroof. I wore my camouflage battle dress uniform (BDU) and black leather combat boots. As I approached the hospital, a military police officer (MP) was guarding the road. I slowed my car to a halt.

"Hurry, ma'am," the MP said with a salute after he noticed my Nurse Corps insignia.

I knew something was dreadfully wrong. I had never been stopped at the hospital entrance by the military police. My blood ran cold.

In the distance, I saw smoke billowing up toward the clear blue sky. I parked and sprinted toward the hospital, barely noticing the scent of the pine trees. I ran up several flights of steps to get a good view from the windows. I stood stark still at a large window momentarily staring at fire and smoke in the distance. Suddenly, a noise jolted me into motion. A voice on the intercom stated: "MASCAL. This is not a drill!"

I ran down the steps to my duty station and waited. Almost immediately, the doors opened, and medics were pushing a gurney bearing a severely burned soldier. Suddenly, there were so many more. Soldiers had first, second, and third degree burns. The smell of burned flesh penetrated my nostrils. I saw full thickness burns of charred black skin. The tension in the air was palpable. High levels of adrenaline permeated the treatment areas and were increasing by the second. I worked side by side with combat medics, doctors, and highly trained Special Forces medics. I administered morphine and placed Foley (urinary) catheters at the direction of one physician who shouted standing orders to nurses. I noticed a chaplain praying fervently for soldiers.

At one point, a severely burned soldier's eyes met mine with intensity. "Ma'am, am I going to die?" he asked.

"No," I said with reassurance. "You are going to be just fine," I said with a smile.

I called for a doctor to come to his bedside. I could see the doctor's urgency in his eyes. As I helped the doctor push the stretcher down the hallway, I noticed the soldier was facing his injuries with bravery and incredible strength of character. *Gallant* went through my mind.

I pushed the soldier's stretcher into the elevator, and the doctor stepped inside to accompany the patient. The elevator doors shut, and I never saw that soldier again.

At one point during the chaotic day, I had a fleeting thought of my now-fiancé, Jeff. That morning, he had told me he was going to get on the manifest to jump. I did not know if he was among those soldiers being treated. Was he part of these casualties? I pushed that thought out of mind and kept going. I had to.

Momentarily, my surroundings seemed to move slowly, and my hearing diminished. I noticed someone's lips moving.

"O negative blood, Lieutenant," he said again, as he passed a cold bag of blood to me. Holding something cold pulled me back to the moment. Moving quickly, I went to the bedside of a soldier whose hematocrit was critical due to significant blood loss.

"Captain, help me hang blood," I yelled.

"Just hang the blood, Lieutenant!" he yelled back.

My nursing school instructors would come unglued seeing me hang blood without a second nurse, I thought. But then my instructors were not Army nurses. Standard nursing care requires two nurses to review a blood product to avoid any mistakes. Not that day.

When I started the transfusion, I could feel sweat running down my back. I knew O negative blood (universal donor) was appropriate to hang, but the initial shock of mass casualties was wearing off, and the realization of the magnitude of what I was facing was dawning on me. *Nothing about this day is normal,* I thought. *Nothing.*

I moved between beds providing care. I saw more than burned charred flesh. Flying debris caused damage to organs and trauma to limbs. These injuries were part of my whirlwind shocking shift. Fresh surgical incision sites, bloody bandages, wound care, and burn care consumed me. My uniform had blood on it. The sweat dripped down my back. My mouth was dry.

I did not have time to talk to any of the soldiers about the enormity of what had happened to them that day. Some asked if I knew whether their buddies were alive.

Suddenly, someone hollered, "Lieutenant, phone call!"

"Take a message," I said. "I'm too busy."

"You need to take this call."

When I got to the phone, I heard it was Jeff on the line. When I heard his voice, I forced back tears. He was okay.

"I won't be coming home anytime soon," I said.

"I understand," he replied.

After I hung up the desk phone, I instantly compartmentalized my feelings and went to a soldier's bedside to administer pain medication.

After working the mass casualty event for more than six hours, I noticed that the sun had already gone down. I was still working, even though I felt my blood sugar plummeting. I was sweating and tired. I brushed back pieces of my brown hair that had come loose from my tight bun. I had a ward filled with soldiers who needed their bags of antibiotics hung to prevent infections.

When I was finally relieved after working well into the night, I looked down at my boots. They were covered in blood. My brown cotton T-shirt was soaked with sweat. My stomach was nauseated from lack of food, and I was dizzy from dehydration.

Slowly, I walked down the hospital stairs out into the fresh night air. I noticed I was alone in the stillness of the night. The stars above me were my only company as I trudged exhaustedly toward my car. A tang in the air from the pine needles was soothing.

As I approached my vehicle, I noticed a Rosary with black beads lying on the ground. I picked it up and put it in my pocket. I wondered if its owner was alive or dead.

While working the mass casualty event, we had no time to think, *How did this happen?* The next day, the magnitude of the disaster settled on me. For another four weeks, I worked extra hours, providing nursing care for the soldiers who remained hospitalized.

Later, a memorial was held for the soldiers who had been killed. I wanted to be present at the memorial to pay tribute to the dead soldiers, but I was working at the hospital. I felt shut out of the grieving process. I thought of charred skin, bloody bandages, and the closing elevator doors. Suddenly, I stood up from the nurses' desk. I shook it off, thinking, *You're a nurse. This is what you do. Suck it up.*

Too Young to Die

Over the next weeks and months, my shifts at work came and went. When I arrived for report one shift, I saw the crash cart by a patient's room. The crash cart holds emergency medication and supplies for resuscitation efforts. Through the glass windows, I could see the ongoing efforts of the outgoing shift.

One nurse was doing chest compressions on a handsome well-built soldier. Another nurse pushed medication into the intravenous line. The patient was stabilized with this medication, and his heart was now pumping on its own. The outgoing nurses left looking haggard. Another nurse and I were assigned this patient, who was fighting for his life. This critical situation was going to take both of our nursing efforts to keep him alive. The soldier was on a ventilator, which maintained his breathing artificially. His heart rate was unstable, so the crash cart remained at the doorway. I took a deep breath, took off my camouflaged blouse, and quickly drank a cold Coca-Cola.

Here we go. It's going to be a long night. Please, Lord, let him live.

Not long into my shift, the soldier's heart rate plummeted again. The cardiac monitor's alarm beeped while the heart beat was audibly slowing. His heart beat fell from 70 to 40 beats per minute. I started doing chest compressions with my hands positioned above the soldier's xyphoid process on his sternum. One, two, three, four, five, six, seven, eight, nine, ten, eleven, twelve, thirteen, fourteen, fifteen went the count. Each time the sergeant and I would stabilize the soldier. But after sixty minutes, his heart rate would fall again. It was an intense night.

My heart hurt for the soldier's family. I updated them on his condition as often as possible. I extended visiting hours, which allowed his family and fellow soldiers to go to his bedside anytime he was semi-stable. His wife was in shock. Her mother stayed by her side and helped watch her toddler, who was now sleeping in a reclining stroller. The soldier's buddies were resolute that they were not leaving. I had only met the soldier that day, but I believed he must have been a fine soldier to garner the love and respect I saw for him that night in the waiting room.

All my efforts were not enough. The soldier died, and my heart hurt.

Later that night, I took a shower at home with tears silently streaming down my face. I really wanted him to live. His body fought to live. He didn't go out easily. I felt incredibly drained. But I had to pull myself together. My next shift would begin in eight hours. That is the harsh reality of being a nurse.

It was hard to fall asleep. I was angry that my patient died so young. He was strong and muscular. It was so unfair. Death was ruthless. It took life whenever it wanted. *And it never gave back.*

Too Much Blood

"Help me, ma'am! Help me!"

Those were the last words of my patient. The monitor flatlined. I climbed up onto the bed, positioned my hands over his sternum, and started chest compressions.

"Sergeant!" I hollered. "We're coding!"

The anesthesiologist arrived within seconds and intubated the soldier. He started bagging the patient. We worked together like a well-oiled machine, trying to save my patient. The sergeant took over compressions while I hung blood. Another nurse administered medications from the crash cart. It was my turn to do chest compressions again. I was up on the bed, counting compressions out loud as I pushed on his chest. Suddenly, blood erupted from his mouth. The projectile blood hit my hair and right side of my uniform. I was covered in blood.

I continued the resuscitation efforts. We had exhausted all avenues of resuscitation. It was over. The doctor called it. He announced the time of death.

I did not want to stop. The patient had said to *me,* "Help me, ma'am."

His last words rang in my head. I was momentarily stunned. I took off my bloody gloves and placed them into the trash. I washed my hands and forearms and watched the blood swirl around the drain. I walked away and quickly drank a cold Coca-Cola at the nurses' station. Then, I started postmortem care on his body that was slowly getting cold. It was unsettling to me to feel cold flesh through my gloves. It was never easy for me. I bathed his body to wash off the blood. I wanted his body to be as dignified as it deserved. *As they all deserved.*

When I finished the hands-on tasks, I sat down at the nurses' desk with my hair and uniform still covered in dried blood. Now I had to meticulously chart—and relive—every detail of the code, death, and postmortem. I picked up a black pen and began to write. I pushed the soldier's pleads from my head.

I wish I could have helped you. I am so sorry.

Change of shift happened just as I finished charting. When I arrived home, I put my uniform in the washing machine to wash out the blood. I would drop it off for dry cleaning later so it would be starched and ironed.

I got in the shower and washed my hair. I watched as the soldier's blood mixed with the water while it circled the drain. I scrubbed my body clean. I felt detached. Apathy embraced me.

When I climbed into bed with wet hair, what happened at the hospital didn't seem real. My mind replayed events. Although my eyes were closed, I could see every part of him. I relived preparing my brother-in-arm's broken body for his family. I felt a hot tear stream down my face as my mind continued to paint the pictures.

I knew I did more than wash the blood off his body. I had felt the life leave his body. As his skin grew cold, I knew his soul had transitioned to the Mansion of the Lord. As I methodically washed each limb, hand, and finger, the stillness of his body that had no fight left was hard to bear. He had fought hard to live. I had changed the blood-stained sheet under his body. The crisp white sheet on the bed looked nice. As I draped a white sheet over his face and body, I had wondered if his mother knew and was weeping. I noticed the gold wedding ring. Was his wife crying? Did children know their daddy was not coming home?

Finally, the waves of fatigue overpowered my thoughts. I fell asleep and didn't wake until my alarm went off for the next shift.

Amputation

During my time as an Army nurse, I saw a wide range of injuries. It was difficult when a soldier lost an eye or limb. I nursed soldiers after gunshot wounds to the abdomen. I hung transfusions on soldiers who had arteries severed and repaired in surgery.

After one traumatic injury, a young soldier had a limb amputated. I received him as he rolled out of surgery. His stump was wrapped in a white bandage. I took a black marker and circled the blood on the bandage. In an hour, I would reassess the drainage. The soldier was on oxygen and very drowsy. I hung antibiotics to prevent infection. Although the soldier looked pale, he was stable.

Usually in these situations, the responsibility to orient a soldier fell on the bedside intensive care nurse. I wasn't sure how I was going to explain to this soldier that his limb had been amputated. I didn't know if he would remember anything that happened because he had been knocked unconscious from the traumatic injury. I prayed for the right words. I hoped the doctor would be nearby when the time arose.

I loved helping soldiers. I loved being a nurse. I took pride in being an officer. I had grown in my abilities, and I kept learning so I could be the best. But sometimes, I just needed sleep.

Turkey

I will be strong and courageous. I will not be terrified, or discouraged; for the Lord my God is with me where ever I go.
—Joshua 1:9

After one particularly tiring shift, I walked in the door and asked Jeff for a hug. He wrapped his strong arms around me, and I laid my head on his chest. It was comforting to hear his heart beating through his chest.

"I had a lousy day," I told Jeff.

"What you do is appreciated," he said.

I knew that nurses had saved Jeff's life a few years earlier when he was in a combat support hospital. In that moment, he told me the details of his medevac.

Jeff had boarded a Navy transport ship in Italy, headed for Turkey. His orders were to provide support for an Airborne unit whose mission was to support the Kurds.

Jeff had been in country for more than a month when his camp took a direct hit from a storm, which raged for more than twelve hours. Jeff and the soldiers with him struggled to hold the tent poles in the ground.

When the storm was over, the tent Jeff was in was the only one standing. There had been massive flooding during the storm, and the damage to the camp was catastrophic. Bivouac tents lay flattened on the muddy ground. The chow hall, supply tents, and the commo (communication) section were wiped out. *All* communication was down. The wooden latrines had been blown away, and the human excrement pit overflowed and contaminated the entire camp. Soldiers were walking in contaminated mud. There was no edible food, and all supplies and unforms were unusable.

Jeff and another soldier erected a makeshift antenna to get radio signals. They succeeded in establishing communication with an American unit in Germany. The closest Turkish airfield was temporarily closed. Vehicles were stuck in deep, thick mud and sat idle.

C130s air-dropped emergency supplies. Under the parachutes were pallets filled with bundles of military clothing, MREs (meals, ready to eat), and medical supplies.

Some soldiers were digging out vehicles from the mud. Others were gathering the supplies from the pallets. Injured soldiers were held in the medical tent, suffering from head injuries, lacerations, broken bones, and concussions.

After unloading pallets and working in the mud for three days, Jeff began to have intestinal cramping and diarrhea. He continued working for another day, even though he was struggling with episodes of vomiting and diarrhea. After twenty-four hours, he collapsed onto a cot in the medical tent. The vomiting subsided, but he had no control over his bowels. He had a fever and was moving in and out of consciousness. The medical tent had no anti-spasmodic medication to administer for Jeff's painful intestinal cramping. His fever climbed to a life-threatening 105 degrees.

In a desperate attempt to cool down Jeff's body, the nurses packed ice at his groin and under his arms. After each uncontrollable bout of diarrhea, he was getting weaker. He was moaning and extremely ill. Even though Jeff was receiving fluids through an IV in his arm, his condition continued to deteriorate.

An older doctor, a colonel, entered the medical tent.

"He has dysentery. Medevac him out of here right now," the doctor said.

Jeff was moved by stretcher to a Humvee that had been dug out of the mud. It took him to a Black Hawk helicopter (UH-60) waiting for him in a field. The Black Hawk flew him to an airport where an Air Force medical airplane was waiting.

On the flight from Turkey to Germany, an Air Force nurse treated Jeff as he went in and out of consciousness. He recovered in an Army military hospital in Germany in an open-bay ward. He lost twenty-five pounds.

When Jeff regained his strength, there were pertinent practical issues to address. During medevac, he was wearing a chocolate-chip-patterned uniform that was air-dropped by the C130, with no nametag nor unit patch on it. Instead of boots, he wore blue hospital flip-flops. He had no money, no military ID card, and no underclothes.

A military liaison drove Jeff around post. A new ID card was issued. Finance authorized an advance on pay. All the while, Jeff was wearing the uniform from the C130 air drop and blue flip-flops. His next stop was the post exchange (PX) to buy proper military clothing and boots.

As Jeff was about to enter, a Sergeant Major stopped him. Jeff automatically went to parade rest.

"You know you are out of uniform!" the SGM questioned him.

After listening to Jeff's explanation, the SGM's demeanor changed from anger to understanding. Jeff bought clothing at the PX, and the military liaison drove him to the airfield. He flew on a military transport from Germany to Italy. He was grateful to the doctor and nurses who saved his life.

"You will not save every soldier," Jeff said gently, after he had finished the story. "All you can do is your best. The rest is up to God." Jokingly he added, "At least the injured and sick have a beautiful nurse to look at."

Laughing, I threw a pillow at him. Jeff knew how to lighten my mood.

Chapter 4: Early Marriage

It's better to be a lion for a day than a sheep all your life.
—Elizabeth Kenny

Those days Jeff was jumping at the drop zone (DZ) as much as possible because he wanted to make the United States Army Parachute Team. He was very talented. On the other hand, I was a novice.

One cold wintery day in November, I jumped from a Twin Otter from 12,500 feet. I arched my back to stabilize my free fall as I had been taught. I was jumping with an accelerated free fall (AFF) instructor because I was still on student status. I was only in free fall for a moment when suddenly I felt a pull from my back. Wham! The round reserve opened unexpectedly, without the reserve handle being pulled. I could not believe it. I was at an incredibly high altitude—11,000 feet—and now at the mercy of the wind because a round reserve cannot be steered like a square parachute.

I saw the Twin Otter doing a normal rapid descent because the pilot flies multiple loads of jumpers per day. I was now descending through clouds. I could not see the ground whatsoever. My hands were getting very cold. I was wearing gloves, but they were not keeping out the cold. Every 1,000 feet up in altitude, the temperature drops 3 degrees.

At 10,000 feet, I was under canopy, and it was 30 degrees lower than the ground temperature. It was cold, and my fingertips became numb. There was absolutely nothing I could do during that parachute reserve ride. Ever so slowly, I descended.

There was a lot of wind, and I knew I was being blown off course. I would never land on the DZ. I was under canopy going through the clouds with limited visibility. I tried to enjoy the ride. I would reach out and try to touch a beautiful white cloud, but it would slip through my gloved fingers as a cold mist.

Finally, I was below the clouds, and I could see the horizon and scenery. I wondered where I would land. When I descended enough to know approximately where I would land, I mentally reviewed the procedure for a water landing. I was approaching Mont Lake. I did not want to drown.

Fear went through me like ice water. I was doing a mental checklist: Release the harness when my feet touch the water. Get to the surface right away. If the parachute lands on top of me, I needed to swim under it to avoid entanglement with the lines and canopy, then quickly swim to the shore because the water would be very cold. I had never dreamed I might face a water landing in November—with no one nearby.

I am a strong swimmer. I can do this.

Thankfully, I landed on the *very edge* of the shore of the large lake—not in the water. What a difference a few feet make. Thank God I was not in the icy cold water. I had been blown approximately ten miles from the DZ. I was so happy to be on the ground. Because I was under the round parachute, the landing had been hard. The wind whipped at me from the lake, and I was cold.

I started putting my parachute into the rig. It was time to walk out and find a road. As I walked, I shook off the reserve ride. I couldn't believe I had been under a round reserve parachute instead of the main square parachute. I didn't know why my reserve deployed. I was just happy to be on the ground. Finally, I came to a road.

An elderly couple picked me up and drove me back to the DZ. Inwardly, I laughed at myself. Here I was hitchhiking again, which reminded me of my teenage years. I was grateful for the warmth in their car. As I shook off the danger of what had just happened, I was pumped to be alive. Upon inspection, my instructor saw my automatic activation device (AAD) had malfunctioned and deployed the round reserve parachute. That jump surely did not go as expected.

Tomorrow is another day, I thought.

Deployed to Haiti

Be courageous. Do not be afraid. God goes with you
—Deuteronomy 31:6

Jeff received orders to deploy to Haiti for Operation Uphold Democracy. We didn't know it then, but he would go to Haiti *twice*. He needed to report to 3rd Special Forces Group in a few hours. We were lying in bed next to each other. I had my head on his chest, and I was listening to his heart beat.

He drifted to sleep easily, and I always wondered how he could fall asleep on a dime. I lay awake, listening to him breathe.

I laid there wishing he did not have to go. When his alarm beeped, he got up and put on his uniform and boots. In the dark of night, we drove to Group. He kissed me goodbye, grabbed his gear, and walked into the arms room. I didn't want to drive away. Another soldier opened the door to enter the arms room, and I saw Jeff holding an M16. The thought occurred to me that he could be shot at in that unstable country. I shook it off and drove away. We were living on a prayer, *again*.

One evening when I was watching the local news, I was caught by surprise. The MASCAL was being discussed. It had been nine months since that long day. The broadcast was showing footage of the disaster. I had never seen the footage before. The news anchor announced *all* the names of the dead. I started crying uncontrollably. I sobbed. I was inconsolable. I felt like someone had punched me in the stomach.

Jeff had been gone over a month. All I wanted was for him to hold me. Haiti felt very far away in that moment. I felt incredibly lonely, and lack of sleep was making me emotional. I had just finished a long shift at the military hospital, and I was exhausted. I wrapped myself up in blankets and cried myself to sleep.

Parachute Accident

If your nerve deny you, go above your nerve.
—*Emily Dickinson*

On one beautiful clear day, I went to jump with Tim, a very experienced skydiver on the United States Army Parachute Team and a videographer of the competition eight-way team. He was instructing me on my last jump to complete my accelerated free fall (AFF) certification.

The Twin Otter slowly climbed to altitude, and I had a great view of the ground and the DZ. The wind drift indicator showed which way the wind was blowing near the DZ. The spotter directed the pilot to fly the airplane to the best location for the jumpers to exit the aircraft based on the wind. No one wants a bad spot, making it hard to land on the DZ.

"Are you ready?" Tim asked loudly over the roar of the airplane engine.

"Yes!" I yelled.

Ready. Set. Out.

We had a great jump.

We were in freefall, which is 177 feet per second, or 120 mph, and lasts approximately sixty seconds. We waved off, and I tracked away to separate and give enough space to deploy canopies.

When I went to pull my pilot chute, I could not find the hacky sack, which should have been on my right side. I reached and tried three times and could not find it. Jeff once told me if I try three times and can't find it, pull the reserve because I would be beginning the ground rush. I pulled the reserve, but at the exact same time, Tim pulled my pilot chute because he didn't see me reaching for the reserve handle. And I didn't know he was pulling my pilot chute because he tracked in behind me.

When I looked up, I had a tangled mess of two chutes above me. I thought about cutting away the main, but the lines of both chutes were wrapped around one another, and I had one parachute partially inflated.

"Jesus, save me," my heart and soul cried out.

I had no control of the tangled mess above me. I was descending toward high voltage transmission power lines.

"Jesus, save me!" I screamed.

"Please, Jesus!" I begged God's mercy one more time.

I had a fleeting thought that Jeff would get notified that I was dead.

"I'm sorry, Jeff. I'm so sorry," I said aloud.

I barely made it over the high transmission voltage lines and descended toward the tall pine trees. I tucked my arms in to protect them as I hit the first branches. I heard the snap of the first branch, and I do not remember the hard hit into the ground after the fall through the pine trees.

Mercifully, I have no recollection of the painful impact when my body hit the ground. I was knocked unconscious. When I opened my eyes, all I saw was white. I heard a bird in the distance and smelled pine. For a split second, I thought I was in heaven.

"Tori!" I heard my name being shouted in the distance.

My gloved hand felt pine needles. I realized I was on the ground, and the white was the nylon reserve parachute covering my face. When I moved my left arm, it was painful. I bent the toes on each of my feet and was relieved to discover I was not paralyzed. I rolled to my side and slowly sat up. The guys had found me in the woods.

I was dazed, and the events that followed are foggy. I remember going to the Army hospital. I had a fractured forearm, which was placed in a cast, and a concussion. My head hurt.

I don't remember who contacted Jeff. But when I returned home from the hospital, he called. He was using a satellite phone from the commo section. I hated telling him what happened when he was so far from home. But I told him that I was fine, even though my fractured arm was killing me, and my headache was intense.

Jeff told me to go to church when I felt better. I was shocked. We were not a religious couple. He shared that he had been reading a Bible in Haiti. He was leaning heavily on God during his deployment. I promised I would go and give thanks to God.

That accident was a turning point in my life. In my most vulnerable moment, I had cried out to God. I do believe God heard me.

Christian Conversion

I started going to church after Jeff's second deployment to Haiti. My conversion to Christianity was simple. I went to church and met a beautiful Black woman named Dolly. She patiently shared the Gospel with me. A metaphorical veil was lifted from my eyes and stubborn heart. I was convicted. In that moment, I had faith in Jesus Christ as my Lord and Savior. I was baptized and started a whole new life. That was the beginning of my imperfect walk with God.

Promotion

While Jeff was in Haiti, I was promoted to First Lieutenant. I took my oath with several military friends in attendance. Major Russ Wyler gladly administered my oath. He was assigned to 3rd Special Force Group, 2nd Battalion. Captain Eric Bush was the second officer present and was assigned to 3rd Special Forces Group, 2nd Battalion, Charlie Company, ODA—361. Jennifer, a fellow Nurse Corps officer, was present to cheer me on. Max, a Command Sergeant Major serving in Delta Force, was the highest-ranking enlisted present for my promotion. I was blessed to have such incredible military people stand with me during my promotion.

I, Tori Hope Dennis, having been appointed an officer in the Army of the United States, as indicated above in the grade of First LIEUTENANT do solemnly swear that I will support and defend the Constitution of the United States against all enemies, foreign and domestic, that I will bear true faith and allegiance to the same; that I take this obligation freely, without any mental reservation or purpose of evasion; and that I will well and faithfully discharge the duties of the office on which I am about to enter. SO HELP ME GOD.

The promotion ceremony was perfect—except for Jeff's absence.

Letters from Jeff

Do not be afraid. Be strong and courageous
—Joshua 10:25

I received loving, hand-written letters from Jeff while he was in Haiti. I checked the mailbox at the end of the driveway every day. I mailed him letters through the Army Post Office (APO). His letters are a window into his heart and reflect his love and vulnerability.

JAN 95

Hello sweety. I love you, miss you, and need you in my life. You are the best thing that has ever happened to me, and I'm thankful for that. I can't even imagine what life would be like without you. I live for you. I'm not feeling that well knowing that you were in that parachute accident. You really need to thank God for watching over you. I sure thanked him. I really would like to see you again, alive. I went to church this morning. That really helped a lot. I thought and prayed for us. I love you so much, Tori Hope. Hope you are taking care of yourself.

We are going away in the next couple of days. We are taking a trip about six hours from here. We will be delivering food, meds, and supplies to nuns at the orphanage. It is only seventy kilometers away and takes six hours. The roads are terrible.

I'll be home as soon as I can. The Sergeant Major in 3rd SF-G(A) mentioned that they were probably going to start sending many of the service units back within the next month. I don't know. If I think June, anything else will just be a blessing. My love for you now is so much stronger than it has ever been. I love you, babe. Well, I just really needed to write and tell you these things. You mean everything to me, Tori. I will always be your man and your best friend. You can depend on me for anything, sweety. This will all be over with before you know it, and we will be back together. Sending all my sweet thoughts. Love you so very much, sweetheart! With the deepest of love, Jeff

P.S. Give Javelin a bone for me. I sure miss my dog.

JAN 95

Hello darling, I'm twelve hundred miles from home and without you. You mean more to me than you will ever know. You are so very important and special in my life. I can't wait to hug you.

You can thank my buddy, Sergeant Alan Davis, for helping me coordinate this surprise. I mailed him money to buy the most beautiful flowers he could find. It was the only way I could get flowers to you.

I hope your fractured arm is healing. Don't do anything to hurt yourself. You've got the rest of your life to skydive. You and I will be skydiving together before long.

We went to Hinche to deliver food to the orphanage. Roads are terrible.

I just finished running three and a half miles. I got your package today. Thanks for the Ivory soap. Thanks for the letter also. Can't wait to get back home. Word is, we may be back to the states by middle March. I'll write again in a few days and let you know how things are going down here. I love you, babe! Jeff

Not Invincible

All I had to connect me to Jeff were his hand-written letters, an occasional short satellite phone call, and television cable news.

Because it was winter, the sun set early, which made my mood a bit gloomy.

On January 13, 1995, I unlocked my door and heard the phone ringing. I was just getting home from working a long day at the hospital. Normally, I took my combat boots off at the door. Not this time. It could be Jeff calling. Wearing my military uniform, hair in a bun, boots on, I raced to the phone.

"Is this the wife of SGT Dennis?" the female caller asked.

My heart started racing. "Yes, this is she."

"I'm calling all the wives for 3rd Special Forces Group. There was a situation in Haiti. I want you to know that your husband is fine."

I dropped to my knees and tried to process what she just said.

I hadn't seen the news because I had been working all day. I quickly turned on the television. Cable news was reporting one soldier killed and another soldier wounded from Jeff's unit. I was glad I received her call prior to watching the news. That was the first American soldier to die by hostile fire since US forces had landed months before in Haiti. He was shot at a military checkpoint on a remote road. The same roads Jeff drove on.

Decades later, I learned that Jeff had seen the Special Forces medic (18D) in his blood-soaked uniform after aid efforts had been rendered.

After that, I did not receive many letters from Jeff. He was driving all over the remote roads of Haiti. I was living on a prayer, yet at the same time, I felt the false sense of invincibility that youth provides. I never believed anything could happen to Jeff.

One cold day in February, I received a short letter from Jeff. I read it as I walked from the mailbox to the front porch.

FEB 95

Darling, Sorry I haven't written. They are really serious about home by mid-March. That will give me time to put my packet together for the United States Army Parachute Team. LT Belvin already told me that I can go try out. I want to make the team this year. I still love you more than anything, sweetheart. I think of you all the time. I'll be seeing you soon. With all my heart, Jeff

Happiness

In March, Jeff flew back from Haiti in a C130. I took him to the officers' club to celebrate. He was so hungry for steak. The chef brought out a rolling table for each patron to choose their size and cut of meat. Jeff had him special cut a forty-eight-ounce filet mignon steak. Jeff said it was the best steak he ever ate, and he ate every ounce of it.

He was glad to be home. He had spent most of his time in Haiti driving on the remote mountainous terrain and over the washed-out dirt roads. The Special Forces teams were spread out across Haiti, providing humanitarian assistance and establishing order. Jeff drove across challenging terrain in a Humvee to the teams who were in rural remote areas. The mosquitoes were a pestilence. The roads were difficult to navigate. The locals could not be trusted. Jeff was glad to be home, eating steak in an air-conditioned restaurant with his pickup truck parked outside.

While we ate, we talked about our future. Jeff decided to submit his application to try out for the Golden Knights. Afterward, the wait began to see if he would be selected for tryouts. In the meantime, we went to the DZ and jumped together often.

One especially beautiful morning, I was so happy to be at the DZ with Jeff. The Twin Otter took off and slowly made its climb to 12,500 feet. The view was always spectacular through the open jump door. Jeff and I exited and were in free fall together. A photographer took our picture. Jeff kissed me in free fall, and that picture is one of our most treasured photos.

We waved off, and I tracked away. I pulled my pilot chute, and "wooosh" my parachute opened. I felt peaceful under the open parachute. I watched how others were setting up to land. I saw the direction of the wind as the orange windsock waved in the air.

I set up for my landing. I maneuvered the parachute downwind, turned for base, then turned for final approach. I flared the parachute and landed. I was ecstatic. It was a great jump. I was glad we had photos taken of us in free fall together and photos of my parachute landing. What a fun day.

I started planning a church wedding to renew our previous wedding vows. Jeff and I had already eloped in a civil ceremony standing before a judge in an old Southern courthouse. The building was picturesque with marble columns and located in a small rural town with cotton fields and cows grazing in pastures. We had worn jeans and Teva sandals.

At our church wedding. I wore a beautiful, silk wedding gown, and Jeff wore a black tuxedo. It was quite a contrast from the day we eloped wearing jeans. We lit a unity candle, kneeled at the altar, exchanged vows and rings, and promised for better or worse, in sickness and in health. Jeff's brother was his best man. All our immediate family was there. It was wonderful to celebrate our marriage.

Jeff had never been to Pennsylvania. We visited the Liberty Bell in Philadelphia and toured Valley Forge, where Jeff loved the Washington Memorial Chapel. We spent time driving around Amish country in Lancaster, Pennsylvania. We had a wonderful time. I loved sharing places with Jeff that were meaningful to me.

For our honeymoon, we stayed in a lake house on Lay Lake in Alabama. Jeff drove a pontoon boat to the middle of the lake and turned off the motor. We sunbathed on the boat in the warm Alabama sunshine while an occasional wake rocked the boat. It was peaceful. In the early morning hours, we sat on a pier together and fished. It was nice to have quiet time with Jeff. He and I were always full speed ahead. Quiet time was good for us.

When we returned to post, Jeff received orders. He was chosen for tryouts! He would report in September for the United States Army Parachute Team's annual assessment and selection, along with twenty-seven other soldiers.

The Golden Knight tryouts are grueling, and after two months, only eight men were remaining. The other twenty had been cut or quit.

One afternoon, the doorbell rang. I opened the door, and Jeff was standing there in a Golden Knight jacket! What a happy surprise! He did it! Tryouts were over. He was on the team.

A short time later, I was seated on bleachers anxiously waiting for the Knighting ceremony to begin. The eight soldiers jumped from the army aircraft flying above the parade field, performed a parachute demonstration, and landed very accurately on target on the parade field. After the spectacular entrance, they lined up and stood at attention. As each man's name was called, he knelt. Then he was ceremonially knighted with a sword that touched each shoulder. This top-notch Knighting ceremony was fitting because the Golden Knights are one of the most elite teams in the United States Army.

I waddled as I walked to greet Jeff because as I was eight months pregnant. He hugged me gently. I was so relieved to see him. It felt nice to have a hug. He had slept at the barracks during tryouts for two long months.

On that beautiful October day, I was so happy. Jeff had accomplished his dream to be a Golden Knight. I was about to have our first baby. We were so happy together. Our world was perfect.

Mass Shooting

The day of the mass shooting at the stadium on post, I was not certain of Jeff's location. That early in the morning, he should have been running the trails near the stadium. News of the mass shooting on post spread quickly. Because we didn't yet have cellphones, I called Jeff's work number at 3rd SFG (A). It rang and rang. I desperately was trying to remember what he mentioned the night before. *Didn't he say he was going to run with his Sergeant Major today? Where?*

I caught my breath. My heart started racing. I shook off the feeling of dread. Eventually, my phone rang. It was Jeff, and he was fine. He had been running with a buddy on the wooded trails doing their own PT less than two miles from the mass shooting.

The mass shooting had occurred at the stadium where there were 1,300 paratroopers in morning formation. Sergeant William Kreutzer opened fire and killed one soldier, paralyzed another, and wounded seventeen others. Several Special Forces soldiers ambushed Kreutzer from behind, stopping him from shooting anyone else. He was arrested by the MPs.

The hospital was busy treating the soldiers who were shot. After that incident, I didn't look at the world quite the same.

Chapter 5: Motherhood

Nine months had flown by. I was happily anticipating the arrival of our baby girl. Now that the mass shooting faded into the background of my thoughts, I was able to relax. Our world felt perfect. Jeff was skydiving at the DZ with the Knights. He was home every night, which was nice. He had missed a lot of my pregnancy while he was at tryouts.

My pregnancy was not planned, but it was a joy nonetheless. Looking at how large my abdomen was now, I couldn't believe I was rucking just seven months before. I smiled remembering it. Jeff and I were doing a ruck march together. He had led the pace, and I followed him with my ruck on my back. We rucked about three miles and were about a mile out from home, when I told Jeff I had to stop. This was uncharacteristic of me.

Jeff put my ruck on his back on top of his ruck, and he walked home. I moved at a snail's pace the rest of the way home. The next day, I was feeling better after a good night's sleep. We went to the DZ and did a skydive together. I had to leave early because I had to report for duty and work the evening shift at the hospital.

When I arrived for work, I told one of the doctors that I felt fatigued. He suggested taking a pregnancy test. I laughed, but agreed. I was standing at the nurses' station when a sergeant handed lab results to me. I was pregnant!

I called Jeff and told him right away. He was over the moon. He predicted it would be a girl. Life as I knew it had just changed. I had jumped from a plane a few hours earlier. In an instant, that ended.

The next day, I called my mom and shared the news. I asked my mom if she remembered the day I was born. She remembered every detail. When she arrived to the labor ward, women were screaming and thrashing around, their extremities banging into the metal side bars of the hospital beds. She could see the women were restrained and tied to the beds.

My mom believed if she could keep her mind, she could breathe and relax her way through labor. When a nurse in a white cap and uniform came to her bedside to give her medication, she refused. When she needed to push, she was rolled into the delivery room. The doctor used forceps to deliver me, held me upside down by the feet, and smacked my bottom to cause me to breathe.

With my mom's next baby, she labored at home purposefully. She arrived at the hospital giving the staff only enough time to catch a baby.

Birth never ceased to amaze me.

Labor and Delivery

The crib was assembled. The nursery was organized. All we needed was our baby. My due date came and went. When I was almost two weeks past my due date, I drank castor oil in orange juice. Castor oil acts as a stimulant to the bowels, which irritates the uterus and causes contractions. I started having mild contractions after the castor oil cleansed my colon. I lost my mucus plug, which is a normal blood-tinged mucus passing that often signals the start of early labor. I was glad the Army hospital had midwives on staff, having so long ago recognized the stark comparison between medicalized hospital births and births attended by midwives.

I remained at home during early labor. I walked outside and enjoyed the fresh air. I soaked in a warm tub and relaxed. Jeff lit a fire in our fireplace, and I sat near the hearth for the warmth on my back. I ate a good meal and drank plenty of fluids.

I instinctively labored using four elements: earth, air, fire, and water. Those elements ground a woman while she is going through the process of labor.

Walking, standing, and swaying connected me to the *earth*.

I loved the fresh *air*. Focusing on slowly *breathing* through each contraction relaxed me, which increased oxytocin and endorphins and decreased adrenaline. Oxytocin creates strong, effective contractions naturally, and endorphins provided me with my own pain medication. Endorphins are chemical compounds that have a pain-relieving effect ten times more potent than morphine. Decreasing adrenaline stops the stress response, which allowed me to have less pain in labor. Breathing and staying calm helps the progression of labor.

Sitting by the *fire* allowed my brain to go primal, away from the thinking mind.

Taking a bath in warm *water* allowed me to relax and decreased my pain. Endorphins took me to a dream-like mental state, which I call "labor land."

When night came, I went outside to feel the refreshing, cold, crisp December air. I sat down on a wooden bench on our backyard deck, gazed at the stars, and thought of the other women around the world who were in labor with me at that moment. In every continent on Earth, women were in labor. It was an incredulous realization.

I went to sleep in my bed, wrapped in a warm blanket, knowing active labor was coming. In the middle of the night, I woke to strong contractions. I felt ready to go to the hospital.

When I arrived at the hospital, I felt a shift from laboring at home. The bright lights were trying to pull me out of labor land. I kept my eyes closed. The doctor wanted to break my water and start Pitocin to increase uterine contractions. My dear friend Marina was my advocate. She requested a midwife provide care for me, and I was assigned a wonderful midwife named Ruth, who agreed with my birth plan to allow labor to progress naturally.

Seven hours passed, and I was stalled at six centimeters. Ruth discussed options. I could choose to do nothing. I could opt to have her break my water, which is called "artificial rupture of membranes." I could agree to augment labor with Pitocin. I chose for her to break my water. As soon as my membranes were ruptured, I felt a change in my pain level. It was now harsh.

Within minutes, I told the nurse I was feeling pressure. She checked and said I was still six centimeters. The nurse left the room.

After a few more minutes, I emphatically told Marina, "The baby is coming!"

Marina left the room and found the midwife. Ruth checked, and I had progressed rapidly to ten centimeters and was ready to push. Ruth suggested birthing in side-lying position because she found women experienced less tearing. When birth was near, I turned onto my side. In a moment, I was holding my beautiful, dark-haired baby girl. When I stole a glance at Jeff, I saw tears in his eyes.

When I think about my first birth, I am grateful for Marina and my midwife, Ruth Cole. I avoided augmentation with Pitocin, and I did not have an epidural nor episiotomy. Thankfully, I did not need stitches at the perineum. The best part was Ruth encouraged me to lie on my side to push. I had no need for Lithotomy position nor stirrups.

Holding my baby in my arms was the happiest time in my entire life. The love I felt was indescribable. When I gazed into her eyes, I felt the purest love I've ever known. Being a mother is the most rewarding gift on Earth. I felt pure contentment. Looking into my baby's soft eyes, I was transformed into a mother.

Goodbye

What will be, will be.—Irviline Marie Reppert

One cold January morning, Jeff put his duffle into our car. He turned the key in the ignition to warm up the car for our newborn. She needed to stay warm on this cold, bitter January day. He was leaving for annual winter training with the Golden Knights, flying out on a military aircraft, the Fokker F27. Our daughter was only six weeks old, but duty was taking her daddy across the country. Once Jeff said the car was warmed up, he carried her out to the car seat. I sat in the backseat next to her. She was sound asleep, snuggled warmly in her rear-facing car seat.

As Jeff pulled into the headquarters parking lot, my heart started to beat quickly. I knew I was returning to duty in two weeks as an Army Nurse, and I was mentally preparing for parenting alone while working full time.

After Jeff parked the car, I moved to the front seat. He took my hand and kissed it. He gently touched my cheek with his hand.

"Take care of my baby. Take care of my family. Our family," he said, looking into my eyes.

"I will," I promised.

That promise in the car on that cold winter morning would keep our family together in the hard days to come. That promise ended up meaning everything to me and carried me through some of the most heart-wrenching moments of my life.

But that morning, we were a husband and wife saying goodbye with the intention of him returning home in two months.

I watched Jeff walk across the parking lot, getting farther away from the car with every step. Tears stung my eyes, and I quickly wiped them away. I did not want him to go, and he didn't want to leave. I kept watching him walk away.

Jeff was wearing black pants and his black Golden Knights team jacket. He walked tall like a soldier, and he looked handsome with his fresh military haircut and muscular arms and thighs. He was very well built and a talented parachutist.

That was the last time I would ever see Jeff walk on his own two feet, completely free of injury.

Nanny

When I walked back into my house, it was strangely quiet. I felt so lonely, even though the baby was with me. I snuggled her into her bassinet. I was missing Jeff already, and he had just left.

I sighed, then the phone rang. I wondered if it could be Jeff. It was my paternal grandmother, Irviline, who announced she was coming to stay with me for at least a month to help me transition back to work. My father was driving three hours one way to bring her. I was so relieved. I had to return to duty soon. I just did not see how I could walk out the door and leave the baby, particularly after I just watched Jeff walk away. Knowing my grandmother was on her way gave me strength. I knew I could do this. And Jeff would be home in a few short months.

Irviline was no stranger to adversity. Her life had been filled with unexpected tragic events, starting with the death of her mother, who had died in childbirth when Irviline was only five years old. The afterbirth came before the baby, which is called a "complete placenta previa." The baby was stillborn, and her mother bled to death. Irviline had been devastated by her mother's death. She wished her mother would have lived to help her with the challenges of life.

Irviline married at age fifteen. She lived on a dairy farm with her husband and his parents. By her sixteenth birthday, she was visibly pregnant. Unexpectedly, she went into labor early. The country doctor came to the farm to deliver the baby, as was commonplace in 1940.

While laboring, she held onto ropes that were tied to the headboard. Clinging to one rope in each hand helped her cope with the painful contractions. The palm of the hand has a pressure point, and women instinctively grab and hold tight because this pressure point reduces pain. Irviline's mother-in-law sponged her off with cool water. After hours of labor, she gave birth to a premature baby girl. Then a surprise happened. She gave birth to a second baby. Her mother-in-law placed them in tiny boxes lined with flannel cloth and kept them warm near the wood stove. She fed them warm milk through a medicine dropper. One twin lived, but the other twin died. That is how life was.

In 1944, Irviline's husband was drafted into the Army. While the war raged on, she worked in a factory while raising her surviving daughter. Family members kept her baby while she worked swing shifts. Irviline keenly understood the challenge of being a soldier's wife and a working mother.

Irviline's husband died in combat during World War II. When she received a telegram from Western Union informing her with regret that her husband was killed in action in Europe, she collapsed onto the front porch. Her father picked her up and carried her inside. She was widowed at age twenty.

"How did you manage, Nanny?" I asked my grandmother.

"What will be, will be," was what Nanny said to me.

Having Nanny with me calmed my anxiety. She told me not to worry about Jeff.

"It does not do any good to worry," she said. Nanny was giving back love that family members gave her so many years ago.

The night before I had to go back to work, she reminded me not to worry about the baby.

"The baby will be fine. I promise," she said.

Early the next morning, dressed in my uniform and boots with my hair in a tight bun, I was ready to walk out the door for duty. Nanny was holding my baby, and she could tell I was ready to cry.

"Now you *know* I am *not* going to let anything happen to your baby," she said.

I knew she was right.

I walked out the front door onto the porch, met by the cold February air. With a long day ahead of me, I had to get my mind together. I wondered how critical my patient would be. I knew I would find out soon during morning report.

"What will be, will be," Nanny's voice said in my head.

United States Army Parachute Team

I had been back at work for a month. Life was busy. Between caring for a newborn and working at the hospital, I had no extra time.

Every evening, Jeff called for a few minutes. We could only speak briefly because long distance phone bills were costly. Prior to cellphones, the phone company billed long distance charges for out-of-state calls. At least we could speak daily, I consoled myself. That was much better than when he was in Haiti.

Jeff was busy, too. The Army Golden Knights jump out of planes at 14,000 feet or 2½ miles above the Earth. Parachutes must be deployed by 2,000 feet off the ground because no low pulls are allowed as per safety protocol. The paratroopers land on a target that is ten feet square, but each demonstrator often lands in the center, which is the size of a pizza. They train hard and jump approximately eight times per day. Jeff had more than 1,000 jumps.

Members of the elite United States Army Parachute Team are rare athletes. They are soldiers, parachutists, and demonstrators. They travel the United States as ambassadors for the Army, inspiring spectators with their breathtaking skydiving and parachute maneuvers.

During training, Jeff and his fellow soldier Matt jumped from the F27 to perform a Diamond track. They popped smoke from their left leg bracket and tracked away from each other. At a predetermined altitude, usually 7500 feet, they turned and tracked toward one another to form a diamond in the sky with the smoke that trailed from their feet. Jeff and Matt were tracking at a speed of 300 mph toward each other. They would pass each other with only ten feet between them.

The Diamond track was the most dangerous of all the skydiving maneuvers. Two years earlier, Jeff's friend, SSG Jose Aguillon, was killed instantly after colliding with SFC Dana

Bowman during the Diamond track maneuver. Dana lived, but had both lower legs amputated. Jeff had served and skydived with Jose in Italy, and his death was a shock. But it did not deter Jeff from serving in the Army as a Golden Knight.

Jeff was an incredibly talented, highly trained parachutist. I never worried about him jumping. Deaths and injuries were very rare.

Chapter 6: The Unforeseen

My hope is built on nothing less than Jesus' blood and righteousness. On Christ the solid rock I stand. All other ground is sinking sand. —*Edward Mote*

Having my paternal grandmother at my home was such a great help to me. In March, my mother-in-law came for a visit. I was lucky to have a good mother-in-law, and we had a loving relationship. She called me Ruth, and I called her Naomi because we loved each other like the women of that Bible story.

Every night, I was up every three hours with a three-month-old baby. When my alarm went off, I went to work sleep deprived.

As I got into my car to drive home from work, I was exhausted. But I was happy to go home to my grandmother and mother-in-law. One day, I was just getting home from work when the phone rang. It was Jeff. His voice was strained. He was obviously in pain. It was an incredibly quick conversation. I learned he was in the emergency room in Yuma. He had been in a parachute training accident and was being taken to a military hospital in California. After he hung up the phone, I regretted not getting more information. I was glad his mother was at my house. I could feel the anxiety rising in my chest. When I went to sleep, I hadn't heard from him. I had no idea what was happening. I was powerless.

I was awake breastfeeding the baby in the middle of the night when the phone rang again. It was Jeff. He quickly explained his diagnosis. He had compartment syndrome, and emergency surgery was necessary to relieve the pressure in his entire foot. Swelling was cutting off circulation to his foot. Compartment syndrome is a painful, dangerous condition caused by pressure buildup of tissue swelling. Only later did I learn that Jeff's calcaneus (heel) bone had been crushed in his foot from the high speed impact with the ground. The catastrophic injury caused the swelling that was increasing the pressure in the compartments in his foot.

A nurse graciously had allowed Jeff to call me before rolling him into the operating room. He was on a stretcher outside the operating room, and she held the phone receiver to his ear. The phone call lasted less than one minute. He promised he would call me later. He was at Balboa Naval Medical Center in San Diego, California. He was so far away. I was on the east coast, and he was on the west coast. He might as well have been on the moon.

After I hung up, my mother-in-law came into the room. She had heard the phone ring.

"Jeff needs emergency surgery," I said and felt the fear hit me like a tsunami. I had very limited information. I visualized the nurses transferring his body to the operating room table. I knew they were washing his skin with cold antiseptics before the surgeon would take a scalpel blade to his skin. The last thing he would remember was the mask being placed on his face. I wondered if our baby's face went through his mind as the anesthesia took effect.

The baby stretched out in my arms, and I snapped out of my heart-wrenching thoughts. I kissed her forehead and handed her to Nanny. I was so grateful to have both Nanny and my mother-in-law with me.

I noticed the time on the clock. I had to report for duty soon. I showered, put on my Army uniform, and left the baby in the capable hands of loving family.

Jeff's first surgery was to relieve the pressure in his foot. The surgeon performed several fasciotomies on his foot to open the tissue to relieve the pressure. His sliced-open foot was elevated on pillows due to swelling. It would take days for the swelling to reduce.

I was granted emergency leave, and I flew with the baby from Fayetteville, North Carolina, to San Diego. When I walked into Jeff's hospital room and saw his overall physical condition, I was surprised. He was pale and thin. I looked at the intravenous bags hanging on the metal pole at his bedside. He was receiving intravenous fluids and antibiotics. Pain medication was infusing on a pump. His foot was discolored purple. I saw multiple incisions in his foot that were left open, revealing his inner muscle and tissue. His hospital food tray remained untouched. He was not eating.

Suddenly, I became nauseated. My hands became ice cold and sweaty. My heart started racing. I was aware that Jeff had surgery prior to my arrival, but I wasn't prepared for how bad he looked. The dark circles under his eyes contrasted with the deathlike pallor of his face.

When Jeff was able, he told me what had happened the day of his parachute accident. The crew chief indicated to the jumpers the winds were twenty-five knots. The jumpers were on jump run. Jeff was assigned to the Black Team, and he was the first out of the plane. He jumped at 14,000 feet. He opened at the usual 2,000 feet. He spiraled down to 500 feet and grabbed brakes. Everything was routine.

Suddenly, the winds picked up and were gusting at thirty-five miles per hour. Jeff had no penetration (forward movement of his parachute) against the strong, steady winds. His parachute was being pushed backward. Updrafts lifted his parachute up, according to his altimeter. The winds were violent. If Jeff continued his trajectory, he knew he would hit a nearby building. His choices were to hit the building or maneuver around it. He knew maneuvering around the three-story building could collapse his parachute if an eddy was strong. When strong winds hit a building, a whirl of air called an eddy forms off the leeward side of the building. He had no choice. He had to maneuver around the building.

The wind collapsed Jeff's square Ram Air parachute as he maneuvered it around the building. In an instant, he was falling straight down three stories. Everything happened very quickly. For a split second, the letters JESUS flashed through his head. He was trained to never give up. He grabbed his rear risers and pumped them, hoping the parachute would open. Suddenly, he was swung like a pendulum straight into the concrete. He had attempted a military parachute landing fall, and his right foot took the full force of the fall, crushing his calcaneus (heel) bone. He had hit hard on his feet, buttocks, and head. The force of the impact bounced his body up and flipped him, and he hit the ground again. His ribs were slammed into a cement curb. Jeff felt the overwhelming intense pain of the forceful impacts, and incredibly he was not knocked unconscious. The wind inflated the parachute and started to drag it. Jeff had the presence of mind to pull the cutaway handle so he wasn't dragged across the ground. He tried to sit up to take off his right boot, but he could not due to the intense pain in his back and ribs.

Tom, a team member, saw the parachute collapse. He saw Jeff hit the ground and was the first to reach Jeff's side.

"You're alive!!" Tom exclaimed.

The Sergeant Major of the Knights was immediately at Jeff's side. He was the highest ranking noncommissioned officer on the team. He and Tom had been in the same vehicle, watching Jeff and his parachute battle the elements.

The Army medics arrived next, jumping out of the Humvee ambulance. The medics positioned themselves to remove Jeff's right boot.

"Let Tom do it," Jeff demanded while gripping his leg in agony. He knew Tom was a highly trained Special Forces medic.

Tom cut off Jeff's right boot. Next, he cut open the fabric of Jeff's jump suit to expose his right leg. The demonstration team guys gathered around Jeff to show support. They knew Jeff survived that precarious parachute collapse against all odds, having fallen from three stories up.

Jeff was placed on a litter, carried to the military ambulance, and taken to a local hospital in excruciating pain. He remained consumed by severe pain in the emergency department. After several hours, he was transferred from the local hospital to the naval hospital by civilian ambulance.

During the three-hour ambulance ride to the naval hospital, Jeff struggled through immense pain. Jeff had to dig deep within himself to find another level, to cope with the pain—the most pain he had ever experienced in his entire life. He told himself that he could do this. He had to. He had no choice. He knew that at the end of the ambulance ride was a navy doctor. There was help on the other side. He had to get through this no matter what. Hold on for the other side. But the pain made this a near Herculean task to cope. It seemed impossible.

During the three hours of nonstop, torturous pain, Jeff endured the agony with the strength of willpower. When Jeff arrived at the naval hospital emergency department, the doctor recognized immediately the critical medical situation. Jeff was catastrophically injured.

The navy doctors immediately tested the compartments in Jeff's foot for pressure readings by placing a needle into his foot. Jeff let out a primal scream that only a man suffering from indescribable pain can bellow. His pressures were extremely elevated. The high pressure constricted the blood supply to the tissue of his foot. Jeff had acute compartment syndrome. Treatment is by emergency surgery to open the compartments. When not treated quickly, permanent muscle and nerve damage results. Jeff had already spent three hours in an ambulance and hours in the first emergency department. The navy doctor knew he had to act quickly because the intra-compartmental pressure was grossly abnormal. The crush injury of Jeff's heel bone from the high speed physical trauma created acute compartment syndrome of the affected foot. The only hope was to perform multiple fasciotomies and leave the compartments open to reduce the pressures. Jeff was rushed from the emergency department to an operating room without delay.

After having surgery, Jeff was taken to a hospital room. When he slept, he woke up startled and drenched in sweat, having dreamt of hitting the ground. He was reliving the parachute accident in his sleep. He would wake up in a state of terror—heart racing and breathing heavy. This dream occurred dozens of times in the first night. He was suffering from post-traumatic stress disorder.

I was stunned into silence after hearing Jeff's story, which was as shocking as the sight of him. I was overwhelmed. I didn't know what to do. I handed him the baby. He hadn't seen her in almost seven weeks. He held her briefly, then asked me to take her back. His foot was elevated and cut open with many incisions. I was glad the baby had no idea her daddy was hurt.

Balboa Navy Medical Center was a nice facility. The naval hospital center was in Southern California. I was taking a taxi from the hotel to the hospital and back. I did not have a car seat, which elevated my stress level. I did not have a stroller, so I carried our baby through the hospital. My arms were so tired. The trip was difficult. I had carried the baby through multiple airports to get to the west coast. I carried her in one arm and pulled my carry-on luggage with the other, which was stuffed with baby clothes, diapers, and wipes. The baby slept in the hotel bed with me.

The trip was difficult on many levels. I was breastfeeding every three hours, and not having anything except bare necessities was wearing me down. I had to ask the hotel for cleaning supplies to clean the bathtub before bathing the baby in it. Even using public restrooms at the hospital was a chore. I had no place to lie the baby. I had to put a blanket on the floor in the stall to lie her down just to use the toilet. I was grateful she wasn't rolling over yet. I had held her the entire trip in the airplane. I changed her diaper on the floor of the airplane aisle with the prayer that no turbulence would occur in that exact moment. I was doing so many things that were unconscionable in terms of safety but were brought about by extreme circumstances. I was on overload.

I really needed help, but I was on my own. I had to suck it up, which seemed to be the story of my life. I was discouraged and tired. I felt the stress in my shoulders, as if I was bearing the weight of the world. I was having headaches frequently. Thankfully, my breastmilk supply never decreased.

Flying with a newborn is not easy, and I was already dreading the return flight home. My itinerary was brutal. The worst part was saying goodbye to Jeff.

I refused to cry when I said goodbye to him. He was still very pale, and he appeared very withdrawn. When I closed the hospital door, I felt hot tears stream down my face. As I walked down the hallway passed the nurses' station, I could barely see. I found my way to the elevator and waited for the doors to open. I wiped my eyes with the back of my hand, while I held the baby with one arm. It was a sad goodbye.

I had no choice. I had to go home. I had to return to work. I had to keep the baby fed and happy. Being a mother didn't stop just because Jeff was hurt. I had to find the strength to carry on, even though I was exhausted. Besides, the baby and I were almost out of clothes, and we didn't have a washing machine.

When I landed in Atlanta for my connecting flight, I made my way to my next gate. Atlanta is a huge airport, and I had to take the sky train to get from one concourse to the other. I carried the baby up the long stairway to the concourse. I walked and walked until I reached my gate. When I read the board, I was thunderstruck. My flight had been canceled. It was the last flight of the evening to my destination. The realization hit me. I was stuck in the airport in Atlanta with a baby. My heart sunk in my chest. *Did I even have enough diapers?*

I noticed three men talking to each other near the canceled flight's gate. They had military haircuts and looked like good guys. I heard one of them say "rent a car." I approached them and asked if they were going to Fort Bragg. They smiled and said, "Yes, ma'am." I explained my situation. The soldiers offered me and the baby a seat in the rental car. They were my heroes.

Before long, we were on Interstate 20 headed east. I knew I should never take a ride with strangers. But my horse sense told me those men were the salt of America. They drove through the night. I arrived home right before the sun rose. I offered them money, but they refused to take it. I thanked them profusely. I didn't have my checked luggage because it was sitting at the Atlanta airport somewhere. I was happy to be home. I gave the baby a thorough bath and went to bed.

The Next Operation

The next few days were a blur. I worked, took care of the baby, and received telephone updates from the doctors and nurses in California. Sometimes I felt like I couldn't breathe.

I worked shift after shift. I was providing nursing care for Army soldiers, and the irony of the situation was not lost on me. I prayed that the Navy nurses were taking as good care of my husband, lying alone in the naval hospital.

The day Jeff had his *second* surgery, I was working the evening shift. The surgery was an open reduction and internal fixation of his foot and heel. The doctor used bone from Jeff's iliac crest (hip bone) to rebuild his foot. The operation was lasting longer than expected.

When I called the operating room, the nurse told me he was stable and the surgery was ongoing. My heart was pounding. My palms were sweaty. Thankfully, our unit wasn't busy. One of my coworkers told me to go home.

"I have your back," he said.

I never forgot his act of kindness and compassion.

I went home, laid down on the couch, and waited. Time seemed to drag on. Why weren't they calling me?

Please, God, let him do well. Please let the surgery be a success.

So many thoughts were running through my mind. Just before midnight, my phone rang. The surgery was over. The surgeon reassured me that Jeff was stable in the recovery room. The immediate post-operative focus would be pain control and preventing infection.

Within two weeks, Jeff was flown home on a military medical transport plane. He was admitted to Womack Army Medical Center.

The acute phase of Jeff's injuries turned to long-term rehabilitation and chronic pain management. When he finally came home, he was using crutches and could not bear weight on his foot.

Now that he was home, we tried to regain some semblance of normality. We adapted. The focus was on immediate needs. Jeff learned to drive with his left foot *without* adaptive equipment. We bought our first recliner to help improve his comfort level. We tried to live life again. The baby was rolling over and sitting up. I took joy in the small things, even though I felt the looming sadness of the sweeping changes that were occurring in our life. I was holding onto hope that Jeff would heal, get well, and return to the Golden Knights. But as the months went by, I became increasingly discouraged and knew that the life we had known would never return. His foot was too damaged.

Captain Dennis

Even with Jeff's ever-present health problems, I continued my duty as an officer in the Army Nurse Corps. I was so proud when I was promoted. My oath was the same as previous occasions, except the grade.

I, Tori Hope Dennis, having been appointed an officer in the Army of the United States, as indicated above in the grade of CAPTAIN do solemnly swear that I will support and defend the Constitution of the United States against all enemies, foreign and domestic, that I will bear true faith and allegiance to the same; that I take this obligation freely, without any mental reservation or purpose of evasion; and that I will well and faithfully discharge the duties of the office on which I am about to enter. SO HELP ME GOD.

There was no celebration this time. I was too tired. And I was pregnant.

Life Continues

This second pregnancy was not planned. At six weeks pregnant the morning sickness began. I woke up, vomited, and went to work. People gave me a lot of unsolicited negative comments.

"This is bad timing," a friend said mournfully.

"All you need is one more," said another person sarcastically.

"You are a nurse; haven't you heard of birth control?" said another.

Why do people tear women down? I felt myself withdrawing from most people. I didn't need unsolicited comments. The baby was growing in my womb, happily kicking.

Nanny was a comfort. She had buried two babies, birthed three others, had a husband killed in war, and had a grown son die in a car accident. She knew life had twists and turns, but the sun keeps rising.

"Your baby is precious. Our lives do not follow a perfect plan. You do not stop living," she said over the telephone.

The pregnancy flew by. One morning, I woke up before the sun came up, craving strawberries. I ate an entire bowl of strawberries with sugar sprinkled on them. They were so good. I was nine months pregnant and experiencing the familiar feeling of labor. I felt menstrual cramping and light contractions as I ate a second bowl of the delicious strawberries. I heated water and put strawberries in the pot. After the strawberries steeped, I strained them from the water. I drank an entire glass of strawberry water. I would drink the rest of the strawberry water in labor. I fell back asleep.

When I woke up again, I knew I was in active labor. I fed my toddler breakfast, bathed, and dressed her. I packed a diaper bag and her sippy cup. I labored at home, folding laundry and washing dishes. I stood, squatted, and leaned forward, all positions that helped the baby descend farther through the pelvis. I walked my toddler over to a neighbor's house and kissed her goodbye. Contractions were intense.

I told Jeff it was time to drive me to the hospital. My doula, Lisa Rowland, and my mother-in-law helped me labor. Jeff stood nearby on crutches. I alternated between squatting and leaning forward over the bed, riding the waves of each contraction. I politely refused to get in the bed until I was ready to push.

Staying out of bed reduced my pain level. When I couldn't breathe through the urge to push, I climbed into the bed. My midwife, Sue, was wonderful. I pushed lying on my side. Side-lying reduces tearing. No stirrups for me. I had the baby less than two hours after arriving at the hospital, and I was home in twenty-four hours.

Our baby had strawberry-blonde hair and blue eyes. Her sweetness reminded me that life goes on. Nanny was right.

Jeff's Amputation

Keep your chin up.—Norma Ritschard

The life we knew before Jeff's parachute collapse was gone forever. The damaged muscle and tissue of his foot were extremely sensitive to touch and painful to walk on, and the purplish hue of his foot looked ominous. The chronic nerve damage was permanent. The rods and screws that rebuilt his foot along with bone from his hip were intact, but he could not walk without extreme pain. He had been referred to an orthopedic doctor at Walter Reed Army Medical Center, where he was now an inpatient. His third surgery was bone fusions to his foot and ankle, which proved fruitless. Soon, Jeff was going to surgery to have his right foot amputated. The procedure was called a Syme's amputation. It would be his fourth surgery since his high impact injury to his foot.

My sixteen-month-old sat in a stroller to keep her off the dirty hospital floor. I lined a cardboard box with soft pink blankets for a crib for my six-week-old. It was on the floor near the IV poles because there was nowhere else to put it. Jeff's room was extremely small. The wallpaper was old and peeling. I tried not to look at the dingy surroundings because my focus was on my precious children and Jeff.

I was under considerable strain when Jeff was sitting on the hospital bed waiting to be wheeled to the operating room. When a nurse walked in to take him, tears started pouring down my face. Jeff saw me crying. He told the nurse to wait. He got off the stretcher and stood on one foot. He held open his arms, and I went to him. He kissed my forehead, held me with his strong arms, and told me it would be okay. He held me for a long moment in a hug that shut out the world.

I would live on that hug for the next two years. That final hug gave me strength. Jeff knew his foot would be amputated soon, but he gave all he had to me—his love. He gazed lovingly at our baby sleeping in the cardboard box. As he was wheeled out of the room, he blew kisses to our toddler. She blew kisses back at him. Then he was gone. The room seemed so empty.

How am I going to get through this?

Hours later, Jeff was medicated heavily when he was rolled back on a stretcher. I met the stretcher in the hallway, holding the baby in my arms. His eyes were closed, and he was drowsy. I followed Jeff on the stretcher to his room. He was as pale as the white sheets that covered him. I was barely aware that I was still holding our baby.

When the nurses moved Jeff from the stretcher to the bed, I saw his amputated leg for the first time. He was wearing a hospital gown, and beneath it I could see his leg wrapped in a white bandage. When I saw his missing right foot, I felt a wave of nausea. I almost vomited onto the floor. I became cold and sweaty. Lacking the strength to stand, I backed up against the wall and used it to hold myself up.

Don't pass out, Tori, I repeated silently in my mind.

I didn't expect this visceral reaction because I have seen bodies of all shapes and sizes, illnesses and injuries. But I was completely unprepared to see *my husband* like this.

The nurses wordlessly and efficiently got Jeff settled, then briskly walked out of the room without a word. Even though I was still standing, I felt detached. The baby moved in my arms, jolting me out of shock into mother mode.

No doctor came to speak to me. No one explained how the surgery went. I received zero communication. Looking back, this is astonishing to me.

Jeff was heavily medicated and remained asleep. It was very late in the evening, and I needed to get the children to sleep. I left the hospital and drove through the dark, congested city streets to my old college friend Ann's home thirty minutes from the hospital. She had graciously allowed me and the children to sleep at her house because hotels in the area were extremely expensive. A hotel bill for multiple nights would likely have been the cost of my monthly mortgage. My friend did not have an extra bed, but I was grateful to have a roof over my head. It was pragmatic to sleep on the floor so I could pay the mortgage.

After a quick hello to Ann, I gave my toddler her stuffed animal and put her pink blanket on the carpet. She seemed eager to stretch out on the blanket and snuggle her stuffed animal, after having been confined to her stroller all day. I laid down on the carpet next to her and breastfed the baby.

I was utterly exhausted. At only six weeks postpartum, I was still recovering from having a baby. I didn't have a blanket nor a pillow. I wished I had thought to bring those items from home. I was cold and miserable. My uterus was cramping, and I was passing clots, which added to my discomfort.

I watched my toddler close her eyes and drift into sleep. Finally, I closed my eyes and fell into a fitful sleep myself.

When I woke up, the previous day's events rushed into my mind. I needed to get to the hospital to be with Jeff. But first I had to attend to practical matters: a shower, buy my toddler breakfast, hydrate myself so I could breastfeed, and feed and change my baby. Because I was afraid my toddler would fall down the flight of steps, I brought the children into the bathroom with me while I showered. Traveling with a newborn and a toddler is difficult under any circumstances, let alone those circumstances.

As I buckled my children into their car seats, I braced myself for the long day ahead. The day was just starting, and already I felt incredibly drained. The children needed me. I could not weaken. I had to remain strong.

As I drove to the Army hospital, I knew that Jeff would be awake. The anesthesia would have worn off, and pain would be his bedfellow. I had not spoken to him since he was rolled away for surgery. I wanted to see him and hold him.

The drive seemed to take an eternity. I just wanted to get there. Traffic was heavy, and I drove slowly while looking for street signs. Impatient drivers were honking, and an aggravated man with road rage shot me the bird and shouted obscenities as he passed. I swallowed a sob. I was overwhelmed. The need to see Jeff propelled me forward.

When I pushed the double stroller into Jeff's small room, he was pale with dark circles under his eyes. He appeared small in the bed. I suddenly felt panicky, cold, and sweaty. I sat down on the hard, uncomfortable hospital chair, holding the baby in my arms. She was rooting at my shirt, wanting to nurse. The IV pump started beeping, indicating that the pump needed to be fixed. I stood and pushed the nurse call bell.

I sat back down to nurse my hungry baby. That began several hospital days that blurred together. The hospital felt cold and oppressive—vastly different from the vibrant, lively medical center that I had trained at just six years before.

My mother-in-law had taken a flight to be by her son's side. She spoke to him in a soothing voice and put a cool rag on his forehead. I was grateful she was there. I couldn't help Jeff the way I wanted to. Whenever I stood up from the hospital chair, I would become dizzy and wanted to pass out. I was suffering from extreme anxiety, which caused me to suddenly vomit. Eating was a struggle because food tasted like sawdust. Thankfully, my milk supply did not decrease. The baby nursed and had plenty of milk. But the situation was taking a toll on me. I was changing diapers on a toddler and a baby. I was waking and feeding a baby through the night. I was so grateful to have a faithful mother-in-law.

I felt detached inside, as if I were not there. Outwardly, I was accomplishing tasks. I was changing diapers in the stroller. I was feeding the baby. I felt a heart pang every time I put the baby into the cardboard box on the floor. I had to put her down at times. It gave my tired arms a rest and the chance to use the toilet. But it was not normal to put a baby in a box. It didn't seem real. I didn't feel present. Events blurred together. Severe headaches pulled me back into reality. They felt like a vice on my skull. Otherwise, I remained in a state of mild shock.

Our experience after the amputation was not a positive one. A few weeks after Jeff's amputation, a foul smell permeated the room from his limb. I knew by the smell that his underlying tissue was infected. I felt despondent, knowing that this could lead to another amputation or overwhelming infection throughout his body. The surgeon took him to the operating room for the *fifth* surgery since the high impact injury occurred. The surgeon performed an incision and drainage, cutting open the stump and cleaning out the infection. The wound was left open because the tissue would need to heal from the inside. The hope was that the antibiotics would work and kill the bacteria.

Due to this setback, Jeff would need weeks of hospitalization for antibiotic therapy and wound care. That would significantly delay his ability to learn to walk again.

As bad news atop bad news compounded in our minds and hearts, I was quickly losing my physical strength. The medical center was only three hours' drive from my mother's home in Pennsylvania, so I decided to go there to allow my toddler to play. She needed to play and run around as much as I needed a good night's sleep. Living out of a suitcase and spending hours in a hospital day after day was harder than I imagined.

When I drove away from the hospital, I felt defeated. I needed my family. After we arrived, my mom cooked hearty meals for us. My grandmother, Norma, held the baby. My toddler had space to run around and play. My grandfather looked over the car, topping off the oil and fluids. For the first time in weeks, I slept for hours in a deep sleep, aside from the nightly breastfeeding. If I ever needed my family, it was then.

In addition to physical respite, my grandmother gave me pearls of wisdom to help carry me through the next phase of my marriage. Her words were a source of strength for me during the years that followed Jeff's amputation.

Norma

My maternal grandmother, Norma, was born in a city hospital to an unmarried woman. Catholic nuns cared for her in an orphanage until she was placed for foster care. Her Mom and Pop raised her as their own, and she did not know they weren't her biological parents until she was sixteen years old.

The black-haired, brown-eyed baby became a strikingly beautiful young lady. She married in 1942, six months after the Japanese attack on Pearl Harbor. While Norma was pregnant with her first baby, the war was raging. Her husband, Frank, was draft age. One day when Frank was working, he saw his father walk in unexpectedly with a piece of paper in hand. His father talked to the foreman and showed him the paper. Frank knew it was a draft notice. His father had come directly from the rural post office to deliver the news, including his date to report. Within days, Frank left for the Navy. After his initial training at the Great Lakes was complete, he was on a train bound for San Francisco. He would be shipping out to the Pacific Theater. Norma faced uncertainty because no one knew how long this war would continue. No one knew when—or if—Frank would come back. Telegrams from Western Union brought heart-wrenching news to mothers and wives every day.

When Norma was seven months pregnant, she went into labor. Her father-in-law drove her to the hospital and dropped her off at the door. She walked into the hospital by herself.

As was customary in the hospitals in the 1940s, Norma had no input regarding her birth—not medication nor procedures. She was lonely in the labor room. Her premature son was born alive and placed in an incubator. She was not allowed to hold him. His lungs were immature, and subsequently he had respiratory distress. He remained in the nursery, and Norma was not allowed to go to see him—let alone touch or hold him.

The doctor told Norma that her son was dying. A nurse with incredible compassion discreetly brought the baby to Norma. The nurse was violating the doctor's orders for which she could have been fired. However, the nurse knew this moment would be a meaningful memory for Norma for the rest of her life.

Norma held her brown-eyed baby boy for a few moments before the nurse whisked him back to the nursery. The next day, Norma was given the news that her baby died. She had expected that but had hoped and prayed that he would live.

In 1943, women remained in a hospital for a week after childbirth. The baby's burial occurred while Norma was in the hospital. He was buried by her father-in-law—sans gravestone. That was an expense only the rich could afford.

Across the country, Frank was told to report to his commanding officer. He entered the office and saw the Navy chaplain standing there. Frank knew someone was dead. It was in this office that he learned his baby son died.

Two years later, wearing a dark blue sailor dress, Norma waited for the train to arrive. On December 22, 1945, Frank came home, just in time for Christmas.

More than a half century had passed since the end of the Second World War. I sat in her small kitchen listening to the familiar sound of her copper tea pot whistling as the water came to a boil. My grandmother brewed hot tea for me while she poured herself a cup of coffee. We sat around her wooden table in her humble Pennsylvania kitchen. The large kitchen window made a beautiful portrait of her blooming azalea bushes.

"How did you manage?" I asked quietly.

"I had no choice," Norma said frankly. "There was nothing I could do about it. I had to keep going. I had to keep my chin up. I said my prayers. I went to church and sung the hymn 'It Is Well with My Soul.' I had to accept there was nothing I could do about the baby nor about the war except pray."

Norma paused momentarily, then continued. "Keep going. Keep your chin up. The children and Jeff need you. It is well with your soul. No matter the trial, peace comes from God."

I knew she was right. I wasn't going to weaken now. I felt a stubborn determination rise in my chest.

After a few days' visit that went too fast, I drove back to the hospital with the children to resume keeping Jeff company, entertaining my toddler, and breastfeeding my baby. This time, we were given a room at the Fisher House. Despite the improved accommodations, my toddler was still not sleeping well.

"Take our children home," Jeff said weakly. "They'll be happier in their own beds."

I was too tired to protest.

I changed their diapers, breastfed my baby, and buckled them into car seats. To keep my toddler happy on the long drive, I gave her finger foods and a sippy cup. I stopped at a local gas station and filled up the tank. I felt uneasy at the gas station because the area was sketchy. I was happy to get back into the car and lock the doors.

The drive from the medical center back to our home near Fort Bragg took six long hours. I was thankful to pull into my driveway at home.

The girls needed their baths. I carried them into the house. The house felt warm because summer had arrived already in the South. I turned on the air-conditioner to cool it down. Fueled by adrenaline and a mental to-do list, I walked into the bathroom to run my girls' bath water. But when I turned on the faucet, nothing came out! My heart sunk. I checked the other faucets. No water flowed.

Coming quickly to the end of my rope, I trudged over to my neighbor's house. She had water. I wondered what my problem could be.

I walked to the mailbox and picked up the piled-up mail. When I quickly sorted through it, I spotted the past-due water bill. I had been gone for so long the water company must have shut off my water.

Oh, Lord, please keep me sane!

I took a deep breath and said out loud, "It is well with your soul."

I put the girls to bed without their baths. The next morning, I drove to the water department and stood at the door, waiting for them to open. After paying the bill and the late fee, I explained to the clerk what had happened to my husband. With a heartfelt plea, I asked if she could expedite the water being turned back on. Mercifully, she sent a worker to my home right away.

I was so grateful. I was able to bathe my children, wash sippy cups, wash baby clothes, take a shower, and flush toilets. God bless that clerk.

The Next Step

You may not control all the events that happen to you,
but you can decide not to be reduced by them.
—Maya Angelou

Several months after Jeff's amputation, I took the girls to a park for my toddler to play. Jeff wasn't walking yet. I was in survival mode, and I often felt overwhelmed and tense. A stranger was making small talk and asked what I thought of the hit movie *Titanic*.

"I haven't seen it," I told her.

In a very melodramatic way, she was aghast that I missed my opportunity to see *Titanic* in the theater. Suddenly, I felt like I was missing out on living. And yet, inwardly I knew what she described was so petty. I was focused on my family, which was the right thing to do. However, feelings of jealousy were bubbling to the surface.

That woman sent my heart and mind into a tailspin. I gathered my girls and our belongings, pushed the stroller to the car, loaded the diaper bags, buckled the children into their car seats, and lifted the heavy double stroller into the back.

Tears came to my eyes. I felt like that woman had punched me in the gut. I was hoping Jeff would walk someday, and she was talking about a Hollywood movie. She had no idea what was going on in my life. I thought she was insensitive and shallow. Somehow the lady at the park had gotten under my skin.

When I spoke to my dear friend Lisa Rowland later that evening, I told her what happened. The next day, she came to my house with a *Titanic* VHS tape.

"Watch it when your children go to sleep," she said with kindness in her eyes. "Call me anytime something upsets you."

My friend expressed that it was important for me to feel some sense of normalcy during this difficult chapter of my life. She was so kind and clever, and her thoughtfulness meant the world to me.

Lisa called me almost every day. She would start the conversation with, "You love your husband because…?" Then I would have to give her a reason why I loved my husband. She kept my motivation up. She prevented me from spiraling down the rabbit hole. I will always love her for that.

While I was beginning to see glimpses of light, Jeff was battling darkness. Although he was present physically, he was detached. I noticed he exhibited the thousand-yard stare. He sat in his recliner with a blank, unfocused gaze.

One night he told me he could feel his missing foot.

"I'm moving my toes," he exclaimed warily.

He was so convincing I looked under the sheet, but of course his foot was not there. It was phantom pain which is a common phenomenon with amputed limbs.

As the days, weeks, and months passed, Jeff spiraled deeper and deeper into depression.

"Take the girls and divorce me," he begged. "You would all be better off without me."

"We were married in sickness and in health," I reminded him.

Jeff had to pull himself out of the darkness as he dealt with the stages of grief. I was battling my own despair. I was grieving too. Divorce was a carrot dangling over our heads.

When I saw a woman walking with her husband, I would find myself jealous that he was walking on two whole legs. I was jealous at the simple sight of a man walking. My head and heart were grieving.

If I heard a woman complaining about her husband not doing dishes or picking up his socks, I wanted to scream. I couldn't handle hearing trivial things. It seemed so ridiculous. I wanted to yell, "Be grateful your husband has legs!" I was in a state of mental anguish. I felt so alone.

One day, I dusted off the shoebox that held all the old letters Jeff had sent me from Haiti. I started reading them one by one. His loving words spoke of his hope for our future family. Some of his letters contained Bible verses. I opened my Bible and read them:

Romans 15:13: May the God of hope fill you with all joy and peace.

Joshua 1:9: Be strong and courageous. Do not be afraid, do not be discouraged, for the Lord your God will be with you wherever you go.

In his letters, Jeff had written about hope and courage. Tears streamed down my face. I needed hope and courage.

I was reminded of the promise I made to him the day he walked away across the parking lot to leave for winter training as a Golden Knight.

"Take care of our family," he said.

That was the last day I saw him walk without injury. And I had made a promise to him. That memory of a strong, muscular man flashed through my head. He trusted me with what was most valuable to him, our family. I was determined to keep that promise.

Jeff's old worn letters from Haiti sustained me for the next two years. And I lived on the hug he had given me right before he was rolled away for his amputation.

Fortunately, both Jeff and I have very bold personalities lit with an inner determination never to quit. That character trait gave us the strength to spit at the carrot every time it dangled over our heads.

Darkness before Dawn

Jeff used crutches for months. His hands and armpits were raw. His left leg was bearing the brunt of supporting his body.

He was missing part of his right hip, which had been used to rebuild his now-amputated foot. His back hurt because two vertebrae had been fractured during his high-impact fall. Physically and mentally, he had reached his low. If Jeff had been able to walk quickly after his amputation, he would not have spiraled down that low.

In the middle of one night, he stood up to go to the toilet. He was half asleep and stood on both feet, except he was missing a foot. He fell. His mind had forgotten he was missing a foot. I peered over the bed to see him on the floor, looking up at the ceiling. I grabbed his crutches and put them next to him. We were both silent.

That night, Jeff had to find and harness his willpower to stay mentally and physically strong through this process. The wait to walk and heal seemed never-ending. He had to learn to walk again. He had to learn to drive again, using adaptive equipment. He needed to learn to stand in a shower using a prosthetic leg. The most basic tasks were daunting. That night, lying on the floor looking at the ceiling, the choice was his.

I watched Jeff's internal struggle. The battle within him was as hard as the physical one. He chose to push through. He fought the doubts and maintained the hope that he *would* walk again. He could get through anything. He would dig deep and find that determination inside himself. Adversity had him lying on the floor in the middle of the night without a foot. He was angry and frustrated.

In the dark of night, I watched Jeff harness the fighting spirit. His only reason to go on was his family—his little girls and me. Having his family to fight for motivated him. He used his arms to push up onto his knees. Using the crutches, he pulled up, balanced his body, and stood on one foot. He crutched to the bathroom. He was off the floor. He found his reason to fight. He chose not to give up.

Walking

Those who hope in the Lord will renew their strength.
They will soar on wings like eagles; they will run and not
grow weary; they will walk and not be faint.
—Isaiah 40:31

While facing physical challenges, Jeff had to navigate the medical board process of leaving the Army. Due to his injury, the Army was medically discharging him. The medical board was a complicated, stressful process.

After Jeff's wound healed, he had an appointment with a prosthetist at Walter Reed to be fitted with his first prosthetic. Jeff anxiously awaited his new leg. He wanted to take his first steps and walk again. The crutches had worn his skin raw and caused blisters in his palms and under his arms.

All he wanted to do was walk. He stood upright on his prosthetic, bearing weight on his stump. He took his first steps. He was walking!

In a crushing blow, it was painful for Jeff to walk on his stump. The infection was gone, but he couldn't bear his full weight on his stump without pain. He needed to use crutches to walk. It was devastating. The doctors recommended that Jeff undergo another amputation. That amputation would be at the traditional below-the-knee area.

Jeff was skeptical because the first amputation had become infected. He did not want another infection. He did not want another negative experience. He wanted to have a good outcome, and he wanted to walk well again.

He wanted a second opinion, which would prove difficult to get because he was still on Army active duty, and soldiers are required to use the military's medical system.

Jeff did not wallow in the mud. He was down, but there was fight in him. He sought a second opinion. A military friend told Jeff to call Ross Perot. Jeff left a message with a secretary at Mr. Perot's office in Texas, but he wasn't really expecting a response. Mr. Perot was known to have a heart to help people, especially soldiers. The military community respected him immensely.

Meanwhile, I was putting in calls of my own—to God. I was spending a lot of time praying. My grandmother advised me to pray, so I did. My hope was in the Lord.

During the first year after Jeff's amputation, I spent a lot of time praying with a prayer warrior named Joy Dunson. Joy was a remarkable woman. She served in the Army Nurse Corps, earning the rank of Colonel. She was a wife, mother, and mentor who gave encouragement to many women. She hosted a ladies' Bible study in her home that met during the week. The ladies prayed for Jeff's recovery.

One beautiful Sunday morning on my way to church, I noticed how beautiful the sky looked—a piercing blue with no clouds. During a group prayer, Joy Dunson along with several women and myself prayed for Jeff. The prayer was fervent and specific: Allow Jeff to walk again and provide a prosthetic that brings mobility to his life.

When I got home, Jeff was waiting on our front porch, balancing with crutches. With one glance, I could tell he was anxious to tell me something. When I opened the car door, Jeff hollered, "Ross Perot called me while you were at church!"

Jeff had *hope* written all over his face. He was exuberant. Ross Perot had personally called Jeff on a Sunday morning! He promised to get Jeff walking again. He promised to call a surgeon he trusted and recommended. Mr. Perot said Jeff was not on his own. He was going to help him every step of the way. Mr. Perot was even going to pay for a prosthetic through his charity. My prayers had been answered.

God bless that man!

I did not know by what design we had to struggle through so much, but receiving help felt like sunshine bursting through the clouds after a tornado. Finally, Jeff and I could see the other side. We just had to get through another amputation.

Second Amputation

Jeff went to Oklahoma for his second amputation surgery, while I stayed home with our two little girls. I decided I was *not* subjecting the girls or myself to the immense stress we endured the first amputation. I was going to keep our home stable and secure. It was what Jeff and I felt was best for our family.

Ross Perot's recommended physician was excellent. Jeff was so optimistic and so happy. The day of surgery, he called and sang to the children, "I'm a little teapot short and stout. Here is my handle. Here is my spout. When I get all steamed up, hear me shout. Tip me over and pour me out!"

Jeff's second leg amputation (*sixth* surgery) went very well. He was walking quickly! Finally, he was on the road to recovery.

But we would face one last hurdle. After walking with a prosthetic for six weeks, he started having sharp pains at the residual limb. The local military physician did an x-ray and diagnosed stump overgrowth. That is the formation of bone spikes (heterotopic ossification) at the end of an amputated bone, which happens occasionally.

Jeff was scheduled for what we hoped was his final surgery to remove the bone spikes. The surgeon performed the resection of the spikes, and the surgery went perfectly. When Jeff recovered from his *seventh* surgery, the physician recommended radiation therapy to prevent any more spikes from forming. Jeff acquiesced and had radiation to his residual limb. It worked. He never had another bone spike.

It had been a long eighteen months since Jeff's first amputation. He had endured seven operations and one course of radiation since his parachute accident two and a half years earlier. BUT JEFF WAS WALKING!

Baby Sister

Love recognizes no barriers. It jumps hurdles, leaps fences,
penetrates walls to arrive at its destination full of hope.
—Maya Angelou

Jeff was walking even better when our third daughter was born. I went into labor when the sun came up. I knew I was in labor. I had menstrual cramping with waves of contractions. I walked around the house, then I walked outside. I smiled as I watched the children playing happily. Jeff stayed with the children, while a friend drove me to the midwifery clinic.

The military hospital clinic was open because it was a Tuesday. I was four centimeters dilated and in labor. Yet I was not mentally ready to be admitted and confined to a bleak hospital room. After expressing my thoughts to the midwife, she consented to let me walk.

My friend drove me home, and my contractions continued in the car like clockwork. I relaxed my abdomen and let the waves envelope me. When we arrived at the entrance to our subdivision, I asked her to stop the car. I got out of the car and walked home. I admired the beautiful blue sky. The air felt refreshing. I walked slowly and stopped with each contraction, knowing the ground supported me through it. I was going inward. I did not notice parked cars or houses as I walked past them. I walked and labored.

When I arrived home, my little ones ran to me.

"Mommy!" they yelled with excitement.

I knelt and gave them hugs.

"Your baby sister is going to be born," I said.

They were excited. I gave them their baby dolls to hold. I ran warm bath water. Suddenly, I vomited. It felt good—a welcome relief. Vomiting is normal in labor. Usually, it occurs the latter stages of active labor when a woman is moving into transition around eight centimeters. Transition is the stage of *transitioning* from active labor to pushing. Contractions are more frequent and the most intense.

I sunk into the warm bath. It felt good to soak in water while in labor. My mother-in-law brought me sweet tea to drink. I labored in the water until I felt pressure at the peaks of each contraction. Then I got out of the water, dried off, and put on my beautiful long blue dress. It was a great dress to labor in because it was loose and comfortable.

Jeff drove me to the hospital. I labored in the front seat, but I was facing backward in an upright kneeling position with my hands holding onto the headrest. I labored and let the waves of contractions wash over me.

Once we arrived at the military hospital, I walked in, stopping in the foyer to breathe through a contraction. While I stood there, I had a fleeting thought that I was standing in the same military hospital where I worked during the mass casualty event. I was no longer active duty, instead my name was on the Individual Ready Reserves list. I pushed away thoughts of having worked here in this building. I was having a baby. I allowed myself to go inward and surrender to labor.

I saw the midwife in the clinic, and I was six centimeters dilated. She admitted me to labor and delivery. I squatted on the floor and laid my head down on the crisp white sheet of the labor bed. I closed my eyes and relaxed. After laboring for another ninety minutes, I felt overwhelming pressure. My friend hollered for the midwife, who came immediately and saw me standing by the bed. She asked me gently and kindly to position myself comfortably in bed. She examined me and said I could push anytime I was ready. I was on my right side. I pushed and birthed a beautiful baby girl in less than five minutes.

The name I choose for her means "strong." Our family was strong and unbroken. Her birth was a happy day.

Jeff and I were ready to rebuild our lives and decompress from the challenges that we had faced since his high-velocity crush injury. I was grateful to God for seeing us through that nightmare.

DD-214

The Army medically retired Jeff from the military. He was deeply patriotic and loved the Army. On Jeff's last day, he received his discharge paperwork, including his DD-214. Jeff had served in 20th Special Forces Group (A), 3rd Special Forces Group (A), and the United States Army Parachute Team.

Jeff's military training had taught him endurance, perseverance, and ingenuity. He had many firsts after his amputations. Learning to walk again was just the beginning. Using the aid of a metal foot device on the floorboard, he learned to drive with his left foot.

With Jeff's Army friends at his side, he had made a skydive *before* his first amputation. His friends knew it was psychologically important to jump as quickly as possible after a bad jump. This jump was done on the sly because Jeff could not walk. Sergeant Alan Davis and another friend carried him to a C-182. They sat Jeff in the door of the plane. When they got to altitude, Jeff jumped. He enjoyed the skydive. He knew he couldn't land on his feet, so he purposefully landed in the pea gravel pit on his butt. His buddies carried him to the hangar and handed him his crutches. Army guys have the backs of their buddies. That jump was a psychological win for Jeff.

After his amputation, Jeff had to figure out how to skydive wearing his prosthetic leg. With ingenuity, he rigged suspension straps to keep the prosthetic secure to his stump. The prosthetic needed to withstand a free fall at 200 mph. The day of the jump, Captain Eric Bush and Sergeant Alan Davis went into the Twin Otter airplane with Jeff. Jeff was at the door. When Jeff came in for a landing, he didn't want to land on his prosthetic leg. Intentionally, he landed on his butt again. After landing, he stood, walked, and carried his parachute back to the hangar. That was a huge accomplishment.

After Jeff had a well fitting prosthetic, he trained as a private pilot. Flying was very therapeutic for Jeff; he said he felt free. Because a pilot uses both feet to push pedals on the floor, Jeff had to gauge how much pressure to push with his prosthetic. He overcame every obstacle so he could have the independence of flying. After many hours of flying and studying, Jeff became a licensed private pilot. Everything he accomplished after his leg was amputated was from sheer determination and bold courage.

The time had come for the military movers to pack us out of our home. My military obligation was finished, and Jeff was medically retired. It was bittersweet. Our military life was over. It was time to move forward and build a new one.

PART II: THE MIDWIFE

Found

For I know the plans I have for you … plans to give you
Hope and a future. —Jeremiah 29:11

Jeff and I had lived a long period of time under chronic stress. Now that he could walk, I was ready for peace and quiet. My hope and prayer was that we would find a farm.

Jeff and I were looking for a one-story home so he did not have to climb stairs. We also needed a walk-in shower, and having a built–in shower seat would be ideal.

One evening, Jeff was speaking to his best friend, Eric Bush, a former Army officer. His aunt, Ms. Brown, worked in real estate. She found a one-story home with a walk-in shower that had acreage. The best news was it was only two years old and needed no repairs. When Jeff and I viewed the farm in Tennessee, we fell in love. It was so peaceful. It was where we needed to be.

That farm in Tennessee became my refuge from the world. I loved the peace and quiet. It was the first time in my life that I had known such peace. The farm had hardwoods, pine trees, creeks, pastures, fields, hunting stands, and a pond. I loved to walk on the trails in the woods, soaking in the sounds of nature. The gently rustling sound of the wind blowing through the trees, the buzzing of the bumble bees, and the chorus of song birds brought a quiet satisfaction and contentment to my heart. While walking, the girls and I would see white ox eye daisies, wood violets, and running cedar.

The farm was therapeutic for me. I was drawn to my garden, which grew and bloomed with herbs, flowers, and vegetables. I loved gathering eggs from my chickens. Using my hands to dig in the dirt was healing and in stark contrast to getting blood on my hands as a nurse.

The spring brought beautiful wild flowers, fawns in the high grass, calves nursing at a cow's udder near the catfish pond, and the sprouting of my seeds in the hoed garden. Spring on my farm was a lovely season filled with renewal of life. As the intensity of our military life faded, I was able to breathe again.

My days on the farm were busy. I loved hearing the rooster crow at the break of dawn. I often walked barefoot to the chicken coop through the wet dewy grass. It felt incredibly relaxing to my feet. I would open the door to the coop, and the chickens would happily free range all day. The flock followed me as I scattered chicken feed into the grass. I enjoyed the early mornings and relaxed as the morning sun warmed my cheeks. When I washed dishes, I watched the chickens through the windows pecking and scratching the ground. The beetles and bugs didn't stand a chance against my dozen Rhode Island Red chickens.

As my girls grew older, they ran to the chicken coop and carefully put the eggs into our wire egg basket. They carefully carried the eggs to me with happy smiles on their faces.

Jeff took the girls fishing in our catfish pond, and I would take them to the little pond where they wiggled their toes in the muddy water and watched the tadpoles swim and nip at their toes. Multiple heads of cow grazed in the meadow, a beautiful sight when I looked out the front window. I enjoyed listening to the mooing and watching the calves frolic.

Wild turkey roamed our property as did deer. The girls learned to hunt deer from the deer stands. Usually, they did their homeschool lessons in the mornings and early afternoons, but on hunting days, they did not have to do their lessons. When they shot a deer, they watched their dad gut it. They learned to drive four wheelers and rode the trails through the woods.

As time wore on, Jeff noticed a pattern to his stump. If he stayed on his prosthetic too long, his stump would flare up. Using a recliner, he elevated his legs at night for relief. Usually, it took three days for a flareup to lessen. Jeff learned to balance walking and resting to avoid flareups. We were adjusting to life with a prosthetic and learning how to manage.

One morning, Jeff was sitting on the side of the bed, putting on his stump sock and prosthetic.

"It doesn't bother me anymore," he said with a sigh. "I don't get angry when putting on a prosthetic now."

That is when I knew that Jeff had overcome a huge obstacle. He was slowly moving forward from the devastating loss of a limb. Other military amputees told us that it usually takes around seven years to mentally, physically, and emotionally adjust. It absolutely took time, patience, forgiveness, and perseverance for both Jeff and me to navigate this complex situation and overcome the grief. Depression tried to pull us under to a place where it would be easy to wallow in self-pity. Anger was hidden under the surface, and on occasion it boiled over in explosive outbursts.

Over time, we learned to replace negative thoughts with positive ones. We were moving through stages of grief to acceptance. We never quit, which was a feat because we had suffered such deep trauma and neither of us knew how to process it.

When Jeff's leg caused him problems, he sat in the recliner and had marathon television time with the girls. They would watch movies together and eat popcorn. He read them *National Geographic for Kids*. They loved the pictures of the animals from around the globe. Jeff loved his daughters and wanted to protect them from the cruelty of the world.

Chapter 7: Birth Center

About two miles from our farm was a small country store where the girls and I would go to buy general merchandise. One warm spring day, I saw a sign on the door advertising a position as a registered nurse at a free-standing birth center, which means it was not part of a larger hospital.

I was thrilled. I applied and was hired to fill the position. In Tennessee, birth center births and homebirths were available to women. Certified Nurse Midwives mainly worked in birth centers and hospitals, while Certified Professional Midwives provided homebirths.

A Certified Nurse Midwife is a nurse who has received a master's degree in midwifery. A Certified Professional Midwife is a direct-entry midwife who achieves certification through the North American Registry of Midwives (NARM).

Unlike most hospital births I had attended, women at the birth center labored out of bed. They were very active, walking, squatting, and sitting on birth balls. They birthed in whatever position was comfortable for them. I watched the midwife adeptly deliver babies on birth stools, in all-fours position in bed, and in side-lying position. Many women chose waterbirths. It was remarkable to watch this midwife work. I loved it. I provided immediate postpartum care for the women who birthed, including assisting with breastfeeding.

In addition, my job involved driving to homes for postpartum visits. Many families in our rural area lived below the poverty level. I would drive through several counties of rural farmland and backwoods to check on newborns and postpartum mothers. I helped women troubleshoot breastfeeding. I performed newborn screening tests, which ruled out genetic, endocrine, and metabolic disorders. I removed cord clamps from dried umbilical cords. While examining women, I assessed their postpartum bleeding and clots known as lochia.

I enjoyed postpartum visits. I became quick and efficient with my assessments of newborns and women. I particularly enjoyed driving to homes that were off the beaten path. I drove through picturesque rural areas that made my senses come alive. Depending on the season, I saw plowed fields and the new growth of cotton, soybean, or corn. Wild flowers displayed their glory at the edge of the fields and roads. Green leaves would turn brilliant autumn colors, sporadically falling to the ground to become crumpled and brown. Fall leaves would accumulate and line the country lanes and occasionally would be carried into an upward circular pattern when a strong wind blew. Driving through the countryside was beautiful.

While passing through rural areas, I noticed Amish driving horse and buggies and smiled. I felt like I was home in Pennsylvania. Might my childhood aspiration to serve the Amish become a reality?

I decided to transition my nursing career to homebirth midwifery. It would take a lot of work to become a midwife. But I was overjoyed at the prospect of becoming a homebirth midwife for the Amish. Maybe my hope would become a reality.

"Whatever will be, will be," I said aloud to myself.

The Letter

I took my examination to become a midwife after completing rigorous training. I would either pass or fail. There is no in-between.

I had to wait weeks for the results. It seemed like an eternity. Each day, I anxiously awaited the postman. One afternoon, I was leaving the house with my three girls when I saw the mailman driving down the lane. I put my SUV in park.

One of the girls hopped out of the car and grabbed the pile of mail. She read the return address on one envelope.

"North American Registry of Midwives," she said. "Is this it, Mom?"

"YES!" I exclaimed as she handed me the envelope from the backseat. For a moment, I held the envelope. I hesitated and stared at it.

"OPEN IT, MOMMY!" shouted my youngest daughter.

I carefully unsealed the envelope with shaking hands.

"Dear Ms. Dennis, Congratulations! We are pleased to inform you that you passed the NARM Written Examination," I read out loud to the girls.

We all hooted, yelled, laughed, and jumped in our seats. I was officially a Certified Professional Midwife. WOW!

Mexican Women

A little while before, Jeff and I had sold our farm and moved to a home in an exclusive aviation subdivision. Jeff was able to land his Cessna airplane on a private runway adjacent to our house. He would taxi the airplane to our hangar. He was living his passion as a pilot, and he was supportive of my midwifery endeavors. Flying gave him a feeling of freedom and peace. In my opinion, it was wonderful therapy for him.

To gain a substantial amount of midwifery experience in a short amount of time, I worked shifts at a very busy birth center. There were two drawbacks. It was a traveling midwife position. And I missed my girls.

The change of scenery was exciting. I quickly became immersed in Mexican culture and the Spanish language. I had learned Spanish in high school and at the university. However, my Spanish was below mediocre. I was far from fluent.

The music was lively, the pueblo-style architecture of homes was beautiful, and the Mexican culture was vibrant and invigorating to me. The landscape was completely different from my home in the lush green of the Tennessee river valley. Here, there was a lot of dust and prickly pear cactus. I rarely saw trees or grass.

I loved the busy birth center with its constant flow of laboring women. Prenatal appointments, one-on-one continuous care in labor and delivery, postpartum care, and newborn exams filled the days. The other midwives and I took turns taking shifts.

The birth center was open for births every day of the week and all hours. The door always remained locked. Women rang the doorbell to be admitted. There were no inductions, so births happened whenever nature wanted. A mother, sister, or mother-in-law often accompanied the laboring woman. Women stayed six hours after birth, then they went home. A mother and her baby returned to the clinic for postpartum appointments at twenty-four hours, three days, two weeks, and six weeks. The birth center stayed busy, and it had several labor rooms.

One day, the doorbell rang, and I welcomed my first prenatal appointment of the day. Prenatal visits had a pattern to them, which helped me adjust to speaking Spanish.

"Cual fue el primer dia de su ultima regla?" (What was the first day of your last period?)

"Seis de Septiembre," she replied. (September sixth)

"Por favor, orine en un vasito." (Please urinate in a cup.)

Her urine was dark so I discussed hydration. It was important for women to drink three quarts to one gallon of water per day. Proper hydration prevents preterm labor and urinary tract infections.

"Necessita tomar mas aqua." (You need more water.)

"Voy a tomar su presion." (I am going to take your blood pressure.)

Her blood pressure was normal, but I educated every patient on nutrition because it's the foundation of a healthy pregnancy.

"Necessita comer proteina." (Eat protein.)

It was recommended to eat eighty to 100 grams of protein per day to prevent preeclampsia (elevated blood pressure).

"No coma azucar especialmente pan dulce." (Don't eat sugar, especially sweet bread.)

"Coma mas verduras crudas." (Eat more vegetables.)

"Las comidas con hierro son: higado, carne, verduras verdes, frijoles, y pasas." (Foods with iron include liver, meat, green vegetables, beans, and raisins.)

The increased blood volume of pregnancy requires more iron to prevent anemia. If a woman is anemic (having fewer healthy red blood cells), less oxygenated blood will be delivered to the baby.

"Voy a escuchar el corazon del bebe." (I'm going to listen to your baby's heart.)

The mother-to-be beamed with happiness when she heard the baby's heartbeat.

"El bebe su mueve mucho?" (Does the baby move a lot?)

"Si," she said. (Yes)

"Voy a medir la matriz o utero." (I am going to measure your uterus.)

I measured her uterus in centimeters, which assesses fetal growth throughout pregnancy.

"Voy a palpar tu abdomen," I said. (I'm going to palpate your abdomen.)

I enjoyed palpating the abdomen for a baby's position in utero, which is called "Leopold maneuvers." Palpating is also used to estimate fetal weight. Leopold maneuvers were done on all women past thirty-four weeks. With the volume of women seen in the clinic, I got good at it.

Es Tiempo Para Empujar (It Is Time to Push)

The birth center was busy and filled with liveliness. It was rarely quiet. Even though the rhythm of natural labor was the same, each woman had her own unique situation.

Late one evening, the doorbell rang. A laboring woman who was wearing a multi-colored dress was at the door in a half squat. I unlocked the door.

"Ayudeme!" (Help me!)

She walked through the birth center's door and immediately squatted. I squatted with her and tossed a towel underneath her. She birthed a baby into my gloved hands. I placed the crying baby in the mother's arms. I helped her stand up. The purplish-white umbilical cord dangled from between her legs up to the baby's navel. I guided the woman to the closest bed, and she laid down on absorbent pads. I dried the crying pink baby with towels and grabbed a birth pack. The cord was clamped and cut. With one push, the placenta birthed easily with minimal blood loss. The beautiful Hispanic woman with long black hair smiled and laughed. She was happy she made it to the birth center in time.

Being at the birth center was exciting because each day brought different experiences. Another day, the doorbell rang. When I looked through the glass door, I saw a lone woman breathing through a contraction while rubbing her abdomen. I let her in to the birth center and asked a series of questions.

"Tiene contracciones?" (Are you having contractions?)

"Si," she replied. (Yes.)

"Ya se le rompio su fuente?" (Has your water broken?)

"No," she said.

"Cada cuantos minutos son las contracciones?" (How far apart are your contractions?)

"Cinco minutos," she said as a contraction started. (Five minutes.)

"Yo la reviso" I said. (I will check you.)

"OK," she answered calmly.

She was five to six centimeters!

"Respire profundo y relajate," I said as I made her comfortable in a birth room. (Breathe deeply and relax.)

She spent several hours laboring calmly, confidently, and quietly on her left side. She was hoping her mother and sisters would arrive soon. When things got harder and transition was intense, I rubbed her back while she stood, leaning forward over the bed. As the birth energy strengthened, she knew she couldn't wait any longer for her family to arrive.

She said, "Estoy listo." (I am ready.)

The next contraction, her water broke, and her baby quickly crowned. The baby birthed easily with the next push. It was a beautiful birth. Soon after, her mother and sisters arrived. They were lively, animated, and vibrant. The room was filled with happiness and joy. Each spoke so quickly, I couldn't understand a word. There was no need. The exuberance said it all.

One evening, I had just finished the last appointment for the day when the doorbell rang. A short black-haired woman indicated her water had broken. Using an amnioindicator, I tested the fluid that was leaking. The swab turned dark blue, which confirmed her membranes had ruptured. She was not having any contractions, and she was well past her expected date of delivery. To facilitate labor, she was given a small amount of herbal tincture, containing black cohosh (Cimicifuga racemosa) and blue cohosh (Caulophyllum thalictroides) which are known to stimulate uterine contractions. Within thirty minutes, her contractions were strong and consistent. I was often amazed at the effectiveness of herbs on labor. Within two more hours, she was holding a healthy baby boy.

Speaking a foreign language can be tricky. During one prenatal appointment, I was palpating an abdomen and explaining the position of the baby to the pregnant woman.

I touched her lower abdomen and with a smile said, "La cerveza esta aqui."

I thought I said, "The head is here."

The lady laughed and said, "No, no, no, no. No cerveza."

Suddenly, I realized what I said. Quickly I said, "Lo siento! La *cabeza* esta aqui!" (I'm sorry! The *head* is here!)

I had said *cerveza* (beer) instead of *cabeza* (head)! She and her mother good naturedly laughed as I finished her prenatal exam. It was a great appointment, filled with laughter, smiles, and grace. She returned a few days later in labor. I made certain to say *la cabeza!*

One evening, I was on call and watching the sunset through the window when the doorbell rang. The posture of the black-haired woman told me she was in hard labor. She never complained, stoically breathing through each contraction. I rubbed her lower back, brushed her hair, and placed cold compresses on her forehead. She and I spent hours together, moving through the waves of contractions. I labored her on the toilet and in the shower. I massaged her shoulders and back while she sat on a birth ball. Suddenly her water broke, and she felt intense pressure. She quickly moved to the comfortable double bed.

"Voy a revisar su cerviz." (I am going to check your cervix.)

I checked her and said, "Es tiempo para empujar." (It's time to push.)

She pushed twice and birthed a baby girl. After she nursed and the baby was content, I helped her shower. I washed the blood off her legs and feet. When she was ready to go home, she motioned for me to come nearer to her. She took off her brightly beaded necklace and placed it around my neck. Each bead had a painted pattern on it. Her quiet mannerisms and gentle spirit had a strength to them. I was humbled, and I got the distinct impression she was giving me a necklace that she treasured.

Another day, I had just come on shift when a *primigravida* (a woman pregnant for the first time) rang the doorbell. She was in labor. I walked with her to a spacious birth room that had a comfortable double bed. She was tense and unable to relax. I asked her what was bothering her, and she bitterly and tearfully said she was not ready to be a mother. She reminded me of a cat cornered up a tree. Her acrid manner and sharp tongue were unpleasant. She was skittish when touched. I quietly told her she could labor without cervical checks. Her body would lead the way.

After that, the woman did a complete turnaround. Her face softened. She stood and labored with her feet planted firmly on the floor. She breathed with each contraction and swayed her body. As I watched, she became a mature woman and mother right before my eyes. She sat on the birth stool and with an open throat allowed her cervix to open. She had a quick labor and an intense determination on her face when she delivered. She scooped up the baby and immediately started breastfeeding, gazing lovingly at her baby. Her eyes said it all.

One morning, I walked into the birth center well rested and ready for the day. I heard a low moan and knew a woman was in labor. I read the chart to familiarize myself with her prenatal history.

When I walked into the birth room, she was breathing through a contraction. I noticed she was wearing a gold necklace with a pendant of the Virgin of Guadalupe. Attached to her brasserie strap was a Virgin of Guadalupe gold enamel pin. After the contraction finished, we exchanged smiles. I placed a cold compress around the back of her neck and handed her a glass of water.

During early labor, she walked. Walking in early labor is beneficial because it opens the inlet to the pelvis. During contractions, she stopped walking to sway her hips. When she tired of walking, I pulled out the stool. I had her position her right foot up on a step stool for ten contractions. Next, she positioned her left foot on the stool for ten contractions. These position changes help a baby descend. When she tired of standing, she sat on a birth ball and moved her hips like she was drawing the number eight, which is called the "Figure 8." As contractions grew more intense, she sat still on the birth stool and hummed. Throughout transition, she squatted on the floor while lying her head onto a chair. Squatting opens the outlet of the pelvis.

As labor intensified, she sat on the toilet, which is a supported squat position that works very well to relax the pelvic floor. Sitting backward on a toilet works too because the laboring woman can perch up on her toes. Women naturally relax their pelvic floor when sitting on a toilet.

Suddenly, the laboring woman grunted in a deep guttural manner—a distinct sound that means birth is imminent. Quickly, I moved her from the toilet to the double bed. While semi-reclining, she pulled back her legs and birthed her baby. She was elated. After she nursed her baby and showered, she kneeled at the bedside. With her Rosary in her hands, she prayed in Spanish.

One night, the doorbell rang, and a woman was standing at the door in labor. I immediately took her into the exam room.

"Ya se le rompio su fuente?" (Did your bag of waters break?)

"Si." (Yes.)

"Quando?" (When?)

"Hace una hora." (One hour ago.)

"Voy a revisar su cerviz." (I'm going to check your cervix.)

To my surprise, the sterile exam revealed a breech presentation. Fetal heart tones were reassuring at 140 beats per minute with good variability and several accelerations. The woman had spontaneous rupture of membranes at home with clear fluid. The problem was the baby's head was not the presenting part. An ultrasound confirmed Frank breech. The birth center rules prohibited delivery of a breech.

"Necesita que ir al hospital. Es necesario tener Cesarea de nalgas." (You need to go to the hospital. It is necessary to have a C-section for breech.)

The tearful woman was not expecting to have a surgery. With the help of a translator, I educated her on what to expect with a Cesarean section.

The woman visibly relaxed after hearing my summarization. She was transported by ambulance to the hospital and had a C-section. Upon discharge, she brought the baby to see us at the birth center. She and the baby were happy and healthy.

Tapala

My time at the birth center was the best experience a new midwife could ask for. A key philosophy that resonated with me was: Time and patience take care of most labors. I was exposed to many Hispanic traditions, and I experienced a variety of birthing situations. I loved the rhythm of natural birth and the tools *traditional midwifery* used to achieve it. I had only one more day at the birth center, and I would be on a plane headed home.

My last night, I was startled out of sleep in the middle of the night. The doorbell was ringing. A woman with long black hair, wearing a turquoise necklace and a brightly embroidered dress, was at the door with her mother.

She said with a grimace, "Duele mucho." (It hurts a lot.)

I brought her into the clinic. Upon exam, I found she was five centimeters with a well applied head to the cervix, which indicates that direct pressure is being put on the cervix to aid labor.

I advised, "Dese un bano de regadera caliente le ayudara a relajarse. Permite que su matriz trabaje." (Take a warm shower. It will help you relax. Let your uterus work.)

The woman stood under the warm water in the birth center's shower room. With every contraction, she relaxed her abdomen and let the contraction come. She stopped fighting them, instead letting them wash over her like waves. Relaxing lessened her pain.

Her mother would gently remind her, "Respire profundo y relajate." (Breathe deeply and relax.) It warmed my heart to watch the love between the mother and daughter. Actually, most of the women who gave birth at the center had their mothers with them. It was beautiful to see the wisdom of one generation being passed to the next.

After the woman dried off from her shower, I tied a long Mexican rebozo around her waist, hips, and abdomen. The textured fabric of the long, colorful handwoven shawl felt lovely on my fingers. When a rebozo is wrapped properly, it provides abdominal support and lifts the abdomen up, which gives belly support and decreases labor pain. Also, the abdominal lifting allows the baby's head to become better positioned in the pelvis.

I rubbed lavender essential oil on her wrists and feet to induce relaxation. She ate rice and beans and drank Mexican horchata. Horchata is a sweet creamy drink made from rice, water, and cinnamon. I dimmed the lights, and she continued laboring.

"Quiere presion en su espalda con mi mano?" (Do you want pressure on your back with my hand?)

"Si!" (Yes.)

The woman liked the counterpressure (strong, steady pressure) I applied to her sacrum. Applying counterpressure with the heel of my hand directly to a woman's sacrum encourages a baby's head to rotate and reduces the woman's pain level.

Early in my time at the birth center, I had learned key words women might say.

Falta mucho. (Will it be long.)

Dios Mio! (Oh my God!)

No puedo! (I can't!)

Mierda (Poop)

Mierda was an important word to listen for because the sensation to poop means the baby's head is putting pressure on the rectum. This pressure suggests birth might be imminent.

Suddenly, my laboring woman started speaking quickly. I caught the word *mierda* and recognized she must be feeling pressure.

"Es la cabesita del bebe," I explained. (It's the baby's head.)

"Necesito que revisar su cerviz," I said. (I need to check your cervix.)

She was almost ten centimeters dilated. She had an anterior lip of the cervix, which meant it was not time to push yet. She needed to pant or blow with her contractions until she was fully dilated.

"Sopla con las contracciones." (Blow with the contractions.)

I alternated her position. She leaned forward over the bed for three contractions, then she moved to her hand and knees for three contractions. While she was on all fours, I had her lift her chin way up off her chest to imitate blowing out birthday candles. This easily remedies the anterior lip.

In fifteen minutes, I checked her again. Success! The anterior lip was gone.

"Es tiempo para empujar." (It is time to push.)

She rolled over and placed a pillow under her head.

"Jale sus piernas hacia arriba y empuje!" (Pull your legs up and push!)

She pushed, but it was not effective.

"Empuje mas fuerte." (Push harder.)

Still no progress.

She turned on her right side and pushed.

"Empuje otra vez," I instructed. (Push again.)

"Si! Si! Si!" I said. (Yes! Yes! Yes!)

She had it now. The head was crowning.

She pushed again, and the head birthed.

"Empuje otra vez por el cuerpo," I encouraged. (Push again for the body.)

The baby was born, and I placed the crying baby into her arms. She started crying too. She smiled and cried at the same time.

When the cord finished pulsating, I clamped and cut it.

"Necesita pujar otra vez para la placenta. No duele mucho." (You need to push again for the placenta. It won't hurt much.)

She pushed, and a placenta delivered fetal side, called shiny Schultz. With Schultz, the placenta separates and presents from the middle and generally has less bleeding. This contrasts with a placenta delivered maternal side called dirty Duncan. With

Duncan, the placental edge delivers first, with the rest of the placenta following. Separation of the placenta happens more slowly with Duncan, allowing more time for bleeding.

I put the placenta into a bowl and examined it. It was intact with no missing pieces.

"Voy a revisar que el utero este duro para que no sangre." (I am going to check that your uterus stays firm so you won't bleed.) With my hand on her abdomen, I rubbed the top of her uterus (fundus). Her fundus was firm not boggy, two fingerbreadths above the umbilicus, and midline.

I smiled and said, "Es bueno." (It's good).

"Voy a examiner su bebe." (I am going to examine your baby.) I performed newborn exams on every baby. Apgar scores, weighing, measuring, and listening to the lungs and heart were part of the assessment.

"Su bebe esta bien! Ella pesa nueve libras!" (Your baby is fine! She weighs nine pounds!)

She had birthed a nine-pound baby—without tearing. No stitches were needed.

"Trate de ammamantar horita." (Try to nurse now.)

"Tiene colostros. Su leche le bajara dentro tres dias." (You have colostrum. Your milk will come in three days.)

In some Hispanic cultures, chamomile tea is given to babies. We educated women not to use this because it makes a baby sleepy.

"No te de manzanilla. Te de manzanilla hace qu sue bebe duerma, y no quiere comer." (No chamomile tea. Chamomile tea makes your baby sleep and not want to eat.)

The mom stayed six hours and was preparing to leave the clinic. She was wrapping the baby in *a lot* of blankets. Most Mexican women wrap their babies in layers of blankets because the baby needs protection against the hot sun, dust, and wind. Also, the babies are considered to have frio (cold) without the help of many coverings.

As the new mom left the clinic carrying the baby in her arms, I heard the grandmothers say, "Tapala. Tapala. Tapala." (Cover her up.) Through the glass doors, I watched the mother walk away, carrying the heavily bundled baby in the ninety degree heat. I smiled and said to myself, "Tapala."

Later that evening as I sat on the airplane wrapped in a handwoven Mexican blanket, my eyes were so heavy. As the waves of sleepiness overpowered me, I thought of the bundled babies and mused, *Tapala.*

Sue's Waterbirth

This true birth story is included with the permission of Suzanne Rickman.

After the high pace birth center, it was nice to come back home. My days were filled with homeschooling my three daughters and attending homebirths and hospital doula births.

I also volunteered my time at La Leche to assist nursing mothers. I met Sue at a La Leche League meeting. She was the La Leche League leader and an advocate for women. I had nursed all three of my daughters, had tandem nursed, and even nursed through two pregnancies. I encouraged women from both my personal experience and through the lens of midwifery.

Sue and I became friends, and she openly discussed her previous birth experience. Her first baby was born premature. With her next pregnancy, she wanted a full-term baby and a serene birth. When she hired me, we discussed the goal of birth without fear. We developed a plan of care that addressed prenatal care, nutrition, and natural childbirth. Sue wanted to have a waterbirth in the hospital, and her wonderful obstetrician approved.

Because nutrition is so important, I discussed it in depth with Sue. I suggested that she eat vegetables of every color. By eating a rainbow of colorful vegetables, a woman will consume a variety of vitamins, minerals, antioxidants, and phytochemicals. For example, green vegetables provide vitamin K and folate and boost the immune system.

High protein intake is important in pregnancy. Because Sue was a lacto ovo vegetarian, she ate vegetables, eggs, and dairy, but she did not eat meat. Eggs and dairy are complete proteins. However, to maximize her complete protein intake, it was important she combine foods. Rice and beans, pinto beans and corn, lentils and rice, hummus with pita bread, and chickpeas and couscous are food combinations that form a complete protein. Quinoa is a complete protein alone and was a great addition to any meal.

I encouraged Sue to soak in Epsom salts throughout her pregnancy. Soaking would help with relaxation, which would calm her fears. Epsom salts also contain magnesium, which decrease the risk of preterm labor.

Because iron is necessary to prevent anemia during pregnancy, I suggested she supplement with a liquid iron called Floradix. It is plant-based, easily absorbed, and does not constipate. I recommended probiotics, which are important to maintain a good balance of healthy bacteria in the gut, which aids in preventing colonization with Group B streptococcal (GBS) bacterium. Having vaginal or intestinal colonization of GBS can be transmitted to a newborn and cause respiratory issues or death. The probiotic strains I recommended were Lactobacillus rhamnosus GR-1, Lactobacillus reuteri RC-14, and Lactobacillus salivarius CECT 9145.

I explained optimal fetal positioning. I suggested using a pregnancy body pillow, which would allow her to comfortably hammock her abdomen while sleeping on her left side. Sleeping on the left side encourages a baby to move into a left occiput anterior (LOA) position. This is the best position for a baby to have when entering labor. LOA gives the shortest labor time and the least chance of rotating into an occiput posterior (OP) position, which is face up. Occiput posterior position has an increased risk of C-section, which makes prevention important.

I recommended sitting on a birth ball instead of a recliner during the last trimester to help optimal fetal positioning. I encouraged scrubbing floors on hands and knees because it assists in promoting face down position.

To decrease Sue's anxiety, I suggested she write down her fears and burn them. She feared the possibility of complications after her previous preterm birth. When she burned her fears, she released them, which was instrumental in conquering her anxiety. She would enter birth without fear. She was confident and empowered.

I hosted a Blessingway ceremony to bless the way ahead for Sue, celebrate her pregnancy, and offer blessings. Sue was given beads from each woman with a blessing. She would string the beads into a necklace and wear the necklace during labor. At the ceremony, Sue talked about the challenges and joys that lie before her. Sue was supported in a calm, peaceful environment. It was beautiful.

Sue next opted for belly painting with henna. She picked a beautiful pattern, and the henna would remain on her abdomen throughout her labor. The goals were to support Sue during this sacred time in life, to fill her with love, and to encourage her. Love feeds a woman during pregnancy. It's as important as food.

Midwives often use herbs to prepare the uterus for childbirth. Red raspberry tea tones the uterus, which allows for an easier, faster birth. I suggested that Sue drink three cups per day of red raspberry tea.

I recommended a blend of herbs in tincture form starting the last few weeks of pregnancy. This combination of skullcap herb, blue cohosh root, false unicorn root, ginger root, motherwort herb, partridge berry herb and red raspberry leaf gradually dilates (opens), effaces (thins), and softens the cervix. These herbs promote shorter labors and decrease pain in labor. This blend of herbs for childbirth preparation is powerful and effective. The herbs contribute to a good Bishop score by dilating, effacing, and softening the cervix.

In preparation for Sue's waterbirth, I networked with the nurse manager of labor and delivery. She was instrumental in promoting natural childbirth options and had garnered the hospital's approval for portable laboring tubs from Waterbirth International.

A few weeks before Sue's due date, there was a tornado in the area, and Sue and her toddler had been confined in a small closet during the tornado warning. After the storm, I did a home visit to check on Sue and the baby. I palpated her abdomen. The baby was lying transverse, which is horizontal instead of vertical. Using optimal fetal positioning, I placed Sue in the yoga child's pose for thirty minutes. The baby turned vertex (head down) and engaged into the pelvis, which means he dropped. I suggested Sue rest on her left side in what I call the "hammock position" to keep the baby there. In the hammock position, she had her left leg straight and her right leg at a ninety degree angle supported by pillows. This position creates a hammock for the belly and encourages the baby to move into the left occiput anterior position (LOA).

On a winter day, Sue started having irregular contractions. I encouraged her to soak in an Epsom salt bath to relax. She soaked while reading books to her toddler. After her bath, she called me to come over and keep her company. She labored calmly and happily in her own home. Candles were flickering in the darkness while she sat on a birth ball in her kitchen. She tugged on a birth rope during contractions and rolled her pelvis in a figure eight on the birth ball to naturally release prostaglandins at the cervix. Prostaglandins are a hormone-like substance that efface the cervix and cause contractions. Using the figure eight birth ball technique to put pressure on the cervix is like a cervical massage, which releases prostaglandins. Sue was moving into labor land, and she was glowing and looked beautiful. The tranquility and peace that permeated her birth space created a loving labor environment.

When we arrived at the hospital, Sue stood at the bedside. The large birth tub was being filled with warm water. The warm water had a temperature of 94 degrees, which was perfect. I placed rose petals in it as we listened to the relaxing, rhythmic flowing of the water into the tub. The bright hospital lights were turned off when Sue and I got into the tub together. I wore a swimsuit, and Sue wore a sports bra. The beautiful beads on her necklace glistened in the water. Sue floated on her back with her legs around my waist. We labored as one. It was a surreal experience.

While kneeling in the water, I performed the double hip squeeze during contractions. The physiological purpose of this technique is to open the sacrum and lessen pain. I repeated to Sue her mantra of "no mind." By keeping the mind clear, she kept intrusive thoughts and fear from enveloping her. She floated nearly pain free in the warm comfort of water. At one point, she was immersed completely in the water except for her nose. She floated her way through transition. When her vocalizations became high, I reminded her to make low sounds instead. Low moaning sounds dilate the cervix. Sue was free: free to move, free to float, free from fear. She was surrounded by love.

When Sue's water broke, her doctor used a flashlight to look at the water. It was clear with no meconium (baby poop). The nurses and I used my waterproof doppler monitor to listen to fetal heart tones. The baby's fetal heart tones were normal.

Sue moved her hips and pelvis, and second stage was here. The baby's head was crowning. Sue and I touched hands as we supported his crowning head and touched his hair. We smiled at each other.

I looked at the doctor because she was sitting in a chair adjacent to the birth tub and hadn't moved. She was lovingly watching the birth process unfold; it was her first waterbirth.

"You do it, Tori," she said smiling.

"Give one good push," I told Sue.

She did, and her precious baby boy was born into my hands in the warm water. I brought him out of the water and gently handed him to Sue. I was mindful not to pull the umbilical cord because it remained attached to the placenta. I rubbed the baby's back, and he let out a robust cry. I don't think there was a dry eye in the room. It was the most peaceful, gentle birth I had ever witnessed. The room was filled with love.

Chapter 8: Hope House

*This true birth story is included with the permission
of Suzanne Rickman.*

A few years later, Sue was due with a baby girl. Waterbirth was not permitted in the local hospital which caused Sue to make a different birth plan. Sue wanted a waterbirth because her prior birth was gentle and idyllic. To have a waterbirth, Sue arranged to birth across the state line where midwives were licensed to provide out of hospital births. She chose to birth at Hope House, a place of refuge where women had the freedom to birth on their own terms.

Hope House was my passion. To create the serenity of Hope House, I painstakingly cleaned and transformed an older home that been built after the Great Depression. Its solid wooden floors were smooth and welcoming. I sighed with contentment as I looked at the lovely home that I had painted and furnished with a larger purpose in mind. I had worked hard to create a home that women could come to and use as their own.

Walking into the enclosed front porch, a woman was greeted by two burgundy wooden rocking chairs with comfortable turquoise cushions. Against one wall of the porch was a welcoming daybed with white sheets and white pillows, surrounded by white netting hanging from the ceiling, making it a lovely space. The windows had turquoise curtains, which accented the light brown floor. The floor's warm earth tone color would serve as a grounding force when a woman walked into Hope House in labor.

Hope House had plenty of room, and each woman could gravitate toward whichever space made her comfortable. I decorated each room in a different style.

In the living room, I had a birth tub, birth stool, birth ball, and sofa set up near the natural gas fireplace. White Christmas tree lights were strung across the ceiling, creating just the right amount of light when a woman labored in the dark while soaking in the warm water.

The first bedroom had an Amish quilt on the bed with an Amish rocker nearby. A second bedroom was decorated in Victorian-style with a dark-purple-and-cream quilt on the queen bed with matching embroidered curtains. The third bedroom had a sleigh bed with a white quilt. Cream curtains with light purple sheer swags gave the room a feminine, dainty feel.

The last birthing room was an open area with a mattress on the floor and a colorful Bohemian style comforter. Sheer netting hung around the mattress. It was a beautiful space to birth in.

Hope House was humble, but serene and calming. I loved it with all my heart.

On a cold January night, Sue went into labor. She called me in the wee morning hours. Before she could get out a sentence, I could tell she was in active labor. I drove immediately to her home. The plan was to drive to Hope House across the state line.

Inwardly, I was extremely frustrated that the hospital policy did not permit waterbirth. Sue lived minutes from the hospital. I was also disgusted that our state did not grant licenses to Certified Professional Midwives. This meant an ambulance attendant could legally deliver Sue's baby, but Sue could not hire a midwife to attend her in her own home.

When I arrived at Sue's home, she glowed like sunshine. Her lovely Irish face and beautiful smile greeted me. We locked eyes, and I knew she was in intense labor. I held my hand on her rounded belly and palpated through a contraction. Sue and I were bonded once again.

Sue waddled to the car because it was time to drive across the state line. She climbed into my car between contractions. The drive felt like an intense race against time to get Sue to her sanctuary of warm water. Sue labored in the front seat, kneeling backward, and holding onto the headrest, with the seatbelt wrapped around her. She rhythmically moved her hips and abdomen like a beautiful belly dancer. Even though the contractions were painful, the only time she verbalized displeasure was when the car bounced across the railroad tracks and she felt jarring in her groin. After I pulled up to Hope House, she made her way into her birth space.

Sue chose the bedroom with the queen-sized bed with a dark purple-and-cream quilt. The pillows were plump, and the dark purple curtains were embroidered with cream thread. The birth tub was in the corner of the room with a hose draped into it. The hose was connected to the faucet in the bathroom. Water was pouring into the tub as quickly as the hot water heater would allow. In addition, I was boiling water in four pots on the electric stove.

Time was not on our side. Sue was standing on the hardwood floor laboring. I knew she was close to birthing. She got into the tub while it was still filling. Her lovely mother and Sue's two sons were sitting on the queen size bed enthralled with the frenzy. The race was on to fill the tub so she could float and to make the temperature of the water feel like a warm embrace.

But the baby had other plans. Sue's baby girl crowned quickly and made her entrance into the water before Sue could float. Sue was semi-reclining in the water, and her daughter was born into my hands as I leaned over into the birth tub.

The baby was born to a mother who loved her beyond all measure. Sue's two young sons had watched their mother have a waterbirth. The moment when the two boys peered over the tub and gazed at their mother holding their baby sister was an incredibly tender birth scene. Their bright eyes shined with love at their mother. Seeing their loving eyes brought tears to my eyes. Their beaming love made my heart happy. Sue's mother was able to share in the birth experience, and the love and bond between three generations was apparent. Sue didn't have the opportunity to float in the water this time, but deep love was ever-present for her. Sue was loved unconditionally.

To the Moon and Back

Each birth has its own dynamics. Social and family issues impact labor and birth. One time, a woman asked me to support her through her labor and delivery. Her circumstances were unusual. Her husband was serving in the Middle East during the war. She found out she was pregnant the day after he left. He wanted her to have support throughout her pregnancy, labor, delivery, and postpartum, so he encouraged her to hire me. I would be her labor coach, and she would birth in the hospital with her doctor. The three of us formulated a birth plan over Skype. It was clear that they loved each other to the moon and back.

A while later, I was carrying groceries into my house, when I received a call from her. She was crying. For a split second, I thought maybe she miscarried. Through her wailing and tears, I pieced together what happened. Two uniformed soldiers had knocked on her door. As soon as she saw them in their perfectly tailored military uniforms standing with stoic faces, she knew. Her husband was dead.

Stress caused her due date to come and go. One afternoon, she passed the stringy jelly-like mucus plug and was having menstrual cramps. She asked me to sleep at her house for a few nights. I agreed. On the first night, she woke me up. She was having bloody show (bloody discharge with mucus) and mild contractions. I asked her where she felt most comfortable. She wanted to go stand outside under the stars to feel close to her husband. She labored for hours looking at the stars. As the hours passed, we watched the constellations move across the sky. She started moving into transition. It was time to go to the hospital. I drove, and she labored.

We had one planned stop. As the sun rose, she walked quietly alone to the grave of her husband, where she left two blue baby booties. When she walked away from his grave, she squared her shoulders. She was truly gallant. Hero was an understatement. I couldn't think of an appropriate word to describe how I felt in that moment.

She was eight centimeters dilated when the nurse admitted her. She was in hard labor and coping well. Within one hour, she was nine centimeters. Suddenly, all contractions stopped. It is amazing how women can stop their own labor. I've seen it happen before. For two hours, she stared silently at the wall. Suddenly, she cried a wail of deep grief.

"I don't want to let the baby out. I feel like I am letting my husband go," she wailed.

"When you were under the stars, did you believe your husband was with you?"

"Yes, he is undoubtedly in heaven. I have that faith," she said.

"It is okay to let the baby out. You can tell your baby all about his daddy."

Her contractions started again. She had needed the time to work thorough her pain.

She quickly moved into second stage. She pushed well and gave birth to a healthy son. She named him after her husband. She was wearing her husband's dog tags. She took them off and let her baby grip one of the tags. My eyes filled with so many tears that my vision blurred. Their sacrifice cut my heart.

"I'm going to get you a golden retriever when you are six! Your daddy loved golden retrievers," she said to her son, who was cradled in her arms.

There was no doubt she would keep her husband's memory alive.

April's Twins

This true birth story is included with the permission of April Howton.

April was a dynamic Irish-looking lady. She was vibrant and energetic, her smile was infectious, and she was a joy to be around. April had four prior waterbirths, and I had assisted in all of them as either her nurse or doula.

April labored very well and made birth look easy. Her labors and waterbirths had a rhythm and tranquility to them. Often in the middle of active labor, she would take a sound nap. It amazed me every time she did this. When her eyes opened, she would say, "It's time to get in the water." She would sink into the warm water and close her eyes. She made transition of labor look effortless while kneeling in the tub with her head resting on its side. The low vocalizations would come as second stage started. Her vocalizations were a combination of a cow mooing and a humming sound. There was a vibration to the vocal sounds as her throat opened in sync with the birth process. Open throat and loose lips allow the birth process to occur without resistance.

April allowed her body to do the work, and her baby would be born into the warm water. She would turn over, carefully lifting her leg up and over the cord. She would receive her baby and embrace it. Water was April's comfort in labor. She needed it.

One morning, April called to surprise me.

"You need to paint my toenails!" she said.

That was our code for, "I'm pregnant!"

The next part came as a surprise. April had just received her ultrasound results from her doctor. She was having twins! We both knew this birth was going to be different. There would be no waterbirth.

April's doctor was a well respected, very experienced obstetrician. Most twins are born by Cesarean section, but April was praying for a natural birth. Thankfully, April had two placentas and two amniotic sacs, which is the optimal twin pregnancy. This information in addition to April's history of a proven pelvis (previous vaginal deliveries) gave her the best chance for a natural delivery of her twins. Her amazing obstetrician agreed to deliver the twins vaginally. She had three straps around her abdomen. The nurses were monitoring contractions and the fetal heart tones of each twin.

April labored very well. Baby A was breech (butt first), and baby B was vertex (head down). She might not have had the water, but she had determination and grit. She sat on the birth ball at the side of the bed near the monitor. As labor progressed, April used a squat bar to help the buttocks of baby A to descend. She alternated between squatting, standing, and sitting on the birth ball.

When April started making low mooing sounds, I knew second stage was here. She was rolled in the bed to the operating room to deliver the twins. Her doctor was prudent. By delivering in the operating room, he could pivot to perform a C-section if necessary.

Baby A was coming—buttocks first. Her little legs were born next. Her umbilical cord and abdomen came easily. The skilled doctor maneuvered the baby to bring one arm. He turned her to bring the other arm. He positioned her to bring the head. This breech birth was textbook. She was born into the doctor's capable, loving hands. He clamped and cut the umbilical cord and handed the baby to the nursery nurse.

Baby B remained in vertex (head down) position, which was perfect. In a few minutes, April had the urge to push again. The baby's head crowned. With one more push, her son was born. The doctor held him in his hands. He clamped and cut the cord and handed him to a second nursery nurse.

April wasn't done. The placentas remained undelivered. With grit, she pushed and delivered the placentas that had nurtured the fraternal twins. Her uterus clamped down, and she did not hemorrhage. The beautiful birth was over.

With a supportive obstetrician, April had delivered her twins vaginally. Even though she delivered in the operating room, people surrounded her with loving warmth. The warm glow reminded me of the warm water that had surrounded April during her tranquil water births. It was incredible.

The birth of the twins was a beautiful symmetry of traditional midwifery and biomedicine. The doctor had granted April the freedom to labor out of bed. She labored upright on a birth ball. She stood. She squatted. She was never obliged to stay in bed. The traditional midwifery positions decreased her pain level and assisted the breech baby to descend. That doctor was nothing short of a saint. He will always be a hero to me.

Epilepsy

This true story is included with the permission of a birthing woman who requested to remain anonymous.

I had an initial midwifery consultation with a woman and listened to her prior birth story. She had a history of epilepsy. Seizure medications can cause birth defects, so she had weaned off her medication under the supervision of her neurologist prior to her pregnancy. During her labor in the hospital, she had a seizure and subsequently a C-section.

With this pregnancy, she wanted a vaginal birth. She did not wean off her seizure medication this time. She was stable and seizure-free on her medication and under the supervision of a neurologist. She was hoping the baby would not have a birth defect from the medication. The ultrasound scans were reassuring and noted no abnormalities. Her obstetrician was more than an hour away from her home because local hospitals refused to allow VBAC (vaginal birth after Cesarean) for birthing women. She had to travel to have the option of a VBAC. She wanted me to attend her labor as her midwife and decide when to go to the hospital.

Her operating room report showed she had a low transverse incision with her prior C-section, rather than a classical incision (high vertical incision- abdominal and uterine). In addition, her report annotated double layer suturing of the uterine incision where the second layer imbricates the first layer. This made her a good candidate for a VBAC.

While she was pregnant, she had a Blessingway. She discussed her fears: Fear of another C-section. Fear of a seizure. Fear of not making it to the hospital. Fear of the hospital. Fear of a ruptured uterus. Fear of pushing. Fear of birth defects from the seizure medication.

Our plan was for her to labor with minimal stress, keep lights dimmed, and stay out of bed as long as possible.

On a Friday evening, her husband called me. She was unable to sleep, and the contractions were coming hard and steady. I immediately went to their home, but only after knocking on their neighbor's door because I mixed up the houses in the darkness of the cold November evening.

When I walked into her home, she was leaning over the arm of the couch in a front leaning position. Her contractions were every two minutes. She was dilated to five centimeters. The baby was low and in a perfect LOA position. She should have no difficulty birthing this baby vaginally. I said it was time to travel.

Her husband started loading the car. When contractions came, I rubbed her lower back and put counterpressure on her sacrum, which brought her relief. An elderly neighbor came to babysit her sleeping daughter until a family member could arrive.

She sat backward in the front seat of the car hugging on the head rest with a seatbelt strapped around her. Whenever I drove behind a laboring woman, I requested their driver blink the hazard lights at the start of every contraction. By doing this, I was able to time contractions. Her contractions were every two minutes.

When we arrived at the hotel less than a mile from the hospital to continue her labor, I had her take a moment to look at the moon. It was beautiful shining through the bare branches of the tree outside the hotel. It was a cloudless night. The cold, crisp air felt refreshing after the long drive.

The hotel was paradise. Her husband arranged for a luxury suite, and it was perfect. She went directly into a warm bath. I put lavender bath salts in the water. I added lavender essential oil and dimmed the lights. Fetal heart tones by doppler were within normal parameters. The water tub was exactly what she needed to relax and dilate during contractions. We took one contraction at a time. She opened nicely. After one hour and forty-five minutes, she started arching her back upward. This is a sign that a baby is coming soon. I checked her, and she was ten centimeters with a bulging bag of amniotic fluid.

"Let's go to the hospital," I said.

We arrived at the hospital, and what a contrast it was from the serenity of the hotel room. The hospital staff buzzed around. The lights were very bright. The nurses told her not to push because the doctor was not there. I noticed the faint smell of lavender and knew that she was wrapped in the gifts of lavender and love.

Her doctor arrived to break the bag of water, after which he told her to push. She pushed effectively, and in just a few push-es was crowning. The baby was about to be born. I was shocked to see her doctor perform a routine episiotomy. It made no sense to me. It was unnecessary.

Her baby was born easily after less than one hour at the hospital. She had her VBAC! She labored for a little more than six hours. This baby was eight pounds and five ounces. He was bigger than her first baby, and there were no birth defects. The baby breastfed on her left breast first, which is preferable be-cause the baby can hear the mother's heart beating. He latched so well. Relief, joy, and happiness flooded the mother. She looked radiant.

Going to Jail

Many women are not in ideal situations when they are in labor. No matter the circumstances a woman was facing, I provided her a respectful and loving birth environment.

One lady with pearly white skin, blonde hair, and bright blue eyes went into labor a few hours before her husband was to appear in court for sentencing. He had been convicted of possession of drugs. She was in labor, and her pain was intense. The muscles of her body were tense, and waves of anxiety were washing over her. She was in active labor, but her dilation was stalled.

Her husband was hoping the baby would be born before he had to leave. She was emotionally unsettled, knowing he was going to jail. He kept watching the clock, hoping. She labored on the birth ball with her eyes closed. Silent tears flowed down her face. He looked at the clock again. He stood, then went to her and gently kissed her lips.

"I'm sorry. I love you. Be strong," he whispered.

Her eyes remained closed. She heard the door shut and let out a wail, which let out her grief. With her emotion released, her labor became a freight train. She dilated, and the baby descended.

Second stage arrived within an hour of the husband's leaving. Pushing was taking effort because the baby was large. With each push, she made progress. I wiped the sweat off her forehead with a cool washcloth.

She moved from the birth stool to the floor. The head emerged, and I saw a nuchal cord, so I quickly reduced the umbilical cord from the neck. With the next contraction, she pushed the shoulders and the body out. The blonde-headed baby girl let out a cry. I placed the baby on the mother's chest. Her silent tears fell onto the baby's head. After a few moments, she took a deep breath.

"The baby's daddy is fine," she said. "He has a bed and three meals. I must survive. No. I must do more than survive. I need to give my baby daughter a good life."

I helped her breastfeed. The baby latched and nursed well. She was quiet for a while watching her baby. She was falling in love with her baby right before my eyes.

She said, "I learned something about myself today. I am strong. I made it through natural childbirth, so I can get through anything."

"You can do anything you set your mind to," I said.

"I always wanted to be a nurse."

"There is a two-year program at the local community college, *and* there are scholarships."

She smiled. Her body relaxed. She had a plan. I knew instinctively that she was determined and would succeed. Three years later, she called me. She was a nurse.

The River

One day, I received a call from a woman who wanted a homebirth. We met at her home for a consultation. She was born with a right arm limb reduction. This birth defect occurs when a fetus's arm doesn't fully form during pregnancy, resulting in a missing limb. Complicating her medical history was a cholecystectomy (gall bladder removal), followed by a long recovery due to complications with a hospital-acquired MRSA infection.

As I listened to the woman's story, I understood her desire to birth in her own home on her own terms. She wanted to avoid the risk of another hospital-acquired infection. Most importantly, she wanted to birth where she felt comfortable and not feel like a medical anomaly.

Her husband loved botany and was fully on board with natural birth. Her gracious, loving, and supportive mother was widowed and lived with them.

Throughout the woman's pregnancy, she followed my nutritional recommendations religiously. Multiple ultrasounds showed a growing healthy baby.

On a lovely autumn afternoon, her mother called and told me she was in labor. It was her first baby, so I anticipated a longer labor. I arrived at her beautiful home, which was on a river. Her home had large windows with a breathtaking view of the water. The flowing river glistened under the afternoon sunshine. The leaves of the trees that lined the bank were afire with color. The brilliant gold, yellow, red, and russet foliage was on full display.

The woman wanted to labor on her private boat dock and enjoy the spacious feeling the river provided. As we walked down the slope to the wooden dock, she stopped every few minutes to breathe with a contraction. Her husband carried the birth ball. Her mother carried the birth ball base, which would keep the birth ball from rolling.

I carried midwifery supplies in case of a precipitous (fast) birth. When we arrived at the wooden boat dock, the woman sat down on the birth ball and listened to the quiet splashing of water against the river rocks. She asked her mother and me to walk along the bank and pick up river glass because she wanted an artisan to make wall art to commemorate the birth of the baby.

As her mother and I walked along the banks of the river, I kept my eye on her labor from a distance. By her body language, I timed her contractions for frequency and duration. Amazingly, we found enough river glass for her art project. The river was lower than usual, so we got lucky. Her mother put the pieces into a canning jar.

The laboring woman watched as the sun set to the west, and the last rays of the sun glistened on the surface of the water. She walked slowly back to her home. Her contractions were frequent and strong. She stopped suddenly and vomited in a patch of grass. I held her hair back while she vomited. I reassured her that vomiting was a normal part of labor, especially as a woman moves into transition.

When we entered the house, I started filling up the birth tub. Her husband had set it up under a skylight. It was a clear night so the stars would be out soon. The woman wanted to labor in the warm water, looking at the stars. Her mother turned on jazz music, which was all part of the birth plan.

When the woman started feeling pressure, she asked her husband to join her in the birth tub. He sat behind her, and she reclined on him. He lovingly wrapped his arms around her. Suddenly, her eyes got big, and she said: "The baby's coming!"

The baby was born into the warm water. I handed the baby girl to the new parents. The father supported the baby at her mother's chest. The mother held the baby close with one arm.

She looked over the baby, counting fingers and toes. She sobbed in relief when she saw the baby did not have any birth defects. The baby locked eyes with her mother. They gazed at each other, immersed in love.

Redemption

On a Saturday, a brown-haired, brown-eyed woman arrived for her first prenatal appointment. She was frank and unflinching while she shared her past. She had spent years smoking crack and subsequently fell into prostitution. There was a ministry where prior addicts reached out to homeless drug addicts. Occasionally, they succeeded in getting someone off the streets for rehab. In this case, a Christian had walked into a crack house and asked her if she wanted a different life. She willingly went to rehab, and her new religion helped her battle her addiction. She described the withdrawal from drugs as torture—a terrible combination of sweating, body aches, nausea, vomiting, and cravings to use again.

Ultimately, she was victorious and started a new life. She went to community college and received her nursing degree. She bought a small farm and built a life. And now she needed a birth free of narcotics to remain clean.

Her due date was approaching any day. A wise midwife once told me to get as much sleep before midnight as possible. I found truth in that statement. My phone rang in the middle of the night. The laboring woman reported that her contractions were every three minutes. Driving on the country road with my window down, I could smell the honeysuckles. I turned onto her dirt drive, grateful she had remembered to place an oil lamp at the end of the driveway—as I often asked families who lived on dark rural lanes to do. It made finding a home easier in the pitch black.

When I arrived, her horses stood by the fence. The moon lit my way to the white door of her small farmhouse. I rapped on the door to announce my presence, then I opened it and walked in. I told all my mothers-to-be to leave their front doors unlocked after they called for me, in case there was an unexpected quick labor. I've experienced running from a car into a home and delivering a baby with moments to spare.

After entering, I called for her.

"I'm in here," she said.

I followed the primal sounds of labor. She was standing on her toes holding on to the back of the couch. A woman standing on toes is a good indicator birth is near. Her body was shaking, indicating the adrenaline surge of transition. There was a bucket on the floor that held vomit.

"It will not be long now," I said to her.

She kneeled to vomit again. I noticed her toes curled up while she kneeled. It was not necessary to do a cervical check. Her toes were telling me everything I needed to know. Birth was imminent.

Her birth plan listed the shower as the preferred place to birth. She pulled off her nightgown and stood under the warm water facing away from me. I noticed her purple line. During early labor, a purple line appears at the natal cleft at the buttocks. As the baby's head descends and the woman's dilation increases, the purple line gets longer throughout labor. This woman's purple line started at her anus, ran up the natal cleft, and reached the top of the cleft of the buttocks, which indicated she was ten centimeters dilated.

As the shower water ran down the woman's body in streams, she stood with her hands on the shower walls to ground herself. As she started pushing, the rhombus of Michaelis in her lower back pushed out in the shape of a kite. I knew the three lower lumbar vertebrae and sacrum had moved backward, increasing the diameter of the pelvis. This process provides the baby with the maximum amount of space to maneuver its shoulders.

I kneeled in the shower stall and looked up. Her perineum was opening farther with each contraction. Her baby crowned, and she held on to the shower walls with both hands and her head. The baby birthed easily into my hands. I handed her the baby and turned off the shower water. I placed a bath towel over the baby. The new mother stood, gazing at her baby.

"I thank Jesus for you. Thank you, God," she said.

She started having another contraction. She instinctively squatted while holding the baby. She pushed, and the placenta plopped onto the floor of the shower stall. I clamped the cord near the baby's navel and cut the cord. I put the placenta into a bowl. I turned the shower back on and sprayed off her perineum, legs, and feet. She walked calmly to her bed, singing a song to the baby. She had birthed without a single cervical check. Her body was her own.

Bible Verses

I received a call from a Christian woman on a hot summer morning. She was in labor and asked me to hurry. It would be an hour drive to her rural farm, and I was hoping to arrive before the baby. She had a history of birthing precipitously (quickly).

As I was putting my birth bags into the car, I called Neysa Brown, my intern midwife.

"Hey!" she said.

"It's baby time!" I said.

Ever since I met Neysa at the hospital a few years earlier, we had become good friends. She was an experienced nursery nurse *and* labor delivery nurse. Most importantly, she was a trusted intern midwife. She instinctively knew what to do and when to do it. There was a harmony to our work together. We were kindred spirits with a passion for birth work.

The drive to this rural farm was a mixture of plowed farm fields and wooded areas. I loved having prenatal appointments at this peaceful, old, white farmhouse.

The woman had encouraging Bible verses throughout her home—painted on the walls, written on sticky notes on mirrors, and hanging on her refrigerator. The baby to come would be the eighth to enter this family.

Her husband was a farmer like his father before him. Their multigenerational family farm had fruit trees, chickens, cows, goats, and a huge garden. Her kitchen often had the sweet aroma from canning. She hung herbs upside-down to dry in the kitchen alcove.

When Neysa and I arrived at the farm, we carried our black bags up the porch steps. The expectant father opened the front door and greeted us warmly. We walked up the staircase to the second floor. The oak steps were beautiful—clearly a labor of love by a carpenter a hundred years before.

We walked into her bedroom to see the windows were open, and the white curtains were moving slightly with each gentle breeze. She was laboring on her left side. Pads on the bed were ready to absorb the amniotic fluid. She was breathing in a controlled fashion. I knew she was close to delivery. I never checked her cervix because instinctually, I knew it wasn't necessary.

"How are you?" I asked.

"I feel pressure," she said quietly.

"Is that feeling at the peak of each contraction or an overwhelming need to push now?"

"At the peak of contractions only."

"Would you like to pray with your husband until it is overwhelming?"

"Yes."

As they prayed together, Neysa and I stood outside the ajar bedroom door with our gloves on. In less than five minutes, he asked for us.

"You ready?" I asked while positioning my hands for delivery.

"Baby is coming," she said quietly.

With one push, she delivered her beautiful baby in one of the most peaceful, beautiful births I ever saw.

Midwifery allowed me to be with women during the sacred, intimate moments of birth. It was an incredible privilege to be a woman's midwife. These precious, tender moments touched my heart.

Neysa and I were blessed to attend two more of the woman's births over the next few years. Each birth was heartwarming. There was a tranquility in this home and on this farm that filled my heart with peace.

War

While American soldiers fought in Iraq and Afghanistan, pregnant women had their babies without their husbands. I arrived one night to a home to find the expectant mother laboring outside under her grape arbor. She was watching her American flag wave in the wind, illuminated by a solar-powered floodlight and standing proudly under the full moon. That flag became her focal point. Her husband was on his third tour, and the war was ever-present in her mind.

The woman was in active labor and remained silent—except for her forlorn vocalizations during contractions. Between her contractions, I heard a mockingbird forlornly singing for a mate. The night melody of the laboring woman and the lonely mockingbird was only broken by the sounds of crickets and frogs. I felt the laboring mother's soul crying out for her husband through her deep moans. A magnificent magnolia tree stood in the yard. She walked to it and squatted by a garden bench with claw legs. She rested her head on the bench.

Her water broke in the yard under the magnolia tree.

She emphatically said, "The baby's coming!"

With gloves on, I delivered the baby under the moon and stars. The mom held her baby and with great joy noticed the gender.

"He has a *son!*" she exclaimed.

In a few minutes, she delivered the placenta, which I placed in a bowl. She walked into the house carrying the baby while I carried the bowl. We went to the bathroom so she could shower and then bathe the baby. She was determined to look her best for Skype. Her husband would contact her when he returned inside the wire from his patrol.

She was in bed with makeup on and hair curled holding his son in a baby blanket when the call came. He saw the blue blanket and matching baby hat first.

"It's a BOY!" he shouted.

Other servicemen cheered loudly in the background. The new mother's face was beaming as she looked at her husband on the computer screen.

Chapter 9: Amish and Mennonite Births

One early Sunday morning, I called Lindsay Crowson, my intern midwife, who was learning skills and gaining clinical hours to become a Certified Professional Midwife. She was intelligent, discerning, and inquisitive. Her background as a nursery nurse and labor-delivery nurse made her a fantastic intern midwife. I enjoyed teaching her. For several years, I had been a preceptor for intern midwives like Lindsay, and I enjoyed passing on the art of midwifery.

"Hurry, Lindsay," I told her. The drive to this homebirth was two hours. Lindsay was driving in from one direction, and I was driving in from another.

I had received a phone call from a Mennonite man asking me to come quickly because his wife was in labor. Mennonite homes had electricity and running water. I asked him to inflate the birth tub with the electric air pump, connect the hose to the bathroom faucet, and start filling the birth tub with warm water.

When I passed the small Mennonite school, I knew I was almost to their home.

I turned left at their mailbox and smiled at a sign that read "no Sunday sales." As I drove uphill on the dirt driveway, I noticed a John Deere tractor in the semi-plowed field. A green willow tree stood alone by the catfish pond. I pulled in and parked next to their black minivan.

When I arrived, the Mennonite woman was laboring in the warm water. She was wearing her white *kapp* (head covering).

"I'm glad to see you, Tori," she said.

"I'm going to quickly set out my supplies, and then I'll listen to the baby," I said with a warm smile.

This was her seventh baby. She initially had two C-sections—the first for placenta previa (placenta covers opening of cervix) and the second for complete breech. I was her midwife for the next four babies, who were born at home in her own bed.

She moaned low and remained in hands and knees position in the birth tub. I leaned over the edge of the tub and with my right hand maneuvered the waterproof wand of the doppler under her immersed pregnant belly. I listened to the familiar galloping sound of the fetal heart tones. The baby sounded good.

Out of the corner of my eye, I saw Lindsay gingerly walk in. I was so glad she made it in time. But I wondered why she was limping. There was no time to find out. The laboring mother was moaning low, *and* she started pushing. I leaned over the inflatable tub with both arms in the water to position my hands at her perineum. I could see the hair on the baby's head as it crowned. To allow her perineum to stretch and prevent tearing, I coached her to cough the baby out.

"Cough. Good, cough again," I said. "Okay, give a small push."

Gently, the baby was born into the water. I guided the baby out of the water face-down. Because the birthing mother was in hands and knees position, I asked her to turn over when she was ready. She carefully turned over and maneuvered one leg up and over the immersed umbilical cord. I handed her the baby, and they both relaxed in the warm water. The attached umbilical cord continued pulsating, providing the baby oxygenated blood.

While waiting for the placenta to detach, I noticed my surroundings. An oak desk had paper, envelopes, and stamps neatly arranged on the desktop. I smiled as I remembered receiving hand-written letters from her throughout the pregnancy.

Handmade dresses were arranged orderly in her closet. Each dress was a solid color. I never saw any clothing with a pattern. Even the baby's clothes were solid colors.

"I'm feeling a strong contraction," she said.

I placed two clamps on the umbilical cord— a sterile plastic cord clamp near the navel and a stainless steel instrument clamp. I cut the cord between the clamps, using sterile umbilical scissors.

"Go ahead and push," I said.

With that push there was a spontaneous expulsion of the placenta. I scooped the placenta out of the water and put it into a large bowl.

I examined the placenta for any missing pieces, which was something I did at *every* birth. A missing piece is cause for concern because hemorrhage or infection can occur from a piece of retained placenta. Her placenta was all there.

I held up a large towel and averted my eyes to create privacy for the modest Mennonite woman as she stepped out of the birth tub. She wrapped a clean towel around her naked body and walked to the shower. After showering and using the toilet, she put on a nightgown, put her hair into a tight bun, and placed her kapp over her hair. She sighed as she got into bed.

"Resting feels nice," she said.

Lindsay had wiped the baby's skin with olive oil, pinned on a cloth diaper, and dressed the baby in a plain Mennonite newborn dress.

I went to the kitchen to steep red raspberry tea. While waiting on the tea, I cut a slice of homemade brown bread and placed it on a plate. Using a ladle, I scooped barley soup into a bowl. Barley increases breastmilk. She was a wise woman to have barley soup ready on her electric stove. I carried the tray of food and tea to the bedroom. The tea would help her uterus contract *and* increase breastmilk production.

While I sat on her cushioned sofa and charted in her medical record, I noticed the oil lamp on the mantel. The living area was a blend of old world and new. The cast iron coal stove stood in a corner of the room with its black stove pipe exiting the wall. An electric sewing machine sat in another corner on a solid oak table. A family photo album was on the coffee table. When I finished charting, I realized it was Sunday. I would be paid another day. Money was not exchanged on the Sabbath.

Lindsay and I said our goodbyes and walked out into the afternoon's sweltering heat. I noticed Lindsay was limping to her car. She followed me to the closest diner so we could eat and talk. I had to hear *this* story. It's not every day a midwife limps into a birth.

While we ate, she shared her story. On her way out the door that morning, she fell down the porch steps and twisted her ankle! She hobbled to the car and started driving, with her ankle throbbing painfully. During the entire drive and birth, she wondered if she had fractured her ankle.

I took a good look at her ankle under the diner's table. It looked swollen and painful. Lindsay had faithfully assisted me throughout the birth with no mention of her painful ankle. She was an amazing woman and faithful intern midwife! I loved having her at my side. She continued her birth work and radiated the warmth and brightness of her personality at every appointment and birth.

Snowy Night

One day, I was surprised to receive a hand-written letter from an Amish woman. She asked me to "stop by" her home if it was not an inconvenience to me. The letter was written on plain white paper and enclosed in a plain white envelope. Her cursive handwriting was lovely. The letter implied she was pregnant without directly saying it. Her letter explained that her Mennonite cousin gave her my address. Through hand-written letters, I was introduced to the Amish community.

Letters from Amish women were short and polite, leaving out pertinent pregnancy information. Discretion regarding this subject was important, and the Amish women preferred to speak in person—and without their children present. When I received a letter, I never knew if the lady who was writing was in her first, second, or third trimester. If I hadn't previously met the author of the letter, I did not know whether she had no children or seven. Many Amish women have seven or more pregnancies. (It was the Amish belief not to use contraception, but rather to rely on the goodness of God to give them children.)

After receiving a letter, I would make a point to visit the Amish community as soon as I could. When I met a new expectant mother, I let her know that if I didn't turn up for an appointment, I was tied up at a homebirth. I had no way to cancel appointments because they didn't have phones. I let them know I would come for their appointment within two days of a missed appointment.

One night after sunset, my phone rang.

"Is this the midwife," asked an English man. "English" was the term the Amish called anyone who was not Amish.

"This is she," I said.

He explained he was calling for an Amish man who had walked across a snow-covered field in the dark. Because the Amish do not have telephones in their homes, Amish men walk to an English neighbor's home to place a call. I asked the caller to relay questions to the Amish man.

"Have her waters broken? Is she having contractions? Am I needed fast? Which farm?"

Then I said, "I will leave immediately, but it's more than an hour's drive."

I grabbed some midwifery bags and walked outside to my car to warm up the engine. The winter night was cold, and stepping into the crisp air woke me from my sleepiness.

I went back inside to grab the rest of my supplies. One of my daughters had heard the phone ring and helped me carry bags to the car. The cold night wind blew through my coat as we loaded the car. I had three black bags, plus an oxygen tank. I thanked my daughter for helping me and drove off. I called Neysa to let her know it was baby time.

When I reached the two-story Amish farmhouse, the warm, soft glow of a lantern shined on the front porch and the oil lamp glowed through the front window. Because Amish do not use electricity, the rest of the farm was dark. The soft glow of lamps from adjacent farms could not be seen because this farm was surrounded by a heavily wooded area.

When I stepped out of my car, the winter air splashed against my face. My boots crunched in the snow. I noticed the large brilliant, full moon above, surrounded by a multitude of stars shining brightly.

For a moment, I took in the beauty and the awe of the scene before me. The snow covered the roof of the barn and sheds. Dark smoke rose from the chimney. The porch to the farmhouse had a light dusting of snow around the edges. A light snow that was falling evoked a sense of tranquility. I sighed. What a beautiful night for a baby to be born. As I walked through the newly crusted snow toward the Amish farmhouse, I shifted my thoughts to midwifery.

Neysa and I walked up the steps onto the front porch, carrying my birth bags and a flashlight. After my quick knock, an Amish man opened the door. He looked relieved to see us.

"I'm glad to see you both. Her pains are strong," he said.

Neysa and I walked into the warm kitchen. We worked well together—as if we read each other's minds. She accomplished tasks without any need for instruction. She was an outstanding intern midwife.

I organized my midwifery supplies on the large walnut kitchen table into three sections. The first section had labor supplies. The second had delivery trays with sterile supplies. The third section had postpartum items.

On the wash stand stood a large bowl for hand washing. I always dumped out the standing water and refilled it with fresh water from the pitcher. I was especially mindful of proper hygiene due to the Amish's lack of running water. The Amish husband filled pails of water during the labor. It seemed every home was different regarding wells. For example, one Amish house had a well hand pump inside the house to provide water at a sink. Another home I delivered a baby at had a well hand pump outside the home off the back porch.

I had met this expectant mother once before delivery. She and her husband were new to the area. She had written a letter to me, and I stopped by her farm. She had a toddler, so her pelvis was proven and capable of a vaginal birth. The toddler had been sent out of the home before we arrived. Amish children were never in the home during births.

The Amish make up their own delivery beds. Usually there are newspapers layered on the mattress and then a mattress protector on top. Over that is a crisp white cotton sheet and absorbent pads. I always brought extra absorbent pads to use. Next to the bed was a wooden seat with a chamber pot. There was no indoor plumbing.

The woman's contractions were coming regularly, but the baby's head was asynclitic (the oblique malpresentation of the head in labor). She was eight centimeters by exam, but there was more cervix on one side than the other. It was time to get out the broom.

Literally, we handed the woman an old-fashion corn-straw house broom. Then I asked the mother-to-be to sweep with it because the side-to-side motion of sweeping resolves most cases of asynclitism.

After the woman swept the house, I changed her laboring position. I had her place her left foot on a stool during a contraction. With her next contraction, she used her right foot.

Then I asked her husband to hold a kerosene lamp at the stairway, while the woman went up and down the steps sideways.

When she tired, Neysa and I took turns "shaking the apple tree." This is done by shaking and jiggling the buttocks and lower back region. This relaxes the muscles and lengthens the ligaments, which allows the baby to adjust the position of its head in the pelvis. All our efforts worked. The mom-to-be started feeling pressure.

Neysa and I moved the delivery tray into the picturesque Amish bedroom. An oil lamp on the wooden oak bureau gave a soft light, yet the corners in the room had shadows where the lamp light didn't reach. Towels and receiving blankets were laying on the double bed readied to dry and wrap the baby. Extra linens were sitting on the dresser to remake the bed after birth. Neysa held a flashlight in one hand and had a neonatal stethoscope around her neck ready to use.

Labor intensified as the woman sat on the edge of the bed on a clean white sheet, wearing her white kapp. A black, blue, and maroon quilt was pulled back and folded over on itself at the end of the bed.

I noticed that her husband was very attentive to the needs of his wife in labor. He sat behind his laboring wife on the bed for the pushing stage of labor. With the next contraction, she semi-reclined in bed, leaning on her husband. She pulled her legs back and pushed. The large head crowned. With the next contraction, the head was born face-down in occiput anterior position—a perfect position. I watched the external movement of the fetal head. I waited as the baby rotated to realign the head with the shoulders and back, which is called restitution. With the next contraction, the woman pushed the baby's shoulders and body out.

I gently put the baby on top of the bundle of receiving blankets that Neysa had quickly arranged on the Amish woman's chest. Neysa dried off the baby. Still working in the dim soft lamp light, I clamped and cut the cord.

The baby boy cried and was soothed by his mother. I saw the cord lengthen, which indicated the placenta had detached from the mom's uterine wall. She gave a good push, and the placenta came easily. At every birth, I examined the placenta meticulously for any missing pieces. Bleeding or infection can occur from a piece of retained placenta. I never had it happen, but I would have transferred a mother to a hospital if it did. I placed the intact placenta (no missing pieces) into a large bucket, which was sitting in the corner of the room.

I checked her fundus. It was firm with minimal bleeding. Because the room was still dimly lit, I put on my bright headlamp so I could do a thorough examination for tears. Thankfully, she did not need any stitches. There was only a small superficial skin abrasion.

During labor, we had steeped dried comfrey, strained it, and kept the liquid warm on the cast iron cookstove. I put some of the warm liquid in a peri bottle for the new mom to spray her perineum after toileting. The rest I placed in a basin for bathing her perineum.

Neysa had the hanging scale ready. It was a soft, flannel cloth sling attached to the metal weighing spring of a hanging scale. The baby weighed ten pounds. The Amish man retrieved their vegetable scale to weigh the baby, which confirmed the weight from our scale.

"The baby is big!" he said exuberantly. He was grateful the large baby was delivered at home without the exorbitant cost of a hospital stay. The chunky baby boy had been delivered safely, and he was nursing greedily at the breast. Watching the baby nurse in his mother's arms gave me a satisfaction of a job well done.

The Amish man put on his straw hat and carried a lantern in one hand and the white bucket in the other. Through the window, I could see the glow from his lantern in the distance at the adjacent field. The ground was not frozen, so he was able to dig a hole to bury the placenta.

After the mother and baby were settled into bed, I pulled the warm hand-tied quilt up around them. I reminded her to rest and do no housework for ten days.

Then Neysa and I walked out into the night air and trudged through the snow to my car. We were bone tired but brimming with happiness. I looked up at the beautiful stars and breathed in the crisp, clean air. The peacefulness filled my heart with contentment.

Amish Days

I had received several letters from Amish women requesting a variety of supplies to pick up if I had the time. The large animal veterinarian office was a few miles from my home. I stopped by and picked up the antibiotic prescriptions to deliver to an Amish farmer for his livestock. One Amish woman needed essential oils, another requested dried herbs, and the last asked for herbal tinctures. My last trip to Amish country I had dropped off Monistat to treat a yeast infection and tea tree oil vaginal suppositories (melaleuca oil) for mild vaginitis.

After dropping the requested supplies off at farmhouses, I pulled into a driveway for my first prenatal appointment and saw a child raking up pine needles. Another child was carrying armfuls of pine needles to a row of blackberries—for mulch. Across the field, the one-room schoolhouse stood vacant. I knocked on the white screen door, and the pregnant woman, speaking German to the children, sent them to the barn and garden.

We went to her bedroom and started the prenatal. As she made herself comfortable in bed, I used the pregnancy wheel (calculator) to determine her current gestational weeks. She pulled up her dress, exposing her abdomen. Using my measuring tape, I measured from her pubic bone to the top of the fundus. It was within two centimeters of her gestational week.

"You are progressing perfectly," I said and smiled.

I skillfully palpated to determine the position of the baby.

"Your baby is head down and facing to the right, which is perfect," I told her.

I placed the doppler's wand on her left lower quadrant and easily found the fetal heart tones. We happily listened to the baby's heart beating, and she laughed when the baby kicked.

Her blood pressure, pulse, and urine were normal. She had no edema (swelling) in her hands, feet, or legs.

With a finger prick, a drop of blood was used to check a hemoglobin level on my portable hemoglobin test meter. She was not anemic. She had been taking Floridex (liquid iron) daily and drinking two cups of nettle tea per week. Her nutritional and supplemental intake of iron was more than adequate.

"I have a bottle of witch hazel and Tucks pads to use on your hemorrhoids," I said handing her the supplies.

"Thank you, Tori. What do I owe you?" she said.

"Strawberry and grape jam would be perfect," I replied.

As she placed a few pints of strawberry jam in a cardboard box, I placed a half-gallon bag of dried organic red raspberry herb on her kitchen table. Red raspberry tea strengthens and tones the uterus for labor, and it was known to reduce postpartum bleeding.

"Drink two cups of red raspberry tea per day," I reminded her.

"I will," she said.

"I brought more dried organic nettle, which will nourish you with vitamins A, C, B, and K and increase your calcium and iron. No more than two cups per week," I told her.

"The nettles give me energy," she said happily.

"Here are a few amnioindicator swabs. If you think your water breaks, test the fluid. If the swab turns dark, your water is broke. Call for me if that happens," I explained.

I carried a cardboard box filled with pints of strawberry jam to my vehicle. I smiled, anticipating how happy my daughters would be when they saw the jam.

There was always something new to see when I dropped in at the Amish farmhouses. In the early spring, there was greenhouse seeding. It was a great way to get the gardens growing early. In May, the children and mothers would pick buckets of strawberries from the large strawberry patches.

Throughout the summer, the women did a lot of field work, harvesting each vegetable as it ripened. Their produce stands were always busy with customers. Tomatoes, potatoes, squash, sweet corn, peppers, and canned blackberry jams were just a few of the items sold.

Sometimes, I arrived while pie crusts were being rolled out on the kitchen table. The smell of spices and apple pies baking made my mouth water. There always seemed to be loaves of warm baked bread on a cooling rack.

In late July, I helped the Amish midwife can tomatoes in her home while waiting on a prodromal labor to move into active labor at a nearby farm. We boiled water and placed the tomatoes in the hot water for a few minutes. Each tomato would be taken out of the water, and the skin would peel off easily. We cored and cut the tomatoes in pieces. The six pounds of chopped tomatoes were put in a pot with spices and a half cup white distilled vinegar. Once hot, we put the tomato mixture into glass jars and sealed them with lids. All the jars were processed in a hot water bath. Our canning was complete when I saw an Amish man walking across the field toward the midwife's farm. He knocked on the door and spoke German to the midwife and then English to me. Her pains were steady. I carried a cardboard box filled with canned tomatoes to my vehicle and drove to the laboring woman's farm. A baby was born by sunset.

One day, to pass the time, the Amish midwife and I decided to make brown bread while waiting for a labor to progress. The recipe called for 1 cup of brown sugar, 2 cups of flour, 1 teaspoon of baking soda, 1 teaspoon salt, 1 beaten egg, and 1½ cups of buttermilk. I mixed the ingredients together, then poured it into a well-greased loaf pan. The Amish midwife placed the loaf pan into the cast-iron stove.

The Amish midwife and I sat on the porch swing until the loaf was baked. She pulled the loaf out and set it aside to cool. We saw an Amish man walking up the path. By his quick pace, I knew his wife was in active labor. After the baby was born, we all shared the wonderful brown bread.

Another day, I sat on a porch, shelling peas with a young Amish woman. She had asked for a visit because she was *not* pregnant. She had been married a few months, and it was on her mind that she wasn't pregnant yet. I broached the subject of cervical mucus.

"Have you ever noticed if your mucus is clear and stretchy, like egg whites, when you wipe with toilet paper?" I asked.

She nodded that she did.

"That mucus helps carry your husband's seed to your womb," I explained. "That is the fertile time."

Eight weeks later, I received a letter from the young woman, asking me to stop by soon. By the tone of the letter, I knew she must be pregnant. I couldn't help but smile.

Another letter brought me to a new farm. I drove down a long dusty driveway for a prenatal appointment and parked between the barn and the house. I saw an expectant barefoot woman, washing a buggy.

When I greeted her, she smiled brightly.

"I'll eat my lunch under that large oak tree while you finish your work," I said, gesturing to a tree.

"Okay," she replied.

I was glad to rest under the shady tree with my brown paper bag lunch. I ate a toasted tomato sandwich along with dill pickles and a salted and peppered hardboiled egg.

She finished the buggy quickly, and we walked together into the house.

"I've gained three pounds over six weeks. Is that okay?" she asked.

"That's perfect," I replied.

Her abdomen measured right on target. Her urine was concentrated, and her blood pressure was slightly elevated. My advice was to drink one gallon of water per day. After resting thirty minutes, I rechecked her blood pressure. It was fine. I suggested she rest between chores and eat extra protein. She had plenty of chickens, so eating three eggs per day would be easy. She had a wrist blood pressure cuff. I told her to check her blood pressure daily and write me if she noticed any elevations. I told her to soak her feet in Epsom salt daily because magnesium aids in maintaining a healthy blood pressure.

"Do you have hops?" I asked.

"No, but my mother does," she replied.

"Drink one cup of hops tea in the evening every other day. It will help your blood pressure," I suggested.

"I will, Tori," she promised.

Her blood pressure was normal the remainder of her pregnancy, and she delivered a heathy baby.

On a cold November morning, I arrived at a farm and saw an Amish woman cutting deer meat. Her husband had processed the deer he shot on their land. She had the meat in a pile on an outdoor table. I picked up a knife and started helping. I cut the meat into small chunks while talking and giving her nutritional advice necessary for pregnancy. Her mother-in-law joined us in cutting the meat. Once the meat was cut in chunks, they would be cooking and canning it.

We had a great conversation about avoiding desserts, eating a variety of vegetables, and eating eggs and meat. Her mother-in-law had chlorophyll at the house and Floradix. I told the newly expectant woman to start those right away to prevent anemia. Because it was her first pregnancy, we discussed nutrition in depth. I explained how anemia can cause a lot of problems in pregnancy and labor.

"Do you use gloves in the garden?"

"Not usually," she replied.

"Use gloves to prevent an infection called toxoplasmosis. Wash your hands and all vegetables thoroughly. Scrub them until the dirt is off," I said.

As I left, her mother-in-law handed me a pumpkin pie to take home. I thanked her and drove to the next farm.

By the end of that day, I was sitting in the home of a physician who had hired me for her homebirth. The home was immaculate with expensive artwork hanging in the living room. She had fine china displayed in an antique mahogany china cabinet. When I entered her home, I left my muddy boots on the front porch.

Some days as a midwife were surreal: I could be using an outhouse in the morning and sitting at the finest dining room table in the evening. But no matter the home, I always treated the women the same.

Popcorn, Amish Style

One balmy summer afternoon, Lindsay and I were driving in Amish country to attend a birth. We passed the one-room Amish schoolhouse, which stood alone in a field with its red paint contrasting against the green grass. We passed several roadside Amish vegetable stands filled with produce and jellies. Cows were out to pasture, making the drive scenic. As I turned left down her lane, I noticed her white sign with black letters that read, "No Sunday Sales."

I parked the car near the farmhouse. I could hear the pigs snorting in their pigpen. Chickens ran across the yard stretching their necks and pecking the ground.

It started raining, which mercifully relieved the humidity. The heat-laden days of summer temporarily vanished with the gentle rainstorm. The dark blue curtains fluttered as the cool air entered the open windows of the farmhouse.

There was a cast-iron cookstove on the side porch, which I thought was ingenious because it kept the heat out of the house when cooking in the stifling summer months. Inside there were two stoves, one in the kitchen and another in the living room.

The master bedroom was on the ground floor off the kitchen. The woman had a large walk-in pantry with shelves lined with canning jars filled with fruits, vegetables, jams, jellies, and meats.

While she labored, Lindsay and I rocked in comfortable, hand-crafted Amish rocking chairs. Each were adorned with hand-sewn, star-patterned, padded cushions on the backs and seats. There was a treadle sewing machine against the wall. Pumping the foot pedal turns a wheel that moves the sewing needle up and down. There is no need for electricity. I wondered how long it took to sew the beautiful cushions I was sitting on.

In the calm evening, the rain gently fell on the metal roof and fallowed fields. The labor and birth were uneventful, beautiful, and perfect.

I placed the newborn baby onto receiving blankets on the mother's chest. The parents saw the baby's gender and smiled at the addition of a son to their growing family.

Once the cord finished pulsating, I clamped and cut it. The mother had a strong contraction and pushed once more to deliver the placenta. She was relieved the placenta delivered so quickly. When the placenta had been delayed with her prior birth, I had administered several drops of an oral tincture composed of angelica (dong quai), blue cohosh, and shepherd's purse. The tincture caused a strong contraction, and the placenta delivered.

"I don't need that tincture this time," she quipped.

"You sure don't!" I said smiling.

Lindsay wiped the baby's skin with a cloth soaked with extra-virgin olive oil, rather than having a bath with water. Delaying a bath prevents a newborn from getting too cold and having a drop in its glucose levels. Olive oil also contains vitamin K, which newborns need to prevent intestinal and brain hemorrhages. Lindsay pinned a soft, cotton cloth diaper onto the baby and dressed him in a dark blue handsewn newborn gown.

Wearing a solid-color long dress, the Amish woman got up from bed and walked a few steps to a low wooden box with a lid. The chamber pot was seated inside the box. While she busied herself urinating, the bed was stripped of soiled sheets and absorbent pads and made again to be ready for her. After she laid down, I assessed the fundus and rubbed it to prevent uterine bleeding. Then I tucked a quilt around her.

The mother unpinned her bodice to breastfeed the hungry baby. There were no buttons on her dress because buttons were viewed as prideful. As she nursed, she had a strong afterpain.

"Nursing helps the uterus contract, which decreases bleeding," I reminded her as she breathed through the afterpain.

While the new mother rested post-birth, her husband asked if we wanted popcorn. What a treat! He heated their cast-iron skillet on the woodstove. Once the skillet was hot, he added blue and red popcorn kernels, then enough oil to cover them. As the kernels started to pop, he shook the skillet and put on a lid. Once the popcorn was popped, he salted and buttered it to taste. The four of us enjoyed a relaxing evening eating popcorn.

When our time came to leave, I wished I could stay. This birth and midwifery experience had brought me great joy. But it was time to head back to our busy English world—where far inferior microwaved popcorn is the norm.

Amish Roads

After a rainy spring night, the sun had come out. I was in Amish country, driving on the back roads and making my way to a farmhouse for a prenatal visit. The car was mired in the long, muddy driveway, and I hoped I would not get stuck. There definitely is an art to driving on the long, winding, unpaved Amish driveways, and sometimes my car would slide through the mud. That day, I was not lucky. My car tires sunk deep into the mud. I rocked forward and backward. I tried again and again, back and forth, aiming my tires in different directions.

With a heavy sigh and a heave of despair, I turned off the ignition, opened the car door, and stepped into the mud, sliding like I was ice skating. My boots were now caked with mud, and they felt heavy on my feet.

I walked down the hill toward the closest Amish house. Smoke was coming out of the chimney, so I knew someone was home. I did not have to knock on the door because a woman saw me coming.

"How are you, Tori?" she asked.

I am sure I was a sight to see with thick mud caked on my boots and dirt splashed onto my light-blue, ankle-length skirt.

"My car is stuck in the mud, and I have a lot of women to see today. Are there any men nearby who can help push my car out of the mud?"

I knew the woman well, and she was more than willing to help me. She told me to stay at her home, then she walked at a quick pace toward the lumbermill. When she returned, she had a smile on her face and reported that men were on their way. I stepped onto her front porch, and sure enough I saw seven Amish men walking toward me at full stride. Wearing their light-blue shirts, black pants, suspenders, work boots, and straw hats, they were a grand sight.

I walked, slipped, and skated back up the muddy road to my car. I inwardly cringed as I got into my vehicle with dirty boots. I knew the red clay mud would be difficult to clean out of my car.

The men positioned themselves around my car. I gave it gas, and within a quick moment, my car was moving back up the lane. Those were some strong young men. I waved out the window and went on my way.

Muddy roads, flat tires, flooded creeks, and bridges out were part of my midwifery practice. Being a homebirth midwife could be frustrating yet exhilarating at the same time.

Amish Outhouses

The idyllic image of Amish life might end for some when the need arises to use the outhouse. The reality for a midwife is after attending a labor for a few hours, the outhouse becomes a necessity.

The Amish outhouses I used were made of wood and had doors that closed with latches. A thin layer of dirt covered the worn wooden outhouses floors. Inside the outhouses were dark—even during the day—despite the fact that the doors usually had a half-moon cutout to let light in and odors out. Toilet paper rolls usually hung on a long nail that was jutting out of the wall of the outhouse. The seat was wooden with a hole to sit on.

In the summer, the outhouses were hot, with pesky flies buzzing about, and quite smelly. After toileting, I washed my hands with soap in a basin of water in the farmhouse kitchen.

On one cold, wintery night, the stars were no longer shining brightly in the sky. The snow was coming down, and it was very cold outside. As I walked to the outhouse, my boots crunched in the snow, and my only light was from my cellphone. Approaching the outhouse, I wondered if the cold temperature and the snowfall would make a difference in the putrid smell that I had become accustomed to when using the outhouses. My hopes were dashed. The below freezing wintertime did little to improve the conditions of using the outhouse—except that I now could see my breath while sitting over the hole. At least the strips of felt around the hole helped to keep my backside from getting an immediate chill, however the cold slowly penetrated the felt. Keeping my cellphone on for a light, I was extremely careful not to drop the phone into the hole.

On days that it rained, I got wet walking to the outhouse, and then I got wetter coming back to the farmhouse. In those moments, I missed the nicety of indoor plumbing.

The funniest thing to me was that once I finished doing my business in the outhouse, I always reached to flush out of habit. Instantly, I would laugh at myself.

Outhouses were nothing new to me because I had used many porta-potties in the army, however the use of one was not the highlight of my day.

As I walked to the outhouse one tiring day, I grumbled aloud, "I need a job that has indoor plumbing."

Just then I saw a bunny hop away into the tall grass. I stood still a moment and noticed butterflies fluttering among the flowers and foraging for nectar.

"Nah, my job is perfect."

Special Delivery

One day on my way to an Amish birth, I realized I left my three black bags at home. They contained *all* my midwifery supplies. I had never done that before or since. This Amish community was more than ninety minutes from my home, and I had been driving awhile. I pulled over and called my husband.

"Can you please fly my midwifery bags to me?" I asked Jeff. "I can meet you at the closest airport."

"Yes, I'll meet you in Mississippi."

While I waited on Jeff to arrive, I thought how blessed I was. Jeff could quickly fly from our private runway to the Mississippi airport.

I was in a hurry to get to a birth and praying I would arrive before the baby. I watched as Jeff touched down the Cessna 150 Aerobat on the tarmac. He didn't shut down the engine. I ran to the side of the plane and grabbed the bags as he tossed them out the door. I gave him a thumbs-up and the hand signal for "I love you" as the roar of the engine made the exchange a quick one. The prop wash blew my long skirt around me as I hurried away from the plane.

As I loaded the bags into the back of my car, I watched the plane take off. Once at altitude, Jeff circled the plane and flew over me. He rocked the wings of the airplane to say "goodbye." I drove off and headed to the Amish farm. It was a beautiful day for a birth. The best part was I made it there before the baby.

The Unexpected

One warm spring day, an unexpected visitor came to my door. Her brown hair was pulled into a bun, and she wore a cream-colored blouse with a navy-blue skirt.

I answered my door in the usual way, "May I help you?"

"I heard of you through the grapevine," the soft-spoken young lady explained.

As soon as I heard her speak, I knew she was Amish, even though she was not dressed in traditional Amish clothing. I could tell she was exhausted, which was confirmed when she said, "I walked here from the bus station."

I ushered the young woman into my warm, cozy kitchen and put the tea kettle on to boil. We could smell brown bread baking in the oven. I made her a bacon, lettuce, tomato sandwich and gave her a glass of water. She bowed her head and silently gave thanks to God.

When she finished praying, I asked, "How can I help you?"

She told her story. She was eighteen and was expected to make the decision whether or not to be baptized into the Amish faith. She did not want to be baptized, and even though she could have stayed in her community, she decided to leave—without saying goodbye to her family.

"I left them a letter on the kitchen table," she said. "It was easier that way."

She hadn't realized how expensive traveling would be and was already short on money.

"Are you expecting a baby? Have you missed your monthly?" I asked.

"No," she said. "I'm not married."

I could see her decision to leave her family was torturing her. The kettled whistled. I stood up and steeped the tea. I handed her a cup of hot tea with honey and lemon.

"I do not want charity," she said. "Could I do chores to earn money for a bus ticket?" She appeared scared, likely because she was experiencing the overwhelming, fast world of the English.

I gave her bath towels and took her to the bathroom. I gave her a tutorial on how to turn on the shower, using the handles for hot and cold water. She did not have any extra clothes, so I found a long skirt and blouse that would fit her. After her shower, I showed her how to use my washing machine. She washed her dirty clothes, then she hung them on the line to dry. I sent her to take a nap in the extra bed in our loft upstairs.

We agreed she could do garden chores and help me in the kitchen for money. For the next several days, we spent a lot of time in the kitchen. I taught her how to bake bread using an electric oven. We made scrambled eggs using a gas burner and copper-bottomed cookware. In the Amish community, she had only used cast-iron skillets. Her eyes longingly looked toward my three daughters who were much younger than she was.

"Do you have younger siblings?" I asked.

"Yes," she said wistfully.

Because she had not been baptized, I knew she was not shunned. She could always go home. I encouraged her to consider returning to her family.

At my home, she slept soundly and ate well. I was glad she renewed her strength. After a few days, she decided to buy a bus ticket to go to her distant Mennonite cousins—rather than return to her Amish family.

I packed several sandwiches in a brown paper sack and several water bottles in a small travel cooler. I gave her an earful of admonitions on how to travel safely. I handwrote my address on several envelopes, placed stamps on them, and told her to write me if she ran into any problems.

As suddenly as the young woman had showed up at my home, she was gone. Her absence left a void. She never shared her family name nor which Amish community she had left. I never heard from her again.

The Dark

One dark cold night, I received a call to come to an Amish farm for a birth. It was the woman's tenth child, so I did not dawdle. The sky was overcast with clouds, so I had no stars or moon to give me light. Because it was so dark, I used my high beams for most of the drive.

I was happy to reach the farm because driving with no streetlights or moonlight created tension in my upper neck as I strained to see. I didn't want to hit a deer on the way to a birth—or a skunk for that matter.

I drove slowly down the long-curved dirt driveway and parked near the front door. I grabbed my three midwifery bags and walked toward the house. I stepped into something squishy, slid, and almost fell backward. Suddenly, I smelled it. I just stepped into horse manure, and it was all over my black boot.

I went to the door and gave my bags to an Amish midwife who had arrived before me, and we had a good laugh. Standing by the back door by the light of a hanging lantern, I used a stick to scrape the manure from the sole of my boot.

For some Amish births, an Amish midwife came, and she either walked or arrived in a black buggy. I enjoyed working with Amish midwives. It seemed each community had at least one woman who was knowledgeable in the old ways of herbs and childbirth. I gleaned as much herbal, cultural, and generational wisdom that I could from the Amish midwives.

The pregnant woman would decide if she wanted an Amish midwife to assist me. I was not part of that decision. The Amish worked that out amongst themselves. Amish midwives do not go to midwifery school or hold a state license, but they are skilled.

To get the chill out of my bones, I warmed up next to the woodstove. I love the smell of burning wood, and that night, it was especially relaxing. The Amish midwife had the bed ready for delivery. I quickly unpacked my supplies.

The expectant Amish woman was standing by her bed wearing her kapp, bodice, and skirt. Her face had the glow of labor. Active labor produces a bright radiant glow around the face from the hormone surge of natural labor.

I asked the woman to lie down for an exam. When I palpated her abdomen, I could tell that the baby was head down. Using my doppler, I listened to the fetal heart tones. The baby sounded great.

"Baby's happy," I said with a smile.

The woman asked her husband to sit behind her on the bed. Then she leaned on him in a relaxed semi-reclining position.

"Are you ready?" I asked.

She nodded. I knew a cervical check was unnecessary. She pulled her legs back and pushed, and the baby was born easily. The Amish midwife tended to the baby, while I delivered the placenta. As soon as the placenta delivered, I rubbed the uterus to keep it firm. I checked it every fifteen minutes, and it clamped down well.

A grand multiparous (a woman who has delivered five or more babies) is at risk for postpartum hemorrhage due to uterine atony (when the uterus fails to contract, allowing the vessels to bleed). The risk factor can be effectively decreased with good prenatal care and proper nutrition. She had taken Floradix and chlorophyll throughout her pregnancy to prevent anemia. She also had steeped red raspberry tea and drank it daily in the third trimester to tone her uterus.

I rocked in their Amish-made rocking chair while she nursed the baby. I found that nursing a baby decreased bleeding significantly. Nipple stimulation or breastfeeding lead to oxytocin secretion, which causes uterine contractions that prevents uterine atony.

When the postpartum mom finished nursing, I had her empty her bladder. A full bladder shifts the uterus to the right, which causes uterine atony, so keeping a bladder empty is imperative.

Because the woman was an experienced mother, I knew the baby was in good hands. But still, before I left, I gave her instructions: Drink a glass of water with every nursing. Empty your bladder often. Continue taking Floradix and chlorophyll liquid supplements. Continue to drink red raspberry tea to restore tone to your uterus and increase milk supply. Nurse the baby frequently.

When I returned to their farm for a postpartum home visit, I remembered to step carefully around the horse manure.

Yeast

One day when I stopped into a home for a six week postpartum checkup, I heard a baby screaming.

"The baby has thrush," the Amish mother said.

I looked in the baby's mouth and definitely saw thrush. Thrush is a yeast infection and appears as white patches that don't wipe off.

"Is breastfeeding painful?" I asked, suspecting she was getting yeast on her nipples from the nursing baby.

"Yes, it is," she answered.

She needed to eradicate the yeast. I pulled gentian violet from my herb bag and poured it onto cotton balls. Then I wiped out the baby's mouth, making certain the baby did not swallow it. I saturated clean cotton balls and wiped both of the mother's nipples.

"Let it air-dry," I said, explaining gentian violet stains the skin blue temporarily. "If you do this twice per day for three days, you will get rid of the yeast."

"Are you having vaginal itching?" I asked.

Because she had the common vaginal symptoms of itching and white discharge, I gave her a seven-day over-the-counter miconazole vaginal insert for herself.

"If you have symptoms after completing the miconazole treatment (Monostat), use tea tree oil vaginal suppositories," I suggested.

"How do you wash your baby's diapers"? I asked.

"I wash them in boiling hot water and dry them in sunshine," she said.

"Perfect. Hot water and sunshine kill yeast," I replied.

The baby did not have diaper rash, which can also be caused by yeast. I explained that over-the-counter clotrimazole or miconazole cream can be used to treat a yeast diaper rash, if her baby did get one.

"No sweets or desserts," I said. "Sugar feeds the yeast."

When I returned to their farm two weeks later, both the new mom and her baby were well. Out of gratitude, she gave me a shoo-fly pie and said, "Now, don't get yeast."

We had a good laugh. Shoo-fly pie is very sweet.

Stubborn Breech

An Amish woman was lying on a black and maroon hand tied quilt in her bedroom.

"I feel the baby's butt down here. Its head is up here. It's breech," I told her while palpating her abdomen.

I referred the pregnant Amish woman and her husband to a local obstetrician for an ultrasound.

The day of her doctor appointment, I arrived to a flurry of activity as she readied herself for town. One for wear. One for wash. One for spare. One for dress. That was the expression I heard regarding dresses. She had already changed into her "best dress" for going to town.

She wore a pleated white kapp and a solid navy colored dress with long sleeves and a full skirt. The bodice of the dress had a second layer of fabric covering it, called a cape, which was worn for modesty. A tied-on clean apron finished the dress. She wore black knee-high stockings that were held up with bands. Her black shoes peeked out from under her long skirt.

She quickly put on a sturdy black bonnet over her kapp. Because it was winter, she draped a plain, heavy, black cape over her shoulders as her husband closed the dampers on the pot-belly stove. He grabbed his black hat, and we walked out into the cold winter air. As she got into the back seat of my car, I reminded her to put on her seatbelt. I enjoyed driving the Amish couple to town just as much as they enjoyed riding in my car.

"Buggies don't have seatbelts," she said smiling.

The ultrasound confirmed the baby was breech, and an external version was arranged to turn the baby that same day. After the Amish woman was admitted to labor and delivery, a medication called terbutaline was given to relax the uterus. Then with ultrasound as a guide and while closely monitoring the baby's heartbeat, the physician deftly positioned both hands on the abdomen and skillfully turned the baby. The baby rotated from breech to vertex (head down). After the successful external version, the fetal heart rate remained normal, with moderate variability and a reactive strip (two accelerations of the fetal heart rate increasing by fifteen beats per minute for fifteen seconds within a twenty-minute timeframe). After two hours of monitoring, she was discharged home. When I dropped her off, I told her to expect the baby in a few weeks because she wasn't due yet.

Three weeks later, her neighbor called relaying she was in labor. She had her baby in the warm quiet farmhouse, the only noise a fire crackling in the woodstove. The baby delivered head first. It couldn't have been more perfect.

One blustery spring day, I drove an Amish couple home to their well-kept farm after their doctor's visit in town. Their wooded driveway opened into a clearing and plowed fields.

The woman was relieved her external version was successful. She did not want a C-section. I tied a white sheet around her waist to keep the baby in place. She was due any day, and it was her sixth baby.

"When you rest on your left side, put a small pillow under your abdomen to keep the head of the baby aligned with your pelvis. I want the baby to drop," I said.

I placed two drops of blue and black cohosh under her tongue. She swallowed the tincture and washed it down with water. I was hoping for labor or at the least a few strong contractions to drop the baby's head into the pelvis. The baby was still high. I did not want the baby turning back to breech.

After saying goodbye to the couple, I stayed in Amish country and made some rounds to other Amish houses. As I drove, I noticed several Amish men walking behind horse drawn plows. Girls were selling jellies, breads, and cakes at the roadside stands. Within two hours, I received a call from an English asking me to return to the Amish farm as quickly as I could. There was strong active labor.

I pulled up in my car to their house again, and her husband met me outside. He helped me carry my black bags into the kitchen, where I quickly grabbed my necessary supplies.

When the laboring woman saw me, she smiled and asked, "Are you ready? There is a lot of pressure."

I smiled and said, "Let's have a baby."

She pushed once, and a healthy, rosy baby was born into my hands. It was a beautiful, peaceful birth. I was glad she did not have to birth in the hospital. She and I were extremely grateful for that successful external version.

Vaginal Birth After Cesarean

I arrived at an Amish farm on a snowy winter day. When I entered the front door, I felt the warmth from the woodstove on my cold cheeks. I had arrived to check on a woman who was in her third trimester and having irregular contractions all day. This would be her eleventh baby. Her last baby had been a Cesarean section for twins who were transverse (horizontal) lie.

All of the woman's other children were out of the house, as was the custom when a midwife arrived. We went to her bedroom, where she made herself comfortable on her bed. I palpated her abdomen. The baby was in oblique (diagonal) lie with the head toward the left hip. Using optimal fetal positioning, I asked her to rest on her left side. I placed a small, hard pillow just above the hip to force the baby to move from oblique (diagonal) to vertex (head down).

Even though the woman was not in active labor, she asked me to sleep at her home that night. She was having irregular contractions with cramping, and considering it was her eleventh baby, I stayed.

When I slept in Amish homes, I slept upstairs, where there were usually two rooms, one on either side of the stairwell. By the clothing that hung on the pegs of the walls, I could tell which room was used by the boys and which one was used by the girls. When I got upstairs and looked out the window, I saw snow flurries falling. It was cold upstairs, and I snuggled under the thick quilts to gradually get warm. I heard the clopping of hooves. In a few minutes, there was the sound of footsteps on the porch. I smiled contentedly to myself. An Amish midwife had arrived. As night fell, I drifted off to sleep, waiting for active labor to grip the pregnant woman.

In the middle of the night, I was shaken awake by the Amish midwife. I sat up and put on my shoes. It was dark—except for the starlight visible through the glass-paned window. The stairwell was even darker than the room. I carefully made my way down the steps. The stairwell opened to a warm living area, which was adjacent to the married couple's bedroom. The wood in the black cast-iron stove was crackling and providing plenty of warmth. The glass oil lamps glowed softly in the darkness.

The laboring woman was in the bedroom, sitting on the edge of the bed. Her labor was quick and intense, and she was already having pressure at the peak of contractions.

I listened to the baby by doppler. The fetal heart tones sounded great.

"Baby's happy," I said.

Suddenly, her bag of waters ruptured. The amniotic fluid was clear and non-odorous, which is good. She had been sitting on absorbent pads, which soaked up the fluid. The Amish midwife and I changed the pads and prepared for delivery. The laboring woman leaned back onto her husband who was sitting at the head of the bed. She pulled up her skirt, pulled back her legs, and birthed the baby's head. I quickly unwrapped the cord, which was around the baby's neck.

With one more push, the baby's body birthed easily. I placed the pink baby onto a receiving blanket and handed the bundle to the outstretched arms of the baby's mother. She cradled the baby in her arms while the baby cried robustly. I noticed how beautiful the postpartum woman looked in the lamplight. She was glowing and beautiful in her dark blue Amish dress. She was so happy she did not need a Cesarean section. She was glad she had the option of a vaginal birth after cesarean (VBAC).

The delivery was calm and peaceful, during which the woman welcomed her eleventh baby into her warm home while snowflakes fell onto the pasture. When the baby was ready to nurse, the mother exposed one breast, and the baby nursed, swallowing warm colostrum.

As the sun rose, the Amish midwife asked if I wanted an egg for breakfast. She put a cast-iron skillet on the woodburning stove.

"The skillet will soon be hot," she said with a smile.

"Absolutely," I replied.

I went upstairs to change into clean clothing. The smell of coffee and bacon drifting upstairs on a cold winter morning made me ravenously hungry.

I was famished. She fried several eggs and sprinkled them with salt and pepper. The bacon was piled on a plate on the table. She sliced pieces of bread from a loaf of homemade sourdough bread and quickly toasted them in the black cast-iron skillet. She poured strong black coffee into cups. Using the indoor hand pump, she filled a pitcher with cold well water and set it on the table. It was a good meal.

While we were sitting at the table, I filled out the birth certificate information. I was careful to mark "no" at the social security number. The Amish always declined that because they believe they should be separate from the world. Before I left the warm kitchen for the long, cold drive home, I drank a cup of strong black coffee.

I walked outside into the cold air and put the car key in the ignition. I hesitated and stared at the keys. It was bitter cold, and I needed to warm the car. But I didn't turn on the ignition. Instead, I sat there for a minute in the cold and reflected on the night's events. She just had a beautiful birth. I slept in a home without electricity while the snow quietly fell from the sky. I worked side-by-side with an Amish midwife. I ate a breakfast cooked in a cast-iron skillet on a woodburning stove. Now I held keys in my hand to turn the ignition of a new Ford.

For a moment, I was held captive by the contrast between nineteenth-century living and the modern world. In that moment, my life seemed surreal. One of the many reasons why I loved being a midwife was that I moved between two worlds. It brought me joy to facilitate medical care for the Amish when a physician was necessary. However, I was very happy to provide experienced midwifery skills in their homebirth settings because the Amish visibly relaxed in their own homes.

Finally, I turned the ignition, and the low fuel light came on. I needed fuel, or I wouldn't make the long drive home. I laughed when the caution light brought me back to reality. This was no time to be philosophical, or I would be needing a horse-and-buggy ride to a gas station.

Amish Clothing

My day had started with an early-morning phone call. Whenever my phone rang at an odd hour, the chances were excellent a woman was in labor. And indeed, a woman was on the line breathing with a contraction. I waited until she was able to speak.

"I'll be needing you, Tori. Come quickly."

When I stepped outside, it was bright, sparkly, and sunny after the night's rain. The grass glistened, and the world felt new and fresh. It was a glorious morning for a birth.

On the way, I picked up April Howton, an intern midwife, faithful midwifery assistant, and Certified Labor Doula. April and I knew each other well because she had asked me to attend the births of six of her children, including vaginal twins. She had a blossoming doula business, and she fit right in assisting my midwifery homebirths.

When we arrived at the old, white farmhouse, the laboring woman was in an inflatable birth pool in her sunroom. I briefly enjoyed the view through the sunroom windows—a field filled with cornstalks and their diesel-powered John Deere tractor sitting outside the barn.

The woman and her husband were multigenerational farmers and had a large family. She was expecting her seventh. Her children said hello to me as they raced out the door, then they skipped down the old gravel path to spend the day at their grandma's house.

April and I weren't there more than twenty minutes when the woman birthed in the birth pool's warm water. My shirt and pants got wet as I leaned over the tub for delivery. The baby had adorable chunky rolls and checked out just fine. Thankfully, I carried spare clothing in my car. I changed clothing and sat chatting while the mother nursed her newborn son. The baby had a great suck and swallow.

It was a beautiful relaxing morning sitting on the front porch with the many birds chirping and singing their songs. I gently rocked in the two-person hanging swing while filling out my charts. I smelled the faint smell of honeysuckles in the air. Soon the smell of bacon wafted through the screened window, making my stomach growl. The woman's husband was making her breakfast while April was attending to the postpartum mother and newborn baby.

I was sipping hot tea and enjoying the farmhouse-style porch swing when my phone rang. It was an elderly farmer who was a neighbor to the Amish. He was passing a message that an Amish woman was in labor. Relaxation shifted to a hustle as I hopped off the wooden swing, packed up our supplies, and started the drive to the next birth. It was a beautiful drive through several rural counties. It would take ninety minutes— unless we got stuck behind a tractor on the winding, two-lane country roads.

When April and I pulled into the dirt lane of the Amish farmhouse, I thought how beautiful the farm looked. The long drive way was lined with oaks, maples, yellow poplar, and pine trees, and a large vegetable stand stood off to the right side. The large front porch greeted me as if it was smiling. Chickens were running in the yard, pecking the ground.

I saw the laboring woman come out of the house, wearing her white kapp with a dark blue Amish dress. Her large pregnant belly was barely hidden under her long skirt and apron.

As we walked up the steps onto the front porch, she greeted us, "I'm so happy you are here!"

I learned she had been in labor for several hours. We went to her bedroom, where the bed was neatly made up for delivery. She laid down, and I palpated her abdomen performing Leopold's maneuvers. The baby was vertex lie and in LOA position. So far so good.

Using the doppler, we listened to fetal heart tones while bees buzzed and butterflies fluttered outside the open window.

The baseline heart rate was in the 130s with fifteen-beat variability and several fifteen-second accelerations. In other words, everything was perfect. The mom didn't have a fever, and her blood pressure was perfect.

"Baby's happy," I said.

While I sat in their handmade rocking chair and charted, Lindsay Crowson arrived. She had been delayed because a bridge was out, and she had to drive miles out of the way on curvy country roads. GPS was rarely accurate in Amish country. Over the years, I had drawn my own map with all the unnamed roads and marked with the names of Amish family farms.

During active labor, the Amish woman swept the wooden floors with a broom. The movements involved with sweeping helps the baby's head descend in the pelvis. After using the broom for an hour, I saw her labor shift.

Thank you, broom, I thought and smiled.

The woman went to the bedroom and leaned forward on her bureau. This was her second baby, and labor was moving quickly.

The Amish midwife who had joined us occasionally spoke encouraging words in Pennsylvania Dutch to her. Their language was a variation of the German language. This language has been preserved by the Old Order Amish. Many of the Amish in the Southern states had great-grandparents who moved South from Pennsylvania during the 1940s.

The afternoon grew hot, but the breeze through the open windows would bring momentary relief. During the peak of the heat, the laboring woman got into to bed. She was ready.

I sat on the end of the bed with gloves on. April listened with the doppler with every contraction. When the baby was crowning, the woman pulled back her legs, and we had a baby. Once again, I got soiled from the birth.

The baby girl gave a loud cry and had Apgar scores of 8 and 9. The baby was doing well. Babies are scored at birth from 1 to 10. Points are given for color (pink, blue, pale), heart rate, cry, tone, and respiration.

Lindsay put the pink baby girl in our flannel scale sling and hooked it to the hanging scale.

"Nine pounds, fifteen ounces!" I exclaimed. Everyone cheered and reveled at her size.

While I was cleaning up after the birth, carrying a water pail up the porch steps, I stumbled and spilled water all over me. My clothing was drenched from my chest down. I had to laugh. What a sight I was!

Because I was already wearing my spare clothing from my car, the Amish midwife handed me a dress that had been hanging on a wooden wall peg. I went upstairs and changed. Because the Amish clothing was secured with pins, not buttons or zippers, I needed the Amish midwife to help me dress.

When I came back down the stairwell, I peeked my head around the corner. April and Lindsay burst into laughter. The Amish laughed too. The Amish do not have mirrors, so I didn't know *exactly* how *Amish* I looked. I laughed too. I never knew what each day of midwifery would bring.

After we left the farm, April, Lindsay, and I were famished. We had missed supper, and the sun had set. We stopped at a McDonald's—the only place nearby that served food. We were enjoying our food and still laughing at my attire. Apparently, I looked quite conspicuous because the other customers kept staring at me, which of course, renewed our giggles. Then my phone rang.

"This is Tori speaking," I said.

A third lady was in labor! I couldn't believe the timing. But that is how midwifery rolls. After I hung up, I started laughing at my circumstances. I was sitting in McDonald's, eating a Big Mac, wearing Amish clothing and flip-flops, and in desperate need of a shower. But we needed to get to our third birth of the day …

The Hustle

… it was time to hustle. I had just enough time to get home, strip off my Amish clothes, shower, and redress. Quickly, I was on the road again.

When I arrived at Hope House, I turned on the window air-conditioner. Even though the stars were out, it was humid and sticky. It felt nice to be in the air-conditioning because I had been hot and sweaty in the Amish homes most of the day.

When the expectant mother arrived at Hope House, she was in hard active labor. She labored on the porch at the day-bed. We opened the windows on the porch because she wanted to listen to the crickets' soothing melody. She was in labor land, and I didn't disturb her.

April and Neysa arrived to assist me. Neysa's home was closest to Hope House, so I had called her to attend the birth.

When the laboring woman started a low moan, I asked, "Do you need to empty your bladder?"

With a nod, she walked to the toilet. An empty bladder is prudent before starting the second stage of labor (pushing). A full bladder can impede the descent of the baby, cause inefficient contractions, and increase the laboring woman's pain.

After toileting, the laboring woman walked onto the enclosed porch and pushed involuntarily. Her husband helped her as she naturally moved into a supported squat to push. April put absorbent pads under her. Neysa was monitoring fetal heart tones. I positioned myself on my knees to deliver the baby.

The woman smiled and asked, "Don't the crickets sound lovely?"

We all agreed. She smiled, then pushed. I supported her perineum while the baby crowned. She was birthing her baby while in an upright supported squat position, which was fine with me. I always worked with whatever position the laboring woman instinctively used. The baby was born easily, and I unwrapped the cord. I stood and handed the baby boy to his mother. She was standing and empowered. Women are strong.

I drove home, fighting off sleep. I rolled down the windows and turned on music to stay awake. When I walked into my house, I smelled bacon cooking. I was reminded of the smell of bacon that wafted through the screen window yesterday. I was torn between going to bed and eating breakfast. I decided to eat bacon. My husband laughed at my disheveled appearance.

"Last night, you came home in Amish clothes," he reminded me.

That memory seemed so long ago. Smelling the food made me ravenously hungry. As the warm food hit my stomach, my body responded with waves of sleepiness. I placed my cellphone on the nightstand, thinking, *Please don't ring again.* I crawled into my bed and fell into a deep sleep—even though the sun was shining through the window.

Forty-One Weeks

One day, I stopped in for a prenatal appointment at the home of an Amish lady who was more than forty-one weeks pregnant. (The current interpretation of Naegele's rule is an estimated due date for pregnancy of forty weeks—a rule fraught with limitations.)

She opted to encourage labor with my castor oil recipe, which had been given to me years ago by an aging Amish midwife. Castor oil causes bowel movements, and the intestinal motility causes an irritable uterus, which initiates labor contractions.

Over the years, I found that castor oil works well when a woman has a good Bishop score. I went to the store for the castor oil and vanilla ice cream the recipe requires, while the expectant Amish woman went to her cellar for homemade canned peaches. When I returned, we combined three scoops of vanilla ice cream, peaches with its syrup, and two ounces of castor oil.

"I'll stop back in to check on you after I make my rounds to other pregnant women," I told the expectant woman. My plan was to start my faithful labor-promoting herbs once she started cleaning out her bowels.

Next, I drove to the home of a Mennonite lady. She had a long winding driveway with pasture on either side, in which horses stood eating at hay feeders. I noticed her goats had their ears pointed forward, which indicates a happy goat. Rhode Island Red chickens were pecking at the ground. I heard the snorting of the pigs as I passed their pen. The woman had a large, well maintained vegetable garden.

After I parked my car, I grabbed my prenatal bag and walked toward the front porch. Tall sunflowers were growing in neat rows adjacent to the porch and seemed to welcome me.

The expectant woman opened the door and smiled her greeting to me. She was barefoot and had her hair in a bun under her white kapp. Her dress and apron were similar in style to the Amish. Her home had hardwood floors and a coffee table to take our hot tea. Her Bible lay on the end table. The cover revealed it was written in English, whereas the Amish read from the German translation of Martin Luther. Unlike my Amish families, her house had electricity, indoor plumbing, and running water from a well, and it was furnished with modern electric appliances. The aroma of freshly baked bread made my mouth water. Canned jars of pickles, salsa, and strawberry jelly lined a kitchen shelf.

I had been her midwife for five previous deliveries. She had called and asked me to stop in because she was full term (forty weeks). She laid down on her bed, and I measured her abdomen and listened to fetal heart tones. So far so good. Upon palpation, I felt the small parts of the baby and determined that the baby was OP (face-up).

"Spend a great deal of time on your hands and knees, scrubbing the floor," I said. "That will flip the baby to OA (face-down). Scrub the floors of every room while alternating the scrub brush from hand to hand. Crawl backward while scrubbing. Don't move forward. Those movements will turn the baby over."

The expectant mother's sister was visiting. "Could you please review my fertility temperature charts because I missed my period?" she asked.

"I'm happy to help," I replied.

The young woman had only been married three months and was uncertain how to interpret fertility charting. When I saw her chart, I knew she was pregnant.

Taking a basal body temperature (taken upon first waking) reflects progesterone levels. The first temperature pattern during the follicular phase is *before* ovulation, reflecting a slightly lower basal body temperature. The second pattern is the rise in temperature *after* ovulation during the luteal phase. If you see a third temperature elevation, it is the rise in temperature due to implantation of the embryo into the uterus (pregnant!). Sometimes a chart does not show the third rise. However, if you see eighteen days in a row of elevated temperatures after ovulation, a woman is pregnant.

I explained the temperature shifts and told her, "You're five weeks pregnant!"

She was ecstatic!

Western medicine is very reliant on urine pregnancy testing. Simple things, such as temperature charting, are rarely taught or used to aid women in their healthcare. I have found these tools to be quite helpful. It is especially helpful when waiting for labor. A basal body temperature *drop* when nine months pregnant is an indication that labor is imminent.

After that home visit, I returned to the first Amish farm of the day and found that the castor oil had been successful in stimulating the woman's uterine contractions.

I brought in my birth bags. From my bag of herbal tinctures, I pulled out my faithful blend of blue and black cohosh. I put two drops of the tincture under the woman's tongue. She held it in her mouth, then she swallowed it with a glass full of water. Every fifteen minutes for the next two hours, I gave the herbs. By the last dose, the woman was in strong active labor.

I arranged my supplies and settled in for labor. I called labor-and-delivery nurses Lindsey Crowson and Neysa Brown, who said they were on their way. I hoped they would beat the incoming storm. The dark, fast moving clouds were blowing across the sky. I stood on the dirt path that led to the outhouse and watched the ominous clouds.

The cool air felt marvelous. I could feel a sudden thickness in the air and so could the animals. Squirrels scurried up an oak tree to their nests. A rabbit that had been nibbling on the grass bounded toward its hole in the ground. We all knew: This was tornado weather.

Neysa and Lindsay made it just before the downpour and powerful thunderstorm. As darkness fell, I wished I had a television for storm updates. We had no way of knowing if we were in a tornado's path. The rain hit the roof with a vengeance.

The expectant woman labored well into the night, oblivious to the thunder and lightning and wind blowing against the house and shaking the windows. She walked the length of the room and leaned against the dresser to rest her head when tired.

Lindsay, Neysa, and I took turns resting in the upstairs bedroom, where the twin beds had beautiful black, maroon, and navy patterned quilts. The layers of fabric were hand tied with heavy yarn.

The rain continued pelting the metal roof, and the darkness outside now made it impossible to see out the glass-paned windows. The dark pressed in around the house. The rain was loud, but when it switched to hail, it was even louder as it hit the roof.

The howling of the storm kept me wide awake, so I went out to the back porch, listening to the wind, watching the lightning momentarily illuminate, and feeling the intensity of the storm. Part of me loved the storm and the incredible magnificence of nature, but my practical side hoped my car would not get stuck in the mud. *Please don't let the winds take off the house roof,* I prayed, remembering how my own home had suffered roof damage when straight-line winds from a microburst hit our house. During that storm, a tornado touched down three miles from my home.

I moved back inside, where an oil lamp shone brightly amid the darkness. The smell of the wood logs burning soothed me. The sounds of the crackling fire, howling wind, and labor mixed together into a nature symphony. I drank hot tea with honey and rocked in the family's rocking chair, feeling the house shudder occasionally from a strong gust of wind.

Finally, the storm subsided as the sun rose. With the sunrise came the pushing. The woman squatted with her heels flat on the floor to open the outlet of her pelvis. After two pushes, she moved to the bed and reclined against her husband. The baby was born easily.

It wasn't lost on me that the pain of labor ended with the bliss of a newborn baby, much like the raging forces of the storm subsided into calm. The woman's husband blew out the flame in the lamp, and a puff of smoke rose upward and dissipated.

Rooster

On a warm, spring day, April and I arrived at an Amish farmhouse and walked up the unpainted porch steps to the screen door. An Amish midwife met us at the door. She smiled and welcomed us in.

We walked through the spotless kitchen and living area into the bedroom. I quickly scanned the room to see a dark quilt folded down on the bed and several absorbent pads and clean, folded sheets ready for the pending delivery. The window was open, and the curtains moved with the breeze. I could see a row of tall sunflowers through the open window. A lamp was on the dresser ready for nightfall. In the corner of the room sat a wooden box seat with a porcelain chamber pot.

A contraction was in progress, so I waited to speak. The woman looked lovely laboring. She wore her kapp with its strings falling loose onto her shoulders. She was barefoot, but wearing a navy dress. She stood on an absorbent pad, which was collecting clear amniotic fluid. Her water had broken twelve hours earlier with very few contractions. After taking herbs, her contractions started.

Suddenly, I heard a ruckus in the kitchen. I ran out to see what was happening. A rooster was chasing two hens! The hens flew up onto the long walnut kitchen table and flapped their wings. *How did they sneak into the kitchen?* A hen knocked a pie plate dangerously close to the edge of the table. I lunged for it, but the hen tipped it over. A scrumptious apple pie was now splattered across the floor.

In an intense chase, the rooster ran circles around the hens, doing his mating dance. Feathers were flying as the pursuit occurred in the confined kitchen. The Amish midwife snatched one of the hens and tossed her unceremoniously out the screen door. The rooster ran to the door, so she gave him a swift kick out the door. I smiled, then together we cornered the other hen. I carried her outside and sent her flying over the porch rail.

There were feathers everywhere in the kitchen. The hens and rooster had run across the table, wooden benches, and floor.

The chickens' feet must have been covered in manure, which is now throughout this kitchen, I thought. The previously spotless kitchen now needed a thorough cleaning.

The Amish midwife put the spilled food into a bucket and carried it to the pigs. She wiped the kitchen table with a rag soaked with vinegar. I grabbed the broom and swept the feathers into a pile. I neatly swept them into a dustpan and dumped them over the porch rail. While I returned to the laboring woman, the Amish midwife scrubbed the floor and washed the dishes.

Within less than one hour, the kitchen was spotless again. The midwife walked across the lane to her farm. She returned with a large box filled with two apple pies, three warm loaves of fresh bread, and glass plates full of sliced tomatoes and cucumbers. She unpacked the box and adorned the nine-foot kitchen table with the food.

The house was quiet again, except for the galloping sound of the fetal heart beat when April used the doppler. The baby was doing well. The woman labored standing upright, while we sat quietly rocking. No matter what occurred during labor or how a birth progressed, I tried to normalize the situation and blanket the room with calmness. After another hour passed, the woman stifled a moan and leaned over the bed. After the next contraction, she got in bed and semi-reclined.

I checked her, and she was complete. "Push any time you are ready," I said encouragingly.

With one push, the baby was born. The birth was serene. While April assisted the Amish woman and newborn baby, I charted at the clean kitchen table. I chuckled when I thought about the hens perching themselves on the table previously.

A little while later, when I walked down the steps of the porch to leave, the rooster was waiting. The aggressive rooster either perceived us as a threat or wanted to assert himself as dominant over us. He was likely full of testosterone because it was mating season. The rooster tried to fly at me and beat me with his wings.

I was tired and having none of it, so I grabbed a stick and showed no fear. The rooster took one look at me and ran the other way.

"I thought so," I mumbled to myself.

Horse Flies

On a pleasant, spring day, I attended a long labor on an Amish farm. As usual, when I arrived, the farmhouse windows were open with the curtains flittering in the gentle wind. As the woman labored, I sat by a window rocking, taking in the gentle breeze.

When I heard the familiar sound of grunting, I walked into the bedroom and sat at the end of the bed. I put on my gloves and patiently waited for the baby to crown.

Suddenly, a horse put its face through the open window! Just as quickly as it put its head in, it pulled its head back out and trotted off.

No one in the room had time to react because the baby crowned and was born with the next push. While the baby spontaneously cried, I stole a quick glance at the window. The horse was not there, but I didn't have time to think about it because the afterbirth (placenta) was coming. It delivered intact, and I plopped it into the empty plastic bucket that had been provided by the Amish man.

Within minutes, dozens of black flies hovered near the placenta. I put a towel over the bucket to act as a lid, wishing I had plastic wrap. I hadn't noticed a single fly in the home until then. The woman's husband immediately carried the bucket outdoors. From the window, I saw him grab a spade from the shed, then he dug a deep hole and buried the placenta.

While I drove home, I smiled thinking about that horse. Suddenly, I thought of the pesky flies, and my stomach became nauseated. When I got home, I added a box of plastic wrap to my birth supplies.

The Pig

When I served the Amish and Mennonite, I was often given gifts—rocking chairs, quilts, vegetables, jellies, and bread. One day, I was given a pig and a cow. I was NOT putting a pig into my SUV to get it home.

When I walked into my house, Jeff asked me, "How bad is the vehicle?" He knew it always needed a car wash and a vacuum when I came home from the Amish.

I sensed the opportunity to hit him up for a favor.

"Jeff, I need a favor," I said sweetly.

"I can't wait to hear this," he joked.

"Do you have access to a cattle hauler? We now own a pig and a cow."

"What are we going to do with a pig and a cow?"

"Butcher them."

"Roger that."

Jeff borrowed a cattle hauler from a friend, hitched it up to his pickup, then drove to the Amish home. He and the Amish man managed to lure the pig and the cow onto the hauler. Jeff and I drove in his truck with the hauler in tow to a Mennonite butcher.

"It is easier when you bring home vegetables," Jeff said.

"Bacon will taste better than vegetables," I said.

Jeff laughed, "Yes, ma'am."

Pitch Black

Midwives travel at any hour, though it seems to be most often at night. The body produces more oxytocin at night, which stimulates labor, and melatonin levels peak in the evening, which promotes relaxation.

In Amish country, there are not many streetlights like in town or the city. In the country, there are long stretches of woods and fields. Depending on where a home was located, I would ask for the husband or a family member to make the home easy to find in the dark, fog, or rain. I requested that the Amish put a lantern on the ground at the end of their unmarked driveway. In suburbs and in the city, I told families to tie a balloon at the mailbox or front door.

I have gone to many homes unknown to GPS. When driving to them in the pitch dark, lanterns led my way. In those cases, I asked the husband to place lanterns at *every* turn on the off-grid roads.

Sometimes, whether or not I made it to a home in time to catch a baby came down to a matter of minutes. Those simple tricks of the trade saved me from missing many births.

On one such occasion, I was driving slowly in dense fog. It pains a midwife to have to drive slowly, particularly when she's on the cellphone with a mom who's breathing and panting in labor. That night, when I heard the woman on the other end of the phone grunt, I knew pushing was imminent.

When she couldn't talk anymore, her husband got on the phone. I could hear her in the background, on the toilet, panting.

"How long for Tori?" she asked breathlessly.

Thank goodness, her husband had marked the five turns on the country roads well. Because he knew the weather was not in my favor, he had placed *two* lanterns at every turn. Those lanterns lit up the turns like lighthouses light up the shores for ships' captains.

"I just passed the fifth set of lanterns," I told the husband on the phone.

"She is driving the last mile, darling!" I heard him relay to his wife.

I arrived just in time. When the woman saw me, her smile beamed like sunshine. She moved off the toilet onto an old, worn, patchwork quilt on the floor.

Women often birthed on the floor, and I positioned myself according to their birth position. Squatting, kneeling, bending, and twisting were just part of the midwife's job. I moved to accommodate their position no matter how uncomfortable I was momentarily—unlike in most hospitals where the laboring woman is in Lithotomy position for the provider's convenience.

The woman let out a loud moan and birthed a black-haired baby into my hands. The baby cried robustly.

I noticed her husband had hung a LED lantern on a nail in the wall in the bathroom. After I had cleaned up, I asked him about it.

"If the power went out, I wanted you to be able to see," he said.

I smiled. Sometimes lanterns were just as important during a birth as a midwife's hands.

Smoky Amish Farmhouse

I arrived for a birth one day before dawn to find a thin, Amish woman in active labor. She was wearing her navy blue bodice and skirt, covered with a navy apron over. The only weight she gained was in her belly, which was shaped like a basketball.

Her husband was out in the barn, milking the cows. Necessary pre-dawn farm chores were attended to, and the birth of a baby fit right into the rhythm of the farm.

After performing her initial assessment, I sat near the stove charting and waiting for labor to progress. I was rocking in the family's Amish rocking chair made of hickory sticks and oak slats when the Amish midwife arrived.

While the Amish midwife was busy making the bedroom ready for delivery, I noticed that the black stove needed more firewood. I walked outside to the wood pile and grabbed a few pieces of firewood. I came back inside, opened the stove door, and put the firewood in. I opened the damper—I thought.

Suddenly, smoke filled the room and stung my eyes. The Amish midwife came quickly into the room when she smelled the smoke. She quickly adjusted the damper and opened windows. Soon the thick smoke dissipated. I hadn't opened the damper! I had closed it—a mistake I wouldn't make again. We all had a good chuckle, and the laugh was on me. The new logs were putting off heat, so the Amish midwife set the water to boil on the stove.

The good news was the laboring woman's laughing intensified her contractions. Laughing can help move labor along, due to the effects of relaxation and endorphins.

"I'm glad you are here to deliver my baby—not to cook a meal on my stove," the woman chided me.

"One day at dinnertime, I burned three pizzas in a row at my house in my electric stove, because pregnant women kept ringing my phone," I said and laughed at the memory.

The woman laughed so hard she moved right into transition.

I stood and got my supplies ready. The Amish midwife opened the kitchen door and hollered in German toward the husband in the barn.

When the husband walked in from the kitchen, he was surprised how quickly the labor was moving along.

"The midwife tried a new idea, and it worked quickly!" the woman said.

He was puzzled, but before she could explain, a pain focused her attention inward. Her husband took his place behind her on the bed. She semi-reclined onto him. The baby was born easily into a smoke-free farmhouse.

By that time, it was daylight, so I didn't need to wear my head lamp. I could suture by the bright morning sunlight streaming through the window. I sat in a wooden chair at the end of the bed and did the repair, which only required a few stitches.

Horse and Buggy

One cold winter day, I was in Amish country, and my car was stuck in mud—again. An Amish midwife drove me in her horse and buggy for house calls.

The cold air was nippy, but the wool lap blanket across our legs was warm. I felt my toes getting cold in my boots. I was impressed with the Amish midwife's driving skills. When we arrived at each new farm, I carried my prenatal bags into each home and performed the necessary appointments.

Riding in the buggy was so relaxing. Life slowed down, and I felt my muscles relax for the first time in a long time. The hypnotic clop clop clop of the horse's hooves calmed my tired mind.

Traveling that slowly allowed me to take in the surrounding fields, trees, fences, and picturesque Amish homes. The buggy was drawn by one horse with blinders near its eyes that forced it to look straight ahead, preventing it from being spooked by cars speeding by. The Amish midwife had a carriage-driving horsewhip.

I learned a lot on that buggy ride. I needed to slow down while driving and in life in general. I needed to take time to smell the roses. I was overworked, and my phone was always ringing.

That evening, when we rode up to my car, I saw that the Amish men had pulled it out of the mud. I dreaded getting back into my car. But I had to return to my life in the fast lane.

It wasn't long before the fast lane became overwhelming after my mother and father died within two years of each other. During that time, I received a letter from an Amish woman that touched my heart. She wrote warm condolences, and I found her perspective and words comforting.

"Hello, Tori, I'm sorry to hear about your father passing away. Time moves on, and sometimes it seems almost unreal how fast the parents, uncles, and aunts get older and pass away one by one. We must accept it—even though it is hard. Life goes on, and we too get older. If we can, look at the bright side—how nice it is for them to be in heaven where all is peace."

Chapter 10: English Births

During my time as a midwife, I could be at an Amish home in the morning and an outdoor birth with non-Amish English by the evening. Life as a midwife was a whirlwind. One balmy day, I walked to my car to drive to a birth. The cicadas' high-pitched sound was deafening, as loud as I'd imagine millions of bees buzzing. In the South, the cicadas emerge from their slumber every thirteen years. Only the males sing. They vibrate their tymbals very fast, making a beautiful high-pitch chirp. I find that sound relaxing—the song of summer, but some people cannot stand it.

I wondered how my laboring lady would react. She was in labor at the height of the cicadas' singing, and her baby was coming earthside with them.

When I arrived at a yurt in the back hills of Tennessee, a beautiful woman was sitting outside on a wooden deck. I could tell that she was harnessing the energy of the loud cicadas, rather than allowing it to annoy her. She sat crossed-legged, humming a tone in melody with the cicadas that reminded me of a monk praying in a Buddhist temple. I knew that she was in labor land, and I did not disturb her.

I set up my delivery supplies on a picnic table outside. It was a beautiful, blue-skyed day. The woman's husband readied the bed inside the yurt. The woman was using a birthing technique called "hypnobirthing," which is a wonderful method of pain management. She was laboring so well, I found it difficult to time her contractions.

Suddenly, she moaned low. She moved to a squatting position. I placed a towel on the ground under her. She pushed, and then a gush of clear amniotic fluid poured onto the towel and ground.

"Your forewaters broke. Everything is fine," I said.

She pushed again, and the baby's head crowned. I was on my knees with my right shoulder lying on the ground, looking up. I placed my hands at her perineum to deliver the baby. The head delivered occiput anterior.

"Head's out," I told her.

I watched the external rotation of the head.

The woman pushed once more, and the baby was born along with more amniotic fluid. It is quite common for hind-waters to wash out with the baby.

She remained squatting. I handed her the baby. The cord dangled from her introitus and remained attached to the baby's umbilicus. The cord was pulsating, bringing blood to the baby. The baby starting crying, which is always a heartwarming sound at births.

After twenty minutes, I could tell that the woman felt another contraction. She pushed out the placenta, and it plopped onto the towel between her legs. I placed one cord clamp and cut the umbilical cord.

Her husband took the placenta and placed it into a pre-dug hole. Then, he planted an apple tree over it, filling dirt around the roots of the tree. We watched as he lovingly watered the tree with buckets of water.

He returned to his wife and smiled adoringly at her and the baby. He picked up the baby and cradled the precious bundle. The woman stood and walked across the yard to their outdoor shower. She stood on flat stones, lathering up soap with fresh water from a bucket. Then she turned on the shower to rinse off. She dried off and put on panties and a cloth menstrual pad.

Then we bathed the baby with warm water and dried him thoroughly. We wiped him down with olive oil. She put a cloth diaper on him and carried him into the yurt.

I tucked the new mom into her bed and helped the baby latch on to nurse. He nursed well, so I left the happy family of three alone in their yurt. It was a beautiful day.

Acupuncture

I met a lady for preconception counseling and listened to her heart-wrenching story. She had struggled with infertility for five years and had used fertility medication, which did not result in pregnancy.

I suggested she read the book *Taking Charge of Your Fertility* by Toni Weschler. She agreed to chart her basal temperatures and share them with me monthly. She was willing to take Vitex (chaste tree berry) liquid tincture orally. As she had been diagnosed with polycystic ovary syndrome (PCOS), I suggested myo and D-chiro inositol capsules with a 40:1 ratio (inositol is an important supplement because it improves insulin resistance.) I suggested she use Pre-Seed fertility lubricant because it helps protect sperm quality.

Within two months, I received a phone call from her. She was pregnant and over the moon. She wanted me to be her midwife.

Her pregnancy flew by, and she was now forty weeks. She opted to see her acupuncturist for labor induction. I drove to her house before daybreak the day of the appointment. She and I walked in her pasture. She was focusing on nature to get in the right frame of mind to relax for acupuncture. We watched the sun rise together and listened to the birds as the day awoke.

The traditional Chinese acupuncturist placed thin needles on specific points focused on labor induction. The hope was this treatment would initiate a release of oxytocin.

After the woman's treatment, we returned to her farm and took a walk in her herb and vegetable garden. The July weather was getting hot, but it was not too hot. The rosemary, basil, and lavender looked beautiful. I placed jasmine essential oil on her abdomen and lavender on her wrists. She smelled the aroma on her wrists. She visibly relaxed. While we walked, I gave her blue and black cohosh liquid tincture to hold under her tongue and swallow. She started having contractions. She stopped at an old oak tree. She touched its bark and commented about the strength of an oak tree. She put both hands on the trunk of the tree and swayed back and forth.

I heard her hum with a contraction. It was time to call her husband home from work and to set up supplies for her homebirth. We walked back to her home and got her settled on a birth ball. Her husband and her sister were on their way.

I set up the portable birth tub and spread out a tablecloth on the floor next to the tub. The tablecloth was flannel backed on one side and vinyl on the other. I found placing the table cloth flannel side up absorbed fluids well and protected the floor.

The laboring woman used the beautiful birth art on the walls as her focal point. She had painted several spectacular canvases. One was a sunflower that was exactly ten centimeters in diameter, which represented complete dilation of the cervix. Another canvas had a woman with a pregnant belly gazing at the moon. A third canvas with abstract painting showed a baby's head crowning right before birth. The house was filled with the woman's art. It was an amazing birth space.

Her husband quietly came through the door and went immediately to her side. He helped her off the birth ball, and they stood staring at the sunflower she had painted. The room was silent except her low humming during each contraction.

I quietly arranged my birth supplies, gathered towels to warm on the heating pads, and arranged the sterilized instruments. Two Rochester-Pean curved clamp, two Mayo curved scissor, and one umbilical cord clamp lay on the sterile tray lined up orderly like soldiers.

The laboring woman wanted to take a shower before getting into the birth tub. When she stepped into the shower stall, her water broke. The amniotic fluid was clear and had no odor. I listened to fetal heart tones while she stood in the shower. The baby's heartbeat was normal.

"Baby's happy!" I said smiling at her.

The woman walked with a towel around her from the shower to the tub. She climbed into the portable tub and sank into the warm water. The room was silent for thirty minutes.

The silence was broken with her low moan.

"I feel like I need to push," she said breathlessly.

Her sister placed a cold washcloth on her forehead. I checked her while she reclined in the birth tub. I told her to breathe through her contractions until she was fully dilated. She was not quite ten centimeters. She was so close. I had her flip to hands and knees because that position remedies the small amount of remaining cervix, which is called an anterior lip.

In five contractions, she was complete. She reclined in the tub and started pushing. She did not make progress with the first few contractions. She moved to the floor and semi-reclined onto her husband. I placed a *cold* compress at her perineum.

"Push at *this* spot," I said.

She nodded, and I removed the compress. A temporary cold compress directs a woman where to push. Cold is a distinct sensation.

The woman pushed and made immediate progress. After three strong pushes, the baby crowned. After another strong push, her baby was born.

I dried off the baby with a towel and handed him to his mother's outstretched arms. She was crying. She had waited years for this baby.

While she held and kissed her baby, I watched for postpartum bleeding and waited for the placenta. After twenty minutes, she had a contraction. It was time.

"It's time to deliver the afterbirth. Push one more time," I said.

The new mother pushed, and the placenta came. Her fundus was firm but shifted to the right.

"Let's go to the bathroom. I need you to empty your bladder." I put a few drops of peppermint into the toilet water, and I held the tincture of peppermint under her nose. She smelled the mint and started urinating. Peppermint works well to stimulate urination post birth.

After the woman used the bathroom, her husband tucked her into bed. Her fundus was firm and midline. She nursed her baby while I charted.

When she finished nursing, I swaddled the baby and handed him to his daddy. While he rocked him in the rocking chair, I walked the new mother to the shower. She used lavender pure-castile liquid soap. It smelled heavenly.

She dressed in a nursing nightgown, panties, and cloth menstrual pads. I tucked her into bed, and she nursed the baby again. I encouraged her to nurse every two to three hours and keep the baby warm. I advised her to urinate and drink fluids every time she nursed.

"Tori, please don't leave yet," she said.

"I can stay," I replied.

Suddenly, I had an idea.

"Would you like a salad made from freshly picked garden vegetables?" I asked.

"That would be wonderful," she said.

The hot July sun was overhead while I picked tomatoes, peppers, cucumbers, spinach, and lettuce. I washed and chopped the vegetables and put them in a large bowl. I added olive oil, vinegar, feta cheese, apples, and grapes.

"This is perfect!" she exclaimed happily when I handed her the bowl of salad.

"You started the day outside. You needed something from outdoors. You've come full circle," I explained.

She was quiet for a moment. Suddenly, she spoke from her heart.

"You will always be my friend," she said.

"Always," I replied.

Wrong Baby

Women choose homebirth for a variety of reasons. During the initial prenatal visit, I asked each woman *why* she wanted a homebirth. Common answers were: It is my religious conviction. My mother had a homebirth. I do not want a hospital–acquired infection. I want a VBAC. I want a waterbirth. Sometimes the reason was different and incredulous. *I was handed the wrong baby.*

That is uncommon in hospitals, but it *does* happen.

"When I looked at the sleeping baby's face, I immediately knew it was *not* my baby," one woman said with tears streaming down her face.

After comparing the mother and baby bands, the nurse confirmed the mistake.

"I was frantic, wondering *where* was *my* baby. I could feel my heart pounding in my chest. After I called my husband and mother crying, I stared at the hospital door *waiting for my baby*," she said.

After an agonizing wait, her baby was brought to her. She vowed never to birth in a hospital again.

I was pensive as I drove to her home on a warm, sunny afternoon. She was in labor. The main challenge would be helping her cope with pain. With her previous four births, she had received epidurals for pain management.

When I arrived, it took a few tries, but I successfully managed to parallel park my car in the tight space on the busy city street. I saw Amy-Suzette parking her lime green convertible Volkswagen Beetle. She and I met on the paved sidewalk and walked to the old historic home together. Amy-Suzette had worked labor-delivery as a nurse and was passionate about evidence-based birth. She worked hard and was a wonderful intern midwife.

We walked through the black wrought-iron gate and went up the steps onto the porch. When we walked through the refinished antique door of the historic Victorian home, I didn't hear the sounds of labor. She was in active labor with minimal pain. She had taken birth preparation herbs for several weeks, and she seemed to be having just that—a gentle labor. I was impressed with her dilation of six centimeters.

She stood swaying back and forth during contractions. When the contractions finally got intense, Amy-Suzette rubbed her lower back. Once the birth tub was filled, the laboring woman sank into the warm water. We quietly watched her labor. Her long black braided hair was beautiful. She suddenly felt intense pressure.

"The baby is coming!" she exclaimed.

I delivered the baby in the water and handed her the baby.

"It's a boy!" she said amidst tears.

Once she was showered and tucked into bed, she expressed how intense the pain had been during the last few minutes.

"I never felt a baby come out before. My epidurals had masked that pain. But I would do this all over again. Thank you."

She was glad to be in her own home, with her own bed, pillows, blankets, and recliner. She loved the privacy homebirth provided. She felt safe. She relaxed, knowing she would not be handed the wrong baby. She knew her baby was safe, snuggled next to her.

Before I left, I gave the woman a croqueted blanket as a gift. I made it with soft baby blue yarn.

"It's beautiful," she said as she gently laid it over the sleeping baby.

When I closed my car door and started the ignition, the gleam of my croquet hook caught the corner of my eye. The croquet hooks and balls of baby yarn were in the small wicker basket on the passenger side floorboard. I smiled, thinking, *I will have to start a new baby blanket.*

A British Midwife

One summer, a lovely young lady named Rebecca Wagner came from England to shadow me. She was currently working in the maternity settings of Oxford, England. She stayed at my home, and my family and I enjoyed her company very much. She was a wonderful house guest.

Jeff took Rebecca flying in his Russian Yak-52 Warbird airplane. Jeff had trained in aerobatics with a former World War II pilot, and he was very skilled in barrel rolls, loops, and other aerobatic maneuvers. Rebecca had so much fun flying over the Tennessee River and seeing the Wilson Dam, the tallest lock in the world. Jeff took the plane right down to the water level and tipped the plane to a forty-five degree angle to the water. When he flew higher, he did barrel rolls.

"Jeff did a death-defying plunge toward the ground, then pulled up into a loop," Rebecca told me. She had the time of her life!

During Rebecca's stay, we alternated between fun and work. I gave her a tour of Hope House and shared its history and mission to allow women to deliver their babies there if they needed a place to stay. I supported extended stays at Hope House because some women drove hours to cross the state line to receive homebirth midwifery care that was sadly unavailable in their area.

"What a lovely birth space. The bright décor is an incredible bohemian style!" she exclaimed as she viewed the first birth room.

Rebecca proclaimed the next bedroom was "fit for royalty" with the grand purple décor and original hardwood floors.

"How dainty!" she said as she admired the sleigh bed in the last bedroom.

I turned on the string of white lights, which surrounded the birth tub in the large living room.

"Ah. What beautiful fairy lights!" she said in her British accent.

Her smile and vivacious manner were contagious.

In the kitchen, I showed Rebecca my fresh herbs hanging upside-down to dry—currently, lavender and rosemary. I opened my herb closet, where I kept several shelves of purchased dried herbs and liquid herbal tinctures.

Rebecca smelled the aroma of each dried herb while I explained their purpose as it related to the childbearing year.

"Nettle leaf smells like freshly cut grass. Nettle has vitamins A C, D, and K and minerals calcium, phosphorus, potassium, and iron. It has more chlorophyll than any other herb, prevents anemia, and reduces the risk of postpartum hemorrhage. Nettle strengthens the blood vessels, which I believe reduces the risk of preeclampsia. Drinking nettle leaf tea or using Floradix, which contains nettle, are two ways to receive the benefits of this nourishing herb," I explained.

Rebecca smelled the large bag of red raspberry leaf, which had a mild herbal scent.

"Red raspberry leaf tones the uterus and is rich in vitamins A, B complex, C, and E, and calcium, phosphorus, and potassium. It prevents anemia, reduces risk of postpartum hemorrhage, and reduces pain in labor by toning the muscles of the uterus," I said.

"What do these liquid herbal tinctures do?" Rebecca asked.

"The birth preparation tincture contains blessed thistle, red raspberry leaf, false unicorn, motherwort herb, blue cohosh, ginger root, bayberry root, skullcap, wild yam, and partridge-berry herb. Used the last month of pregnancy, it ripens the cervix, facilitates a good Bishop score, tones the uterus, and shortens time in labor," I explained.

I handed her the blue and black cohosh liquid tinctures.

"The judicious use of cohosh will bring a baby for postdates women," I stated.

The last brown glass bottle on the shelf was an anti-hemorrhage tincture.

"This tincture contains blue cohosh, yarrow, motherwort, shepherd's purse, and alfalfa. It is used as a preventative after the baby and placenta are delivered. Blue cohosh is an oxytocic herb, which contracts the uterus. Yarrow is a stypic herb, which stops bleeding by contracting blood vessels. Motherwort prevents bleeding and is a uterotonic that increases uterine contractions. Shepherd's purse reduces postpartum blood loss. Alfalfa is high in vitamin K, which is an essential vitamin needed to reduce the risk of hemorrhage," I said.

"Do midwives use medication?" Rebecca asked.

I explained the individuality of each state's law to Rebecca, because England operated under the National Health Service. Hope House was in a state where midwives had licensure to *administer* medication specific to the practice of midwifery.

Administration of medication by a midwife included Rh Immune Globulin, Pitocin (postpartally), Methergine (postpartally), and Cytotec (postpartally), and lidocaine for perineal repair and prophylactic ophthalmic medication and vitamin K intramuscularly for newborns.

With modern medication and knowledge of traditional herbs, I was able to bridge the gap and blend traditional midwifery with evidenced-based care. My midwifery practice blended both worlds and brought balance to birth.

Driving

Rebecca shadowed me during prenatal appointments at Hope House. I allotted two hours for each visit with each pregnant woman. I went over nutritional education and herbal information and conducted a prenatal exam. Rebecca was amazed that women traveled as far as three hours to have midwifery services. I explained that midwives cannot deliver babies in homes in certain states, which is a disgrace. That's why some women have to drive long distances to receive midwifery care.

Blood pressures, urine dips, weight, fundal height, palpating position, fetal heart tones, and cervical checks (upon request) were part of the prenatal care. I spent hours reviewing nutrition, optimal fetal positioning, herbal teas and tinctures, and vitamins.

Regarding nutrition, I stressed consuming 75 to 100 milligrams per day of protein to reduce the risk of preeclampsia. Colorful vegetables were next in importance, then low-glycemic fruit. High glycemic fruit have more carbohydrates and calories and should be a rare treat.

During one appointment, I pricked a finger, drew a hemoglobin (Hgb) level, then evaluated the drop of blood with a hemoglobinometer. The woman's Hgb was low at ten, which prompted discussion of choices on how to raise her level. I liked a Hgb level to range between twelve and thirteen during pregnancy. I discussed the benefits of liquid Floradix, which is plant based. I recommended chlorophyll or wheatgrass. All are beneficial in treating anemia. We discussed high iron vegetables and greens, such as spinach, brussels sprouts, peas, kale, asparagus, and broccoli. I stressed the importance of cooking in cast-iron skillets, which increases iron intake. When I saw the woman six weeks later, her hemoglobin was normal.

Early the next morning, Rebecca and I drove two hours to an intentional religious community, a Christian commune of approximately fifty families in the community. The group was set up to keep separate from the world, but they did preach the gospel to the locals. We drove through a rural wooded area until we came to a glade where the small homes of the commune were located. When I stepped out of the car, I reveled in the incredible tranquility of the backwoods rural area. It was so peaceful.

That day, I did a prenatal exam on an expectant woman who desired a vaginal birth after cesarean (VBAC). I encouraged her to use a rebozo for abdominal support to lift her abdomen up and inward because achieving optimal fetal positioning is key for a successful VBAC.

"Do you have evening primrose oil in capsule form?" I asked.

"Yes, I do," she said.

"Take it orally every day. It is known to ripen the cervix. Also, start the herbal labor prep tincture at thirty-five weeks, which will dilate your cervix and give a good Bishop score before you go into labor."

I walked out of her home into the hot humid Southern summer with a huge smile of contentment on my face. I truly loved being a midwife.

It was a ninety-minute drive to the next appointment—a postpartum check-up. The ride took us to a remote rural area on a worn dirt path with grass growing between the tire tracks. When we came out to a clearing, the sun shone on a white farmhouse. The family was of the Pentecostal faith.

Short Bible verses were stenciled onto various sizes of painted wood and hung on the walls throughout the home. These inspirational wall hangings made the home a peaceful and encouraging place to visit.

I weighed the baby using a cotton sling and hanging metal scale.

"The baby is gaining well!" I said joyfully.

Babies should gain their birth weight back by two weeks, and thereafter gain at least three to five ounces per week. By six months, birth weight should double. By one year, birth weight should triple.

"Do you have any tips on increasing breastmilk supply?" asked the breastfeeding mother.

"The best way to increase supply is by drinking a tea made from a blend of herbs. Fennel seeds, red raspberry leaf, nettles, and blessed thistle increase supply. Summer McCreless of Mothering Herbs sells the best lactation tea blend," I stated.

When Rebecca and I stood to leave, we were gifted beautiful wooden blocks with Bible verses mounted on them. It was a lovely end to a long day.

Shadowing in Amish Community

The next afternoon, Rebecca and I had the opportunity to visit with a Granny Midwife. As we drove past several Amish farms, I explained that the Amish are known for simple living, plain dress, and a deep reluctance to adopt modern conveniences. The Amish don't like to be photographed because it is viewed as vanity and idolatry.

Once we arrived, Rebecca and I spent several hours speaking to the elderly Amish midwife about her experiences. Instead of using a doppler to count fetal heart tones, she used a fetoscope, which does not need batteries, so it was practical for the Amish midwife. She also had a traditional wooden Pinard horn to listen and count a baby's heartbeat. The wide, flat end is placed on the pregnant belly, and the sound travels through the hollow wooded core to the smaller open end and the naked ear of the listener.

The elderly midwife explained that to turn a breech baby without an external version, she put a hot water bottle at the woman's bottom and a cold towel on her abdomen. The baby will move its head away from the cold toward the warmth down below.

When there was a shoulder dystocia, she tilted the mother onto her side and then back to McRoberts position to release the shoulder.

The Amish midwife successfully managed to keep blood pressures within normal ranges with daily doses of hops tea. To induce labor, she used blue and black cohosh and ginger. Nettle tea was used post birth to increase breastmilk and because it is an excellent source of iron for an anemic post–birth woman. She used cotton root bark and shepherd's purse herbs if there was heavy postpartum bleeding.

The granny midwife was a joy to talk with. I admired her aged, wrinkled hands that had touched so many lives.

We left the granny midwife's home and visited an Amish home that was painted on both the outside and the inside. The walls were off white and the wood trim was a distinct blue color that I had noticed in Lancaster County, Pennsylvania, farm houses as a child. Most homes in this southern community hadn't been painted inside because the families were still establishing themselves. This home was lovely and organized.

Another Amish home was partially finished on the inside. It was tidy, but some areas of the walls showed two by four studding.

"There are rich and poor even in the Amish communities," Rebecca observed. I agreed with Rebecca that depending on their trade, how old they were, and how long they were established in an area influenced their wealth.

I had a scheduled appointment with a woman in her second trimester. When I knocked on the door, I saw multiple children at the kitchen table. Amish children do not learn English until they are school age. Regardless, I knew not to use words like pregnancy, baby, or midwife because the children did not know their mother was pregnant, nor did they understand how babies are born—let alone made. The Amish kept pregnancy and childbirth private from their children. The woman spoke in German to the children, and they obediently went outside. Her prenatal appointment was easy and straightforward. She gave me a basket filled with vegetables, and Rebecca and I left for the next farm.

We stopped into the most picturesque Amish home in the area—a white farmhouse with red wooden barn buildings adjacent to it, surrounded by carefully-cut grass, bountiful vegetable gardens, and a tidy row of blackberries.

We spoke to the Amish woman on her lovely porch out of reach of her teenage children's ears. The woman was learning midwifery skills from me, but she hadn't studied much lately because she had been busy jarring up jams, mucking the stalls, and canning cucumbers and tomatoes. I knew that she would make a fine midwife someday.

Our next stop was a grand-multip. I checked her hemoglobin, and she was not anemic. "What herbs are you drinking?" I asked.

"Nettles and red raspberry, and I'm drinking liquid chlorophyll," she answered.

I praised her efforts. She sent us to another farm that needed me to stop in. They had left word with her to request that I come. This was common, and I never knew how many farms I would visit in a day.

On the way to the next farm, we passed the one-room schoolhouse. There were no little heads studiously bent over their desks because school was out for the summer.

The heat was oppressive, making us feel hot and sticky. I knocked on the screen door, but she had heard my car coming.

"Come in, Tori," she said. I introduced her to Rebecca, and she welcomed us to sit down in the rockers. The rocking chairs were comfortable, but my sweat saturated the back side of my shirt because it was now the hottest part of the day.

The woman explained she was having some pain on her lower right side. I sent her to the outhouse, and she returned with a urine sample in a glass jelly jar. Her urine tested normal. Because an abdominal palpation was necessary, we went into her bedroom, and she shut the doors and curtains. Her vitals were normal. Her fundal height matched her gestational weeks of pregnancy. Fetal heart tones were normal. My conclusion was she had pulled a muscle and was having round ligament pain. She worked hard on her farm.

"Please lift less weight over the next week," I suggested. "Also drink one gallon of water per day."

After we left the farm, Rebecca commented on the oak wall clock that hung in the living area of the farmhouse. When the house was quiet, the ticking could be heard. It was the type of clock that needed winding once per week. The Amish keep their clocks on Standard Time and don't observe Daylight Savings Time. I was fascinated to learn from Rebecca that England observes a time change, but they call it "British Summer Time."

"The ticking of their clocks and the crackling of the fire in the woodstove are a beautiful part of Amish births," I said. I was keenly aware how fortunate I was to be a midwife for the Amish.

Farm Midwifery Center

The following week, I was driving Rebecca to the renowned Farm Midwifery Center in Tennessee, where she was going to attend midwifery classes.

Years before, I had attended midwifery lectures by author and midwife Ina May Gaskin. I was blessed to have learned from such an intuitive midwife. I attended lectures on vaginal breech, twin deliveries, the delivery of the head over an intact perineum, and using the Gaskin Maneuver to resolve shoulder dystocia.

I loved the class on how Amish traditions affect birth, which was taught by Carol Nelson, another incredible Farm midwife. She gave us a tour of her local Amish community, which included an interview with an Amish midwife.

Nostalgia flooded my heart as I remembered Ina May Gaskin's smiling face as she handed a single red rose to me at a midwifery event in Alabama. The beautiful rose was a gift of recognition because I and many others were fighting for legalization of homebirth midwifery in Alabama. The fight for licensure in Alabama would continue for years, with midwives eventually prevailing.

I dropped Rebecca off at the Farm, wishing her well and holding back the tears in my eyes. She had been a joy, and I hoped to see her again someday. England seemed far away in that moment. I watched Rebecca walk away, knowing she had a beautiful life ahead of her.

As I drove home, I remembered the most beautiful breech birth I ever attended. The homebirth setting was filled with tranquility. A fireplace gave off a warm glow. Rocking chairs were padded comfortably. It was lovely. When the laboring woman was fully dilated, she moved into a semi-reclining position with her bottom at the edge of the bed. She continued laboring for more than one hour—even though she was fully dilated. This is important in a breech birth to prevent head entrapment because the head is birthed last. (The head is larger than the buttocks.) She was birthing on a queen-sized bed with warm bedding. She had several strands of white lights adorning the ceiling and the walls of the room.

After one hour, she had the overwhelming need to push. Once she pushed, the baby's buttocks came first. With each push, the buttocks presented farther and farther out of the vagina. The first leg delivered easily, and then the second came like clockwork. A warm blanket was placed over the buttocks and legs. The cord was pulsating at a strong 120 beats per minute. Because the baby's hands were above the head, it was necessary to rotate the shoulders and reach in and bring the anterior arm down. The next step was to rotate the other way to bring the other arm down and out. Momentarily, the baby was let to hang to allow flexion of the head (flexed head-chin to chest). Quickly, the baby's hairline was visible, and it was time to deliver the head. With the right hand's fingers on the cheekbones, and the left hand below the occiput, the baby's head was deftly brought down then up. The baby was born easily. It was a beautiful and incredible homebirth.

My thoughts went from breech to the Gaskin Maneuver. When in Guatemala, Ina May Gaskin observed indigenous midwives directing a woman into all-fours position. This position change spontaneously resolved a shoulder dystocia. Ina May brought the technique to America, and it was the first obstetrical procedure named after a midwife.

I could hear her voice in my head, happily lecturing how to resolve a shoulder dystocia:

"If the anterior shoulder is caught above the mother's pubic bone after the vaginal delivery of the head, flip the woman to all fours," she taught.

I sighed as I remembered the many babies I brought earthside with my hands. I knew Rebecca was going to learn a lot during her stay at the Farm and that she would support many women and babies when she returned to England. The art of midwifery was being practiced all over the world as it has been for millenniums. *That* was a profound thought.

As I drove alone, I felt a void. I deeply missed Rebecca. The ringing of my cellphone stopped my brooding. I felt that familiar rush of adrenaline as a woman was breathing through contractions on the other end of the phone. Instantly, I stepped on the gas and headed to Hope House.

Chapter 11: Hope and Determination

I hurried to Hope House to set up my delivery tray. A Guatemalan woman was in labor with her third baby. She was married to an American missionary and had recently moved to the United States.

The woman stood, walked, and sat on the birth stool during labor. She was strong and stoic. She carried her Rosary beads tightly in her hands. She said her prayers while moving her fingers to each bead on the Rosary. Her labor progressed well, and she went to bed to push. She pulled her legs back into McRoberts Position and birthed her baby. Suddenly, she put her hands onto her breasts and vigorously rubbed them. She was overzealously performing nipple stimulation. The baby was crying and doing well, but she didn't make eye contact with the baby. She continued to rub her breasts for minutes.

When the umbilical cord lengthened, I asked the woman if she was ready to push to deliver the placenta. She pulled back her legs and pushed. Once the placenta delivered, she visibly relaxed. She picked up the baby and starting nursing on her right breast, while continuing vigorously rubbing her left breast. Finally, after several fundal checks with a firm uterus and minimal bleeding, she stopped rubbing.

After the woman was settled in for the evening, she confided in me. When she was in labor the first time in Guatemala, she labored in a ward. The beds were lined up, and each woman had a mosquito net around her bed. She watched a woman next to her hemorrhage to death during the delivery. When she asked her mother how to prevent that from happening, her mother said prayer and rubbing the breasts. I understood now why she was so forceful with her nipple stimulation. Sometimes, midwives don't learn the full picture of emotional trauma until after the birth is over.

Telephone Deliveries

On rare occasions, I talked husbands through the birth of a baby and the placenta by cellphone. Because there were very few midwives in my area, I covered a radius of two hours from my home in all directions. Sometimes I traveled even farther.

One day, I had been at a location with no cell service. I received a voice mail approximately thirty minutes after the original call. Thirty minutes doesn't seem like much, but it is when it's a woman's tenth baby.

Immediately, I called back, and when the husband answered instead of the patient, I instantly knew that a baby was imminent.

"Please describe what you are seeing," I said.

I could hear the woman in the background saying, "The baby is coming!"

"Grab a towel and catch the baby," I told the husband.

He did. Then he put me on speaker phone.

"Rub the baby and dry the baby off," I directed.

I heard the baby cry.

"Can you describe the baby?" I asked.

"The baby is turning pink and moving," he said.

"Slowly move the baby to the mother's chest," I said. "Be careful not to pull on the umbilical cord because the placenta is still attached to the uterine wall."

"Okay, the baby is on my wife's chest," he said.

"Cover the baby with a clean, thick bath towel," I said.

During that entire conversation, I was driving toward their home, very mindful of traffic and redlights.

Suddenly, the new mom had a very strong contraction.

"You are going to need to manage the delivery of the placenta," I said. "Find a large bowl."

"I have a large Tupperware container," he said.

"Place another towel on the floor under her buttocks to catch the blood," I advised.

The mother pushed, and the placenta delivered easily with the fetal side first, called shiny Shultz. I directed the husband to place the placenta into the Tupperware container.

"Do you see any blood flow at her vagina?" I asked

"No," he said.

"You will arrive in five minutes," my GPS announced.

I heard the husband laugh shakily. "I will never be so happy to see someone in my entire life," he said.

"You have an incredible birth story to tell," I said.

Babies arrive when they want—in any weather, at any time of day, and sometimes before the midwife arrives.

Overdue

I went to a rural home that had two large oak trees in the front yard. I parked and carried my prenatal bag to the door. I knocked and was greeted by a jolly woman with a large belly. She was forty-one weeks (one week past the estimated due date).

I palpated her abdomen and believed the baby was over ten pounds. After discussing options, she decided to encourage labor by using castor oil and herbs.

She drank the induction shake, and within the hour she was on the toilet. Every fifteen minutes, I dosed her with blue and black cohosh for eight rounds. Contractions were regular but tolerable.

She and I walked outside and stood under the old oak tree. The breeze felt good.

"I need to go inside," she said suddenly.

She climbed into bed and leaned on her birth ball. Active labor had gripped her. Neysa arrived and helped me set up the birth supplies.

I asked her husband to fill up the large bathroom tub. It was her fifth baby, and her contractions were already coming every two minutes. Labor was moving quickly.

She got in the tub and audibly sighed as she sank into the warm water. The buoyant deep warm water flooded her brain with pain-inhibiting endorphins, which relaxed her and slid her mind into bliss.

Her husband lit candles and dimmed the lights. I checked the fetal heart beat using the submersible hand-held doppler probe. A calming silence filled the room.

Darkness had come, and the night was still. I heard an evening whippoorwill calling from an old crabapple tree in the yard. In the birth room, the only sound was her husband speaking quiet, private words into her ear.

She felt a pop. I used the flashlight to see the amniotic fluid with particles of vernix floating and mixing with the clear bath water. She felt pressure.

"Where do you want to birth? In the tub? Or on the quilts on the floor like your birth plan stated?"

Without answering, she stood up and moved to the floor. Her husband dried her off with towels. I turned on a table lamp, which provided enough light to see, but was not glaring.

She pushed, and the head turtled, which was an indication of a looming shoulder dystocia. With her next push, the head was born. The head slowly restituted (turned).

"Go ahead and push," I said.

She pushed, but the shoulders were stuck.

"Turn over. Go to your hands and knees," I said.

She flipped over immediately.

"Push," I said calmly.

She pushed, and the baby didn't budge. I reached with my right hand to dislodge the shoulder. I was unable to move the shoulder. I was able to reach the baby's hand and gently pull the arm out. The rest of the baby came easily.

It took less than one minute from the delivery of the head to the delivery of the body, which is within the normal parameters for the situation. I placed the baby on the quilt on the floor, and Neysa quickly dried the baby off with towels. I told the birthing mother to talk her baby. Baby's respond to their mother's voice.

Neysa listened to his heart and lungs with a stethoscope.

"Everything is perfect," she said with a smile.

The baby started crying loudly and remained attached to a pulsating cord providing rich oxygenated blood.

His mother was still in hands and knees position. I passed him between her legs up toward her chest.

"Here is your baby," I said.

She moved onto her side and held her son with tears streaming down her face. She tenderly kissed his pink forehead.

"It's a boy!" she exclaimed.

I cut and clamped the now flaccid cord. She handed the baby to her husband. He and Neysa swaddled the baby with warm blankets, while the birthing mother squatted to deliver the placenta. She pushed, and the placenta came easily. She stood and walked naked to the shower. After a refreshing shower, she sat on the toilet and urinated. Using a peri bottle, she squirted an herbal blend of comfrey, plantain, and violet over her perineum. This liquid herbal blend aids in healing abrasions and sutured tears. She would use this same blend over the next few days as a sitz bath.

In her breastfeeding nightgown, she walked to her bed, and I covered her with a warm comforter.

"The baby had an Apgar score of 8 at one minute, 9 at five minutes, and 10 at ten minutes. He is doing great!" Neysa reassured her.

Neysa weighed the baby in the cotton sling scale.

"He is 10 pounds and 8 ounces!" Neysa exclaimed. We all admired his pudgy cheeks.

He latched well and nursed greedily. While the mother fed him, she talked about her birth.

"It was not the easy birth I envisioned. But I was able to change positions and push my son out with the midwife's help. My friend had a baby last month. She was pushing on her back with her legs in stirrups. The room was filled with nurses as the doctor struggled and pulled on the baby. Nurses pulled her numb legs up and back to her shoulders. Her legs were numb due to the epidural. The nurse pushed on her abdomen to shove the shoulder under her pubic bone. The doctor cut two episiotomies. Her baby was finally delivered, but its arm didn't work. There is damage to the arm from the delivery that might be permanent. Her baby was taken to the nursery for days," she recollected.

She continued, "I am happy with my birth. Those few moments were scary. But you both handled it calmly and with the room blanketed with loving warmth."

Inwardly, I gave thanks to the Guatemalan indigenous midwives and the American midwife Ina May.

Tornado Warnings

Living in the South, the weather commands respect, due to frequent tornado watches and warnings. Tornadoes can rip through a community without much warning. Several times per year, the sirens went off, warning a tornado was spotted on the ground. When a siren went off, we could hear it from miles away. Because tornadoes are unpredictable, sometimes people are caught in the wrong place at the wrong time.

During one tornado watch, Neysa and I found ourselves in an old Victorian home with a wrap-around front porch and a hanging porch swing. Inside, the home was spectacular, with a stunning staircase, timeworn hardwood floors, and hand-carved crown molding.

We entered the woman's bedroom to find her close to delivery. She was standing next to her antique four-poster bed, leaning forward onto pillows. I spoke quietly to her, so as not to disturb her labor. Neysa placed pads on the floor under her.

She was a multip, and her labor had progressed rapidly. She felt pressure and was involuntarily pushing. When the body pushes involuntarily, the uterus is doing the work and the laboring mother cannot control it. The baby is coming! With gloves donned, I positioned myself for delivery, kneeling behind her. The forewaters protruded from the perineum. The baby crowned. Suddenly the head was born, and the membranes ruptured, causing clear fluid to soak the pads on the floor. I reduced the nuchal cord while watching the baby's head complete its external rotation. As soon as the rotation was complete, the baby was born into my hands. The cord dangled between the birthing woman's legs. I was kneeling on the floor, holding the baby.

When the cord ceased pulsating and was flaccid, I clamped and cut the cord. Delayed cord clamping has evidenced based advantages for babies. It improves immunity and circulation and increases iron levels. A baby receives extra blood while transitioning from the intrauterine to the extrauterine environment.

Neysa wrapped the baby in a receiving blanket and placed him on the bed in front of the mother. The mother gazed at the baby, but she was intently focused on the harsh contractions she was experiencing. She remained standing, leaning forward over the bed. A gush of blood ran down her legs, indicating the normal detachment of the placenta. The cord lengthened, which is another sign of detachment. She pushed, and the placenta plopped into the basin I was holding.

I cleaned the woman's legs and feet with warm, soapy water and dried them with a towel. She laid down in the warm bed, and her husband handed her the baby. She placed the baby on her breast and closed her eyes.

The afterpains are intense for multips. The more often the uterus has stretched, the harder it needs to work to stay firm and return to its normal size, The process is called involution, and it is normal for the uterus to cramp for several days. She breathed through several contractions as if she was still in labor. She placed a dropperful of herbal tincture—made with yarrow, motherwort, black haw bark, and crampbark—into her mouth to lessen the afterbirth pains. She swallowed it and drank a glass of water.

Later, walking down the wooden steps of the old staircase, I wondered how many babies had been born in this historic Victorian house. *If only walls could talk.*

Neysa and I were driving home from the homebirth when the weather turned ugly. We had known there was a tornado watch for the entire day, but we were unaware of the tornado warning as we were driving in the car. The rain and wind picked up, and the sky was getting dark. We tuned in to the weather radio channel and heard of a tornado sighting on the ground just north of us.

Suddenly, cars were pulling over to the side of the road, with both headlights and hazard lights on. We pulled over under an overpass. Due to the blackened sky and torrential rain, we could not see the tornado. We continued listening to the radio as the car rocked with the wind gusts. The windshield wipers were useless against the stormy downpour. Next hail fell from the eerie, greenish-gray sky. I could hear my heart beat in my ears. It was as if time stood still while we held our breath. The downpour seemed to last forever.

When the rain lightened up, we could once again see through the windshield and I breathed a sigh of relief. After what seemed an eternity, the storm blew over us. We could see the horizon and were grateful for that. Neysa drove the vehicle to the closest exit, where we pulled in to a hamburger joint and ordered food.

We both agreed that we hated tornado weather. According to the radio news, a tornado had touched down in the town a few miles to the north of us. Thankfully, we were unscathed—except for the jitters.

The life of a midwife is as unpredictable as the weather. I never knew from one day to the next what would happen.

The Swimming Pool

When summer arrived, I would open my backyard pool to pregnant women for one-to-one prenatal sessions. In chest-deep warm water, a pregnant woman would back float with pool noodles while being continuously supported by me, as I gently moved her around in the water. This Watsu technique promoted deep relaxation as the woman closed her eyes, trusting me fully to pull her safely through the water. Her body was massaged by the moving water. I encouraged relaxed breathing while I moved her in different patterns in the water. In the end, she would rest in complete stillness in a back float.

The pregnant women reported that the supported back float reduced stress. Most importantly, it helped them face their fears. It also engendered trust between them and me.

I encouraged swimming, art, and journaling as effective methods of facing any previous trauma or fear. Some women painted artwork and would decorate their labor space. Other women wrote a list of fears and burned them in a ceremony.

One woman chose Watsu for labor. When I arrived at her home, she was in her swimming pool with noodles under her knees and arms. The patio was covered, giving protection from the sun. A gentle sound of flowing water came from the outdoor water fountain. Her backyard was a tranquil oasis and a perfect birth space. Her husband had a comfortable birth tub inflated on the patio, and a string of soft lights hung from the ceiling.

I donned a bathing suit and waded out to the laboring woman carrying my doppler in one hand. Fetal heart tones were perfect. I gently moved her through the water during contractions. She relaxed, breathed, and cleared her mind.

As labor intensified, she gravitated to the patio. She labored standing and rocking her hips. Her husband spoon fed her watermelon and frozen yogurt between contractions. As the sun set, she climbed into the birth tub. The string of lights provided light and brought a sense of tranquility to the birth space.

She was calm and quiet until her eyes opened wide.

"The baby is coming," she said loudly.

"Go ahead and push if you want," I said soothingly.

She pushed once, and her baby was born into warm water with lovely white lights hanging around the tub. It was a peaceful birth space filled with love.

The Physician

One day, a medical doctor from Alabama came to tour Hope House and interview me. She wanted to understand why women chose homebirth and to ascertain whether midwives could deliver safe care. She was writing an article and rather than cling to assumptions, she wanted to have open dialogue and see the reality of midwifery and homebirth. I agreed to the interview with no expectations of a positive article. I had never met her before, nor did I know if the interview would go well because the medical establishment was often hostile toward the practice of midwifery.

When the doctor arrived, she admired the large wooden sign hung on the old barn. The horse shoes on the sign spelled out HOPE. During the long interview, I shared the story of Hope House and the plight of women who clung to hope.

I explained to her that Hope House gave women hope by providing refuge for women seeking homebirth. Because it was illegal for a homebirth midwife to practice in Alabama, women traveled across state lines to their midwife.

It wasn't just our *location* that provided hope. Hope House welcomed women with limited financial resources. I remembered my roots and my blessings, and I did not turn my back on the poor. I believed every woman should be able to birth with hope.

The philosophy of Hope House was Hold On Pain Ends. In a literal sense, this was true for each contraction and for labor itself. Additionally, it was a metaphor for any momentary hardship a woman was facing in life. In the most important sense, it was Hope Eternal.

I welcomed the doctor into my humble Hope House, wondering what she would think of the simply furnished home. We walked onto the front porch. The open windows brought a breeze in from the pasture across the street. One of my daughters and I had painted the cement porch floor a welcoming, warm sandstone color. Two burgundy rocking chairs sat by the windows. A daybed with turquoise bedposts had white mosquito net draped from the ceiling around it. The bed was made with white cotton sheets and adorned with turquoise throw pillows. The décor reminded me of the American Southwest.

We entered the living room, which looked cozy with its cast-iron stove. Hope House was always ready for a birth. The inflatable tub was in one corner of the living room, and a string of white lights hung across the ceiling. When a woman labored, the warm glow from the soft white lights gave just enough light. The inflatable tub had individual clean liners for each woman who birthed.

Because most doctors are unfamiliar with waterbirth or water labor, I proceeded to explain the benefits of warm water during labor, which include pain relief, relaxation, and a shorter labor. It's been called a "midwife's epidural." To support waterbirth safely and skillfully, I attended a waterbirth seminar through Waterbirth International.

I explained waterbirth thoroughly from a provider's viewpoint. The water temperature needs to be warm enough to be comfortable to a laboring woman, but not so hot as to cause the baby's heartbeat to rise. A woman should shower and have clean feet before entering the tub. During pushing, if a shoulder dystocia is suspected, a woman can turn over onto hands and knees in the tub, or she can move to the floor and assume all fours.

The next room we entered had a mattress on the floor with a colorful, soft, silk comforter. Beautiful silk curtains fell from the ceiling to the floor, surrounding the mattress. The curtains could be tied back around the four corners of the mattress, or they could be left untied to create the feeling of a nest. Having the mattress on the floor allowed a woman to feel grounded while laboring. Soft white lights were strung along the ceiling. It was a beautiful room, reflecting the style of India or West Asia. Women gravitated to this room to ground themselves.

Another bedroom I showed her had a cast-iron queen bed. The deep purple-and-cream quilt gave the room a royal appeal. On a wood dresser, I had two trays lined with sterile drapes. The sterile instruments and sutures were lined up in orderly fashion on top of the drape. The trays were portable and could be carried from room to room. I explained that a woman had the freedom to birth in any room at Hope House. The laboring woman chose which room she wanted to birth in, often wherever she found herself pushing. I simply had to move the sterile trays.

An oxygen cannister and resuscitation equipment were tucked in a corner ready to use if necessary. A wooden birth stool sat on the hardwood floor. I found it a remarkable tool. Birth stools helped open the pelvis, which facilitates descension of the head. It is also a practical way to deliver a placenta. The birth stool is empowering. A birth ball sat in the corner. Birth balls aid optimal fetal positioning during labor. A glass oil lamp stood ready on the mahogany table to be used in the event of a power outage.

Because I provided prenatal appointments and postpartum appointments in homes, I had to have midwifery bags ready to go. I also had a delivery bag for homebirths. I showed the doctor my black bags, which were divided into compartments and very well organized. Each bag had several plastic sleeves with small pockets to keep items easily accessible.

My delivery bag contained small pockets that held essential oils, herbal tinctures, and dried herbs. Larger compartments held the doppler, stethoscope, blood pressure cuff, thermometers, amnioindicators, sterile gloves, gel, and olive oil. A second large compartment held IV fluid, catheters, tubing, tape, and gauze. Several sterile packs of instruments and suturing material filled the center of the bag.

The prenatal bag had a glucose monitor (glucometer), hemoglobinometer, GBS swab test kit, stethoscope, blood pressure cuff, thermometers, amnioindicator swabs, sterile gloves, urine dip sticks, doppler, gel, measuring tape, and herbs.

The postpartum bag had birth certificate registration forms, cord clamps, infant stethoscope, flannel cloth hanging baby scale, erythromycin eye ointment, thermometer, measuring tape, vitamin K shots, and infant CPR resuscitation equipment (Ambu bag and mask).

A shoulder bag carried a full oxygen cannister with masks and cannulas for both mother and newborn. The shoulder bag made transporting the oxygen tank easier.

I explained how I monitored a baby's fetal heart rate without hospital monitors. Using a hand-held doppler, auscultation assesses fetal heart rate and establishes a baseline. Midwives listen for rhythm (regular and irregular), variability, accelerations, and the timing, depth, and duration of any decelerations. While listening, one hand is placed on the abdomen to assess frequency, duration, and intensity of contractions. The fetal doppler can be used in all different laboring positions. It is used during water labor and water birth. No straps around the abdomen are necessary. A doppler can give the same information as a cardiotocography in hospital.

After the tour, the doctor and I sat on the sofa and arm chairs adjacent to the cast-iron stove. When she asked me to share my story, I described growing up near the Amish in Pennsylvania and how I respected their choice to live according to their cultural beliefs, including birthing at home. I summarized my journey from the neonatal intensive care unit (NICU), to serving as an Army Nurse, to settling on a small farm in rural Tennessee. I shared my passion for midwifery, which intensified after working as a RN in a rural birth center. I chose to earn my credential as a Certified Professional Midwife with the intention to support homebirth. My midwifery practice provided comprehensive and empowering midwifery services.

I explained that after performing hundreds of home visits as a midwife, I appreciated the value of health care in the home versus the office. Visiting families in their homes gave me a unique picture of the challenges that each family faced. I spoke of a variety of situations that could be encountered in home visit appointments and ways to successfully overcome the challenge.

For example, one day I arrived at a small farm, and a pregnant mother with a ten-month-old baby met me at the door. She had a lovely front porch and a tidy living room. I asked to wash my hands before examining her. She said her kitchen sink was not working because a pipe broke, and they did not have the money to fix it. I washed up in the bathroom and noticed the tub was piled with dishes. She had four children, which made a family of six. With three meals a day and young children, dishes are a challenge under the best circumstances. While asking her prenatal questions, I noticed the baby had a heat rash when she changed his diaper. I sat on the couch while she breastfed her baby.

Kindly and politely, I asked how she was managing showering and washing dishes. Because it was late spring, her husband, herself, and children were using the outdoor shower at the old barn, and she washed dishes in the tub. She was not regularly bathing the baby in the tub because she struggled keeping the tub empty. Tears fell down her cheeks. She said her husband worked so hard, but money was tight.

I drove to a nearby tractor supply store and bought a small, round galvanized tub and a bucket. When I returned to her homestead farm, we set up the galvanized tub on the front porch. We tied a clean sheet on the porch rails. She carried a few buckets of warm water and poured them into the little tub. The sheet kept the breeze from blowing directly on the baby. She washed him in soapy water while singing to him. After the bathing was done and the baby was diapered and in clean clothes, she was able to dump the tub of water over the porch edge. When I left, she was smiling. I was smiling too, knowing her pregnancy would have a bit less stress.

I also described my experiences at off-grid homes, areas where cellphones did not have reception and dirt roads did not have names. I told the doctor about one summer day when I parked my car at the end of a dirt road. I carried my black bags down a dirt path the width of a deer trail. After a quarter of a mile, I came to a shack with tin sides and roof. I hollered "Hello?" because I had an uneasy feeling. I was afraid that I was not at the correct home.

When I heard a baby cry in the distance, I knew I *was* at the right homestead, so I continued down the path. Near the creek, I saw a firepit and a nursing mother. She smiled at me as I approached her.

The well was not dug yet, and she was using boiled creek water to wash dishes and laundry. She and her husband bathed in the creek.

I knew that it was imperative that she successfully breastfeed because boiling creek water to mix formula and wash bottles would be unacceptable. Having no refrigeration complicated things further.

I worked with the baby's latch, and I returned every day for three weeks to make certain the baby was gaining weight. I taught the mother a variety of breastfeeding positions, such as football hold, cradle hold, and cross cradle hold. The baby was thriving. I gave a gift of a wicker laundry basket that could serve as a bassinet. She loved it.

When I visited two years later, a beautiful log cabin had been built, a well had been dug, and solar panels powered a small refrigerator. The husband had built a large smoke house made of stones. A small stone fireplace piped smoke in to the smoke house. Hanging hams were being slowly smoked with hickory chips. A bucket of cold well water with its dipper sat on the back porch. I sunk the dipper into the bucket to fill it and drank the cool water slowly. What good water! The homestead was lovely.

Her husband gifted me a wooden birth stool he built for my birthing women to use. He always gave me a dozen fresh eggs as a parting gift. He would carry my bags down the worn path to my car, while I carefully carried the eggs. They were very grateful for the help I gave them in their early struggle to establish a homestead. As a parting gift, he gave me goose grease, which is the fat of the goose cooked down. Goose grease is used as an old remedy to treat the symptoms of sore throats and colds. Honey with goose grease is taken like cough medicine. Goose grease can be rubbed on the chest to ease congestion. Goose fat contains twenty percent palmitic acid, which is a known anti-inflammatory. What a wonderful gift.

I continued to share stories with the doctor because she genuinely was interested in community health. One warm spring day, I arrived at a single-wide trailer, where I noticed a 4x8 sheet of plywood propped against the wall. I stepped up on the concrete blocks that served as steps, then I rapped on the door.

A jolly lady holding a baby opened the door. While examining the mother and baby, I saw a rat dart along the wall and dive into a hole in the floor. When I asked the mother about the rodent problem, she pointed at the hole in the plywood floor.

"The trailer is old, and water damage caused rot in the floor," she said.

Luckily, her husband was not hurt when he stepped through the floor, creating that hole.

That day, her husband was chopping wood for a neighbor in a barter, and then the neighbor was lending him a circular saw for a week. Her husband would be replacing their entire floor, and he couldn't go to the expense of purchasing a circular saw.

In the meantime, the mother was in a battle with the rodents.

"Can I see your dressers?" I asked. She had a solid wood oak dresser. I removed the smallest dresser drawer, then she and I created a makeshift bassinet out of it that could be carried from room to room.

When the mother washed dishes, she could keep it on the counter next to her and when she showered, it could be in her view on the bathroom sink counter. Having the baby in eyesight was imperative because both rats and snakes could enter through the hole. Her husband was working hard, and the problem would be fixed soon. In the meantime, she had the dresser drawer she could use for the next week.

When I returned for the next postpartum home visit, I saw tremendous progress. There was new plywood flooring throughout the entire trailer. The trailer was scrubbed clean. The white crib was assembled and adjacent to their bed. The rodents were gone.

Many families struggled but persevered through hope and determination. I explained to the doctor that sometimes women gave birth at a relative's home if it had more amenities than her own. At the start of autumn, a woman birthed at her grandmother's large farmhouse. When we scheduled a postpartum visit, the new mother asked that I come to her home instead of her grandmother's farm.

I arrived at her home on a cool, crisp fall morning. The leaves were turning brilliant colors. I had driven several miles through a wooded area, enjoying nature's glory. The surrounding pastureland looked like a scene on a postcard. The concrete block home was plastered with white stucco. When I knocked, a man hollered to come around to the back. The newborn baby lay in a stroller, wrapped snuggly in a blanket. The postpartum mother was hanging out laundry. I noticed she was using an old Maytag wringer washing machine. My grandmother had owned one, and I had seen a few at Amish homes. Her husband had retrofitted the washer to use propane because their electric had been shut off. They didn't have the money to pay the bill.

Even though the husband worked hard, money was scarce. When I asked the mother about practical matters, she said the well pump was powered by solar so they had running water and the use of an indoor toilet. A cast-iron stove served as both a heat source for the home and a method to cook. They cooked on an outdoor grill as well. She was using a spring house at the creek to keep perishables cold.

From a practical standpoint, all was well. The mother and the baby were thriving, and she had all her needs met. She waved goodbye as I got into my car, and she returned to her laundry.

For many families, my job description blurred between midwifery and public health nurse. I did what I could. I remembered how Ross Perot helped Jeff and me. I was paying it forward.

I explained to the doctor, who was still listening intently, that most of the women who sought my care were low income. One afternoon, I was brought to tears. I had just wrapped up a prenatal visit for a lady who was due any day. I used a generous sliding scale, and in her case, I waived all payment.

"Goodbye," I said, standing on her porch turning to leave.

"Can you wait?" she said. She went back into the house and came out with a long knife. Then she walked into her large overgrown garden, looking over her vegetables up and down the rows. I saw her face light up, and she cut the vine to a zucchini.

She proudly carried it to me. When she handed it to me, she said, "This is perfect. It is small, so it will not be bitter. It is plump and firm, without blemishes or soft spots." She handed that zucchini to me with joy on her face as if the vegetable was a diamond. It reminded me of the story in the Bible of the widow's mite.

I held back my tears. The woman gave me the best she had. The expectant woman was the diamond.

As my conversation with the physician neared an end, I summarized my practice standards. Using a health risk assessment, I provided homebirths for women who were low-risk and willing to eat well. Optimal fetal positioning, labor support, and breastfeeding support were of paramount importance. Collaborative care with physicians, when necessary, rounded out my practice.

I explained how women could improve their hemoglobin if they couldn't afford supplements. Consuming meat separately from milk will provide optimal conditions for iron absorption. Iron does not absorb well when combined with calcium. Additionally, foods in iron absorb better when combined with foods high in vitamin C.

Lastly, I described my philosophy. As a midwife, I worked in the trenches. I remembered what it was like not to have a car. For this reason, I used my own car to pick up Amish women and accompany them to ultrasounds and obstetrician appointments. I remembered what poverty felt like—all too well the feelings of desperation. Therefore, when I saw a family in need, I chose to help. I summarized my practice in one word: HOPE.

After the physician left, I reflected on our conversation. My interaction with her was positive. She seemed a kindred spirit. I wondered what she thought.

Recently, I had a negative interaction with an obstetrician who shook his finger at me as if I was a child. While he acted like an overgrown bully, I stood my ground and kept my composure. I was not intimidated. After a tough childhood and years in the Army, that man's arrogance and aggressive posture did not unnerve me. I would continue to serve underprivileged women, and his opinion of midwives would not stop me. I was used to criticism and the negative campaign against the legalization of homebirth midwives.

The doctor who interviewed me shared publicly her perspective of our conversation. Her words brought me to tears. In my life, praise has been rare. She wrote that I was a saint, she hoped that I was typical of the midwifery profession, and she hoped there were more midwives like me. I was humbled by her words.

Certainly, I am not a saint. I was physically exhausted taking call 24/7 and juggling life outside of midwifery. It was hard being a wife, mother, and midwife.

The physician likely had no idea how her encouraging words would carry me forward. She saw value in my work. That perspective was balm to my tired soul. Slowly, I was growing weary. An overwhelming depression mixed with anxiety was trying to drag me under. It was an ongoing battle within myself. A darkness was trying to pull me into a rabbit hole. I fought it off with every ounce of my being and told myself that I had to keep moving forward.

NASCAR

I carried my cellphone with me everywhere—every day, every hour—and I slept with it within arm's reach every night. When someone calls a midwife, their expectation is to reach her.

One Saturday afternoon, I received a call from a laboring mother who was finding it difficult to speak. She was clearly in active labor and getting into the backseat of her truck to travel north toward Hope House. She had to cross the state line because her state did not license homebirth midwives.

Like many women, that woman wanted freedom. Her preference was to labor upright, walk outdoors, squat, soak in the birth tub, eat, use a rebozo, and use birth balls.

That afternoon's call was like many others. She was on her way. I arrived before her and readied her birthing space. The birth tub was filling with warm water. Organic rose petals floated on top of the water. White lights hung from the ceiling provided a soft glow in the room. The gas fireplace offered a lovely ambiance and warmth. Sterile instruments were set up on the tray and covered with a sterile cloth. Lavender essential oil was diffusing in the air. The birth stool and birth balls were ready for her.

The phone rang again.

"I'm pulling over now," her husband said.

"Please come meet us because she feels like she has to push!"

I calmly asked, "Which road and mile marker?"

When he answered, I ran out the screen door and jumped into my car. I left in such a hurry, the door remained unlocked and ajar. They were ten miles away.

"Keep driving, and I'll meet you at the halfway mark." I said.

While driving, I stayed on the cellphone to monitor her progress. She was not making birthing noises yet. I was on a two-lane road, and I saw their truck pull off on the side of the road. I did a U-turn and parked behind them.

I jumped out of my vehicle and raced to the passengers door. She was reclining and panting heavily. I looked between her legs. The baby was not coming yet. We had just enough time. I jumped into the truck, staying by her side while her husband drove to the birth house. Her brother drove my car, following us on the winding two-lane country road, with driving rivaling NASCAR. Those country boys could drive.

In the meantime, Lindsay arrived at Hope House and found the door open. She was surprised I wasn't there. When she saw a truck pull into the birth house and park as close to the door as possible, she knew birth was imminent. Lindsay desperately hoped I would show up. In the meantime, Lindsay grabbed towels and thought, *Where is Tori?*!

I saw the relief on Lindsay's face as I jumped out of the rear seat of the pickup truck. The laboring woman's mother pulled in behind us and ran hurriedly into Hope House carrying candles. I knew she was tasked with setting up the holy candles because the family was devout Catholic.

The laboring woman let out a deep moan as she got out of the truck. It took great effort for her to walk up the three steps into the front porch. As she walked from the front porch toward the living room, she stopped for every contraction, moved into a standing squat, and swayed her hips. She made it to the filled inflatable tub. She slid into the warm water and sighed. She opened her legs instinctively and started pushing involuntarily. The baby's dark hair could be seen crowning. I coached her to breathe for a moment and not push. It was important to let her perineum stretch to avoid tearing. Next, I told her to give a slight push. My gloved hands guided the baby while protecting her perineum. The baby's head was born in occiput anterior position, which is the normal, face-down position. I deftly reduced the nuchal cord. With the next push, the baby birthed easily and gently into the warm water. I lifted the baby out of the water into the mother's arms. The baby looked around and was calm. In a very touching moment, the new mother stroked her baby's head.

Amazingly, the baby weighed in at ten pounds. But the best news was the perineum was intact. No stitches were needed. Because the events had unfolded so precipitously, everyone was on an adrenaline high. I sat on the front porch, rocking on the wooden rocking chair, watching the sun set with the magnificent colors only nature can paint.

Every fifteen minutes, I checked the new mom for bleeding. Her uterus was firm with minimal bleeding. All was well. The baby was breastfeeding contentedly. Lindsay and I sipped on large cups filled with sweet, iced tea. I felt a breeze come through the screen door and sighed. This moment was perfect.

Patience Is a Virtue

I received a call before dawn. Her water was broken. I asked the normal questions: Time? Amount? Color? Odor? The fluid was clear, and there was no odor. She was only having a few cramps. I told her to drive up to Hope House and settle in.

When I arrived, her husband had vases of flowers on the dining table, on the dresser, and on the wooden bench. It was beautiful.

By sunset, there were still no contractions. We discussed her options. She drank the castor oil shake first. Once the laxative effect occurred, I started the blue and black cohosh tinctures. Every fifteen minutes for two hours she held the tincture blend under her tongue momentarily and then swallowed. She put on headphones and listened to birth affirmations.

She walked outside to open her pelvis and to connect with nature. After a long walk, she sat on a birth ball in the living room and did nipple stimulation on both breasts. Curtains were closed, candles lit, ocean music played. The room was calm and dimly lit.

Suddenly she started crying. Her emotions unfolded. She admitted she was filled with fear. As she released her emotions and faced her fear, her contractions became a freight train. She steam-rolled into transition. I told her approximately 300,000 women around the world were laboring with her at this exact moment. I told her women are strong. *She* is strong.

Labor was hard and fast. Her husband massaged her back and gave counter pressure to her sacrum during contractions. In between contractions, she belly-danced. She moved her hips in a figure eight to help the baby descend.

I filled the tub, and she sank into its warmth. She moaned loudly with contractions. She repeated several times, "I can't do this anymore."

At that point, I checked her, and she was ten centimeters. She was restless. I told her to go where she felt safe. She climbed out of the tub and leaned on her husband. She walked to the queen-size bed, while hanging onto him during contractions.

She pushed once, and the head moved down. After a few more powerful pushes, the baby crowned. I coached her to cough the baby out with the next contraction. I did not want her to tear. She coughed, and the head was born. One more push, and the baby's body was born.

I put the baby into her arms. She kissed the baby's face and love swept over her. Birth is simply amazing.

Sunny Side Up

A woman who was giving birth for the first time (primip) was laboring at Hope House. She was taking walks down the old country road behind the house, enjoying the crisp, fall air. Every few minutes, she stopped to breathe through the contractions. The colorful autumn leaves scattered on the ground danced along the road with the light breeze. The mother-to-be was having back pain with each contraction, so I suspected occiput posterior (OP) position, which means face-up instead of face-down.

We returned to Hope House when she was ready to labor indoors. During a cervical check, I determined the posterior fontanelle was in the posterior quadrant of the pelvis, and the anterior fontanelle was higher. This confirmed the baby was in occiput posterior (OP) position. I suggested the laboring woman position herself on all fours in the warm living room in front of the fireplace. When she tired of laboring on all fours, I had her place one foot on the seat of a wooden chair. Then I encouraged her to walk up and down the front steps. She labored beautifully, spending most of the labor on her hands and knees. She had the glow of a woman in labor.

When the urge to push was overwhelming, she climbed into the warm bed and pulled her legs back in a semi-reclining position. As the baby's head emerged, the eyes were looking up toward the ceiling and not at the floor. The baby was born in occiput posterior position (sunny side up). This is the most common fetal malposition. With one more push, the baby's body was born. Robust cries could be heard throughout Hope House. Incredibly, the baby weighed in at almost nine pounds. Watching women labor never got old. Their strength is a super-power. I loved being a midwife.

VBA2C

Under certain circumstances, I helped women have vaginal births after *two* Cesarean sections. Some of the women had waterbirths, while others birthed on the floor or in their beds.

When this was being considered, I interviewed the pregnant woman and listened to her past medical and maternal history. If a woman had a C-section for a breech baby and then a subsequent C-section due to a hospital no-VBAC policy, she was a good candidate.

However, if there was a history of a vertical incision on the uterus from a prior C-section, VBAC was not an option.

During prenatal appointments, I stressed the importance of excellent nutrition with a high iron and high protein diet. Whole foods with multicolored vegetables were essential. Red raspberry tea, evening primrose oil, liquid Floridex, and probiotics were standard advice. At thirty-five weeks, a course of ripening herbs was started along with eating dates, which help efface and dilate the cervix.

A VBA2C candidate had to be active every day—walking, sitting on a birth ball, or swimming. I stressed optimal fetal positioning, and so sleeping on the left side in the hammock position was important to achieve the best fetal lie and position.

I encouraged creating birth art for release of previous birth trauma. Women could choose a Blessingway to celebrate the path forward. Foot baths were often part of a Blessingway. A basin was filled with bath temperature water, Epsom salts, dried lavender, and oatmeal. I would wash her feet. The loving act of washing a pregnant woman's feet helped her feel safe and loved. The foot bath was relaxing for her. We often set up their birth room or birth space several days ahead, so prayer and meditation could ease the mom-to-be into a nurturing labor.

At prenatal appointments, I listened and gave motherly and midwifery advice. Some women even stopped by my home for hot tea and a chat. I walked with women in late pregnancy on wooded trails or at the park. I kept them company when they needed my presence.

When labor started, many of these women felt a mix of emotions. They were often excited and happy. They were determined to achieve their goals. But even with the best preparation, they felt a hint of apprehension. I would watch them mentally face their fears.

Laboring in water or taking a shower helped relax a woman. When labor got tough, I would tell a woman to go where she felt safest. Feeling safe allowed labor to progress.

Sweat, determination, and hard work embodied these women hoping to have VBA2C. They were warriors.

The Break-In

Once I received a call late in the day from a laboring woman, who was enroute to Hope House from another state. She estimated her arrival would be in approximately two hours, due to heavy rush hour traffic.

When I arrived at Hope House, the front door was open. There were no cars in the driveway. I cautiously entered my beloved home to find broken glass all over the hardwood floors.

The house had been ransacked.

I could not believe what I was seeing. I was alone in the house, and the thought occurred to me that the intruder could still be in the house. I stood still. I heard nothing. I walked from room to room to clear the house. There was no one. I felt violated and angry at the same time.

But I had no time for drama, so I pushed back my emotions. I had to clean up Hope House quickly because a woman in active labor would be arriving. I called my friend Stacie Hunt, a midwife who happened to live near Hope House and also served a local Amish community. She came straightaway and helped me clean the house. We put the birth space back together and had midwife supplies ready just as a car pulled in the driveway.

The laboring woman stepped out of the car and breathed through a contraction. She looked beautiful. The sun was setting as she stood in the stillness of the evening. She breathed and centered herself outdoors after the long drive. I watched her from the window, breathing as she breathed. I centered myself. She labored outside, enjoying the freedom from the confines of a vehicle. I was breathing and calming myself while watching her labor unfold.

When the laboring woman entered Hope House, Stacie and I greeted her with warm smiles. She gravitated to the back bedroom and labored in an upright position, dancing a slow dance with her husband. I filled the birth tub with warm water and sprayed the room with lavender essential oil spray. She and her husband relaxed in the warm birth tub.

The tranquil scene was the opposite of the frenzy that occurred to clean up the ransacked birth house. I allowed the tranquility to wash over me like a gentle waterfall. We had a beautiful birth.

I never found out who ransacked Hope House. But the perpetrator's negative energy and disgusting actions never penetrated our birth space. Stacie and I made sure of that.

Stacie Hunt was a Certified Professional Midwife. Any time I called and needed a second midwife, she assisted me without hesitation. She was worth her weight in gold. We shared laughs, tears, and midwife life together for a season. Hope House brought us together. Stacie's smile and laughter added sunshine into my world. Together, we brought many babies earthside. I will always love her for the unconditional love she gave me. She was a saint.

The Storm

Midwives know that storms and full moons bring babies. My three daughters would watch a full moon rise and tell me that I better go to sleep. They knew my phone would ring. And it always did.

On this occasion, there were storms *and* a full moon. The full moon was high in the sky, with the quick-moving clouds of a thunderstorm headed our way. A laboring woman called and was enroute to Hope House. Her husband would be driving through the torrential rains on winding back roads. Thankfully, the leaves had not started to fall from the trees because rain-soaked leaves make driving conditions hazardous.

The laboring woman was traveling north to cross the state line. The drive was worth it to her. She had a traumatic injury to her leg while serving in the Army. She was a below-the-knee amputee because of it. She did not want the amputation to impact the birth of her baby. When she contacted me, I told her she could birth in water. She was ecstatic.

She crossed the state line in hard labor. I had the birth tub filled with warm water. The delivery trays were ready, and lavender was in the air. As I stood by the screened door, the wind on my face felt refreshing.

I watched as her husband parked the car near the front porch. He jumped out of the car and opened his wife's car door. Sitting in the seat of her car, she put on her prosthetic.

She walked with difficulty and great effort. But she was walking. She was a warrior.

"Your warm water is ready for you," I whispered.

She smiled and said, "I feel pressure."

She walked into the living room on two feet, then she took off her shirt and bra. Sitting on a chair, she took off her daily wear prosthetic. She pulled off her shorts and panties. She stood on one leg and pivoted her body toward the edge of the birth tub. After her husband assisted her into the tub, she visibly relaxed. I turned off the lights, only leaving the white lights that gave a kind, soft glow.

For thirty minutes, there were no contractions. She dozed in and out. Suddenly, her eyes popped open!

"The baby is coming!" she exclaimed.

I smiled at her and said, "Anytime you are ready, push and have your baby."

She pushed once, and he was born into the warm water between her thighs. She lifted him out of the water and kissed him.

"I did it!" she said proudly.

After a few minutes, she had a strong contraction. She pushed once more and birthed the placenta in the water. After cutting and clamping the cord, I handed the baby to Lindsay Crowson, my intern midwife. The attentive husband helped his wife pivot from the birth tub to the chair. She put on her prosthetic and walked to the shower.

When showered and dried off, she walked to the cream-and-light-purple room with the sleigh bed. I completed her postpartum assessments and the newborn's assessments. When I had them tucked into bed for the night, my phone rang again.

The storm and full moon were bringing another couple to Hope House. The Hope House lights were on welcoming them. The cool breeze was still blowing through the screened windows on the front porch. It always felt refreshing to sit and rock on the wooden rocking chairs during storms.

When the woman walked onto the porch, I could see her relax. She looked happy to be out of the car. Laboring while in a car increases the pain of labor. I've never met a woman who said laboring in a car was comfortable.

"Your rocking chairs are greeting me like old friends," she said.

She stood on the porch, breathing in the fresh, clean air. Her contractions were steady and strong. The violent lightning contrasted with the darkness outside. A few seconds after the lightning flashed, the thunder boomed. The woman said she was having pressure, and it was clear to me that she would be birthing soon.

We ran warm water in the old cast-iron tub located in the bathroom because she was birthing quickly. We didn't have time to fill the large portable birth tub. She sank into the warmth and sighed in relief. Her husband kneeled at the side of the tub, gently holding her hand.

The lights flickered off and on. The oil lamps were already lit in case the power went out during the birth.

"Well, I guess if the lights go out, it will just be an Amish birth," said Lindsay Crowson.

Lindsay had a great sense of humor. The couple laughed because they knew we also birthed Amish families.

BOOM! The thunder continued. Every few minutes, the woman had a contraction. She started pushing.

The lightning lit up the bathroom in a rhythm that rivaled her contractions. We felt the strength and beauty of nature as the baby crowned while Mother Nature roared outdoors. The laboring woman's face glowed as she panted and gradually opened her perineum. Her strength and beauty were striking as she birthed her baby into the water.

After I clamped the cord, her husband cut it. I handed him the baby. He dried the baby thoroughly and rubbed olive oil on the baby's skin. Afterward, he swaddled the baby in several warm receiving blankets, which I always had warming on a heating pad.

While the new father was tending to the baby, the new mother birthed her placenta in the water. I scooped the placenta out of the water and put it in a bucket.

"We're going to bury the placenta in our yard and plant a tree on top to mark the baby's birth," the husband told me.

I drained the tub, and his wife showered and put on a nightgown. She walked to the queen-sized bed and plumped up a pillow. Once she laid down, her husband handed her the baby, who latched greedily. Everyone smiled. It was a heartwarming scene of a happy family.

That night, I slept on the daybed on Hope House's front porch. *The storm could bring more women,* I thought.

But it didn't, and I went to sleep, listening to the falling rain.

Police

A few days later, my cellphone rang after midnight. Jeff shook me awake. I grabbed the phone and walked out of the bedroom.

I could hear a woman moaning. When I heard "ding, ding, ding," I knew the car door was open. When the sound stopped, I knew the door was shut and the seatbelt was fastened.

"Tori?" the woman asked.

"I'm here," I replied

"I'm in labor. Contractions are strong and coming every two minutes."

"I'll see you soon."

I knew they had an hour drive, and it was going to be a hard one because she was clearly in transition. I was ready and waiting at Hope House for them. When they did not arrive on time, I wondered, *Was the baby born in the car?* I put that thought out of my head because her husband hadn't called.

My mind went through several scenarios. *Flat tire? Car accident? Having a baby in a car without cell service?*

Then I heard the car pull in and stop at the front door. I could see that the woman was trying hard not to push. I held open the screen door for her, and she climbed the steps and came in. She stopped inside the door. She closed her eyes and had an intense contraction on the enclosed front porch. She took three steps forward and held onto the wooden rocking chair. She planted her feet, bent her knees, and breathed through another contraction. When her contraction was over, she spoke.

"It's good to be out of the car," she said.

I nodded because she had made it to Hope House with not a moment to spare.

"The tub has warm water in it, and it is waiting for you," I said.

We labored our way to the living room, where the large birth tub was ready, with rose petals floating on the surface and lavender essential oil in the air. She stripped off her clothing and sank her pearl-white body into the warm water, immersing herself. She slid under the water after each contraction and slowly came up and rested against the side of the birth tub. The glow from the hanging lights made her wet red hair glisten. When we made eye contact, she smiled at me.

"Tori?"

"Yes?"

"Thank you for creating such a beautiful, safe space." She took a long deep breath in and let it out. "I'm ready. It's time," she announced.

The woman pushed her baby out, then she brought the pudgy baby out of the water. The baby's eyes opened and gazed into hers. It was bliss.

"What a story I get to tell you someday!" she said to the baby.

After the woman was showered, dried, and changed into a breastfeeding nightgown, she told me the story of their drive that night. Her husband was driving a bit over the speed limit because she was moaning loudly in the passengers seat. Suddenly, the lights and siren of a police car lit up their car. When her husband pulled over on the remote road, the officer walked up and asked for his license and registration. The husband handed them to the officer and tried to explain the precarious nature of the situation.

"My wife is in labor!" he said.

The officer seemed to dismiss this as just another motorist exaggerating and making excuses for speeding. He ran the license and registration and wrote out a ticket. This process seemed like an eternity to the moaning woman. Finally, the couple was on their way again.

This time, the husband was dutifully driving the speed limit. The woman described gripping the door handle with Herculean strength. She breathed, moaned, and gripped that handle all the way across the state line. It was a car ride to be remembered. She decided she was going to the court hearing to regale the tale of her labor story to the judge and vowed not to miss one single detail. I would have loved to be a fly on the wall in that court room. It was a birth story to be remembered.

Massage

I loved attending births with midwife Stacie Hunt. She was a joy to work with, with a positive upbeat personality and an infectious laugh.

Depending on the progression of labor, acupressure and massage were options on the table. I would darken the lights in a room, spray a lavender mist into the air, and apply acupressure to the SP6 point on the inside of the leg just above the ankle. Using acupressure on this point for thirty minutes on each leg shortens the length of labor and reduces labor pain.

Labor progresses when a woman relaxes, and Stacie was a master at massage. She would add essential oils to a carrier oil to form a massage oil. Rubbing and massaging the body releases endorphins, serotonin, and dopamine—positive hormones that reduce anxiety and relax a woman. Rubbing both thighs using a deep massage relaxes the perineum. Massaging the inner thighs with light massage improves cervical dilation.

Stacie's masterful touch soothed a laboring woman into labor land. Through observation, I learned Stacie's massage methods and incorporated them into my practice.

After deep massage and acupressure, a woman would comfortably rest in bed. After a good rest, labor would progress. Hope House would welcome a baby earthside to the lovely blend of lavender, clary sage, and jasmine.

Births with Stacie invigorated my midwifery spirit. Because there weren't many midwives in our rural area, having Stacie at my side was a blessing. She was my faithful friend and a smart seasoned midwife. When I needed an extra set of hands, she was there for me. In life, there are few things worth having. A true friend is priceless. Stacie was just that: a true friend *and* priceless.

The Log Cabin in the Woods

One midafternoon, I was driving when the road winded into a wooded area. I had my car windows down, so I could feel the temperature cool when I drove under the canopy of trees. I felt relief from the hot summer sun. I could smell honeysuckle and hear birds singing. Occasionally, squirrels ran onto the road, stopped suddenly, and indecisively darted back and forth until scurrying across the road.

I turned into a bumpy, dirt driveway and drove for about one mile with tall hardwood trees lining either side of the road. I could see light up ahead. The clearing revealed a small log cabin.

After I was welcomed inside, I saw a cast-iron stove that served as a heat source and for cooking. There was a fireplace made of stone. The cabin had running water pumped from a well, powered by electricity from solar panels. A composting toilet completed the necessities of the home. The home was powered by a propane fueled generator and public utilities.

I set up my midwifery supplies on a large, solid-walnut table. As usual, I organized the supplies in three sections: labor, delivery, and postpartum. There were cookie sheets and a bowl for the placenta supplied by the laboring woman. I placed the delivery supplies onto two cookie sheets lined with sterile drapes. The laboring woman chose which room she wanted to birth in, and I followed behind with the cookie sheets. It worked well and gave her freedom to birth.

The cabin had one air-conditioner mounted in a window in the living room. The doors to the living room were shut to keep the cool air in. I found the woman laboring on the floor in the living room, kneeling and leaning forward. She was in active labor, but not transition.

I went to the kitchen and warmed a rice pack in the microwave for a few seconds. Then I placed the rice pack at the woman's sacrum and pushed with counterpressure, which gave her relief.

"I needed that," she said.

She flipped over so I could palpate her belly to determine the baby's position. The baby was head down. I placed the doppler where I expected the fetal heart to be. I heard the familiar gallop of the baby's heart. The assessment was normal.

The woman and I walked in the woods for an hour. Upright positions help a baby descend. We came to a clearing with a large pond with strikingly beautiful ducks gliding effortlessly across the water. It was a lovely place to labor. She remained standing watching the ducks while the sun seemed to make her hair shine. In the distance, I could hear a train crossing a trestle. When we returned to the cabin, she walked up and down the porch steps. When she tired, she leaned forward on the hand-carved wooden porch railings. After the walk, she stood in the shower and let the water hit her lower back. She dried off, then sat on a birth ball for an hour. She felt the need to sit on the toilet. This was always a midwife's clue that delivery was imminent. She sat on the toilet and moaned low.

"Let's walk to the living room. You can lie down on the bear rug," I said.

Her birth plan indicated she preferred to birth in the living room on that bear rug, where she had arranged a plastic picnic tablecloth flannel side up. She had several soft flannel sheets layered next. A warm blanket was folded nearby for after the birth. With every contraction, she stopped walking and semi-squatted. When she grunted, I knew she was involuntarily pushing.

We made it to the bear rug where she laid on her left side and pulled her right leg up. She did not push. She picked up a walkie talkie and told her husband to hurry to the living room. She breathed through each contraction. He walked in, kneeled, and kissed her.

She pushed, and her water broke spontaneously. I rarely used the amniohook to artificially rupture membranes because it increases labor pain for women. Having fluid cushion the cord minimizes the risk of variable decelerations from cord compression. I always despised the early artificial rupture of membranes. It made more sense to wait until transition or pushing, or to allow the rupture to be spontaneous.

The woman pushed again, and the baby's head was born. I slipped the nuchal cord over the head. With the next push, the baby was born into my hands. I placed the baby on the soft flannel baby blankets. I clamped and cut the umbilical cord. I handed the new father his son as was directed in the birth plan.

The new mother focused on pushing out the placenta. She pushed, and the placenta presented in dirty Duncan. I examined the placenta meticulously for any missing pieces. It was all there, so I put it into the bucket.

The family of three bonded with each other on the bear rug. After counting fingers and toes and admiring the baby, the new father picked up the bucket containing the placenta. I knew that he had already dug a deep hole for the placenta.

The baby nursed greedily. As night fell, the husband turned off the air-conditioner and lit a small fire in the stone fireplace, which would be enough to keep away the evening chill. The warm bear rug along with flannel sheets made a comfortable spot to sleep. When I left, the new mother was dozing off. The baby was in a Moses basket next to its mother. Her husband carried my bags to the car, thanking me profusely with each step.

I drove away through the heavily wooded area feeling satisfied. Suddenly, a deer ran in front of my car. I slammed on my brakes and came to a sudden halt, bracing for the "thud." Thankfully, the deer made it across the road without being hit and causing costly damage to my vehicle. Because there were no streetlights out in the woods, my headlights provided my only light. I continued to drive cautiously because I knew dawn and dusk are when most deer are out. It would be a long slow drive home.

Her Hope

These true birth stories are included with the permission of Raygen Catoe.

I met Raygen when she was pregnant with her second child. She said the birth of her first child was traumatic both physically and emotionally. She tearfully recalled the obstetrician cussing at her. In addition, a compound presentation (the baby's hand delivered with the head) made pushing seem insurmountable. She described feeling overwhelmingly vulnerable during the labor and birth because she was exposed from the waist down with a doctor who had an angry attitude. She recollected a bedside manner that was unprofessional, inappropriate, and unacceptable.

With Raygen's second pregnancy, she chose homebirth. She wanted the privacy of her own home. When I arrived at her home in the historic district of the city, Raygen was wearing a long blue dress. Her face was radiant, and I instantly thought how beautiful she looked. As labor intensified, she chose water labor to reduce the pain. In the warm water of the inflatable, padded birth tub, she felt protected. Her husband played the guitar and sang to her. I sat cross legged on the solid wood floor of the historic home listening to the sounds of her labor and the strumming of the guitar. I smelled the aroma of comfrey and lavender herbs, which were steeping on the stove. They would be used for a sitz bath postpartum. The inevitable need to push came. Raygen worked hard. Pushing took a great deal of time and effort. As the baby's head crowned, his forehead came first called a brow presentation. When a brow comes first, instead of his head being flexed with the chin tucked at his chest, a larger diameter is needed to navigate the birth canal. Raygen pushed with determination and strength, and her baby son was born into the warm water. It was a hard birth, but she did it.

When Raygen was pregnant with her third child, she decided to go to the Farm Midwifery Center in Summertown, Tennessee. She hired Stacie Hunt as her midwife, and I would be her doula. As Raygen labored, she and I walked the quiet, tranquil trails at the Farm, occasionally seeing deer and squirrels. When I noticed Raygen's contractions became irregular and spread out, we headed back to the cabin.

Stacie, Raygen, and I discussed the irregularity of her contractions. Raygen was lying still while we talked, and her contractions became stronger. We changed her labor approach to "be still and quiet." It worked. Her labor became a freight train. Her baby daughter birthed so quickly that the second Farm midwife did not make the birth. Raygen was comfortably positioned on the bed, and the baby was born into Stacie's hands. I could feel the love in the room. Raygen was radiant.

Over a year later, I received a call from Raygen. She was pregnant with her fourth child and had decided to birth at Hope House where I would be her midwife.

During her labor, we sat on the enclosed front porch. Raygen looked beautiful sitting on the day bed with the white bed canopy draped around. I rocked on the wooden rocking chair, enjoying the breeze.

As labor got more intense, Raygen immersed herself in the warm water of the comfortable birth tub, illuminated by the hanging white lights. She labored well with each contraction. Her husband, Michael, played the guitar, singing and serenading her. He was very talented, and his music filled the birth space with love. I could have sat there listening to him forever. His beautiful voice transfixed me, and I knew I was witnessing a precious moment in time.

When Raygen felt pressure, she moved from the tub to the large queen-sized bed in the bedroom with the cream-and-purple satin comforter. She chose a bed birth because the memory of the painful brow presentation during her prior waterbirth cast a negative cloud over any thought of birth in water. A son was born to Raygen and Michael in the queen-sized bed.

I had the privilege of being Raygen's doula once and midwife twice. I watched her recover from her first traumatic birth and grow into a strong, determined woman who took each birth as they came. She magnificently birthed on her terms and in her own way.

Give It Time

Trust birth and give it time

A beautiful woman was anxious about her baby's arrival by the estimated due date. She had good reason. Her husband was leaving for a one-year deployment in Afghanistan in a few short days. When I checked her at a prenatal appointment, she was four centimeters dilated and having irregular contractions.

"Sperm effaces (thins) the cervix. Go home and be intimate with your husband. Have a good meal and a long walk and go to sleep. Labor will come."

In the middle of the night, the young mother-to-be called and asked, "Can you sit with me?"

"Meet me at Hope House," I said.

She was having anxiety and needed her midwife. Her contractions were still irregular, so I gave her blue and black cohosh liquid tincture to encourage consistent contractions. It worked. Anxiety was overwhelming her, understandably. I used the cohosh to overcome the power of the anxiety.

I knew being immersed in love would help beat back anxiety. I set up the large, padded birth tub in the living area at Hope House, and she soaked in the warm water with her husband, enjoying priceless time together before his deployment. I lit candles around the tub, which flickered in the darkness. She leaned back on him, and he wrapped his muscular arms around her pregnant belly.

As night turned to day and the sun slowly rose, she entered transition. But the baby was asynclitic and not wanting to descend. Asynclitism is the oblique malpresentation of the fetal head in labor. The head was not in line with the birth canal. It was tilted to one side. It was time for the steps. The woman walked up and down the porch steps to encourage the baby's head to shift. She labored with one foot on a step and one foot on the ground. She climbed the steps sideways. Stair climbing worked. She was ten centimeters at her next vaginal check and +2 station.

While the woman was stair climbing, the tub was drained and refilled with clean warm water. She sank into the comfort of the water and pushed. After one hour of pushing, we changed positions. I knew we needed the widest pelvic diameter, so I asked her to go to hands and knees in the tub. In one push, the baby's head was born. The body came with the next push. It was a beautiful waterbirth.

The new mother had worked hard for this baby. It was a long, difficult labor.

Thankfully, she and her husband had a few days to spend together before their long difficult year began. Sometimes life is just hard.

Mothering

For me, midwifery was more than catching a baby. Sometimes, I became a mother figure for women, such as if their mother had passed away or was in jail or on drugs.

During many appointments, I gave women a listening ear. I gave practical advice on adjusting to motherhood and adjusting to more than one child. I gave suggestions on how to manage marriage during pregnancy and postpartum. Sometimes all a woman needed was a hug.

I opened my home to women for a cup of hot tea and a chat. I quietly listened to many women share their heartaches and burdens. They opened a window into their hearts and tearfully spoke of past emotional traumas or marital woes. Sometimes a woman who sought my care found herself in an unplanned pregnancy. I encouraged them all with my simple words.

"I cannot fix your problems, but I can walk by your side on this pregnancy journey, and if you want, I will walk a little farther with you on your life journey."

My goal was to awaken confidence in pregnant women about their bodies. I would lovingly assist women in achieving a great accomplishment—birth. I empowered them to know that they *cannot* fail at birth. Birth unfolds as it should for each woman, and it is her journey to take.

Ashleigh Reade wrote a letter to me. She knew that serving as a midwife was a battle against the medical mainstream. She was right. I often felt like I was swimming against the current. Her lovely words warmed my heart.

Tori, I wanted to tell you how much you mean to me. You have helped shape me into the mother who I am in so many ways. I know it can be discouraging to be in an area that doesn't respect midwifery. But you are giving mothers and babies the chance at a peaceful beginning that profoundly influences the mother/child relationship in ways that we don't even fully understand yet. Stay the course. Keep up the good work. You are the hand and feet of God and an angel to me. I love you. Always, Ashleigh Reade

I mothered many women. But the truth is these women mothered me in a way they never knew. They carried and propelled me forward to stay the course.

Cartoons

Sometimes early labor stalls. If a woman's mind is racing, her oxytocin won't increase, and adrenaline is more prevalent. I advised women whose labor stalls to watch their favorite movie, one that felt like an old shoe because they've seen it a million times. That works magic.

Alternatively, I have suggested watching cartoons to women who need to laugh. Oxytocin and endorphins rise and adrenaline decreases as they laugh, so the intensity of contractions increases. I could watch the shift from a stalled labor into active labor. When a woman went inward into active labor, I would turn off the television because she was in labor land. Even now, it amazes me.

One autumn day, a woman who had come to Hope House to birth went to walk the old country road for fresh air. The colorful leaves were blowing on the trees in the nippy wind. The waving leaves seemed to cheer the labor on. She had laughed her way into active labor by watching cartoons. Now she walked the old country road, hearing only the sounds of leaves crunching and the whistling of the wind blowing. She stopped to sway her body with every contraction. The whipping wind made the apple red, yellow, russet, and gold leaves dance around her feet. As a contraction ended, she would take a deep cleansing breath. Then she would continue walking without a word spoken. As labor progressed, she swayed her hips in a circular motion like a hula dance.

"I want to go back," she said.

I was chilled by the autumn wind. However, I knew her need to go back was not related to the weather. Her labor had reached a new level of intensity. We returned to Hope House, and she stood by the fireplace to warm up, then she made her way to the sofa.

"I need to push," she said emphatically.

"Do what your body is telling you," I said encouragingly.

She pushed on her side. After her baby was born, she kissed him and looked him over. She swaddled him and placed him next to her. After she nursed him, they both drifted off to sleep on the sofa.

When the baby woke up, I examined him. After the routine weights and measures, she latched him to the breast. I heard clicking noises while he nursed, which did not surprise me as I noticed a tongue tie during the newborn examination. She scheduled a frenectomy (tongue tie revision) with a dentist.

On his first birthday, she returned to Hope House, and we walked the old country road. As she pushed him in a stroller, an autumn leaf fell from a tree into his lap. I smiled to myself and thought, *How appropriate.*

Long Labor

You cannot fail at birth.—Stacie Smith-Hunt

One day when I arrived to a birth, the laboring woman was sitting on a birth ball. Her labor was steady, and throughout, she stood, squatted, sat backward on a toilet, and walked. She did supported squats hanging onto the birth rope, standing lunges, labored with one foot up on a chair, and laid on her left side.

She labored in the hands and knees position for several hours trying to turn the baby from OP to OA. For an hour, she belly danced and swayed. When tired, she leaned forward over the bed. On the birth ball, she moved in the figure eight pattern.

Lights were dimmed, her favorite worship music was playing, and she hydrated. She rested in the labor tub and fell asleep between contractions.

Back pain became pronounced. She climbed out of the tub, and I used a rebozo to attempt to rotate her baby from OP to OA. Her abdomen still had a saucer shape at the belly button, which indicated OP. My rebozo efforts did not work. The baby remained face up.

As labor progressed, the woman grew extremely tired. It had been fourteen hours with limited sleep as she labored through the night. I encouraged her to lie down. She rested for an hour. Her contractions were strong. For pain relief, I did the apple bottom shake, and to open the pelvis, I performed the double hip squeeze (a counter pressure technique that relieves back pain and helps reposition a posterior baby).

She asked for her Rosary beads. She held them and prayed. Within an hour, she was feeling pushy. Her membranes ruptures spontaneously and were clear. With exam, there was caput succedaneum (benign edema on the scalp). Caput occurs from pressure on the head from the birth canal. She was completely dilated at ten centimeters.

During the pushing stage, she tried every position to get the baby to descend, remaining strong and uncomplaining. She squatted, stood, kneeled, put a foot up on a chair, and reclined in bed in McRoberts position. She pushed on hands and knees, seated on the toilet, and upright in a supported squat.

In one last effort, I directed her to hands and knees again. While pushing, we used the clothespin technique (double hip squeeze). There was still no descent.

After two hours of pushing, I decided to transfer her to the hospital due to minimal descent in second stage. The laboring woman was exhausted from pushing.

"You cannot fail at birth. You will either birth from above (C-section) or birth from below vaginally," I told her encouragingly.

We arrived at the hospital, and it was confirmed the baby was face up. Because the baby was in posterior position, the doctor attempted a manual rotation. The baby would not turn. Next, he tried vacuum extraction. The baby did not descend at all. After twenty-four hours of labor, she birthed from above in a C-section with a supportive obstetrician.

I helped her breastfeed in the recovery room. The baby latched well.

She shared her perspective with me:

"We cannot control birth any more than we can control the tide. Some babies need to be born by C-section. I am at peace with God's will. During the C-section, I was able to praise the Lord and feel joy at His presence. God does not leave us or forsake us."

When I left the hospital, I repeated Stacie's lovely quote, "You cannot fail at birth."

Compound Presentation

Lasondra Passarella was a wonderful labor-and-delivery nurse. When she walked into Hope House for her first labor there, she was awestruck. She said the scene before her was beautiful. A Moroccan woman was sitting on a colorful silk comforter, which was bright like the colors of India. The comforter was on the large floor mattress with a silk canopy hanging from the ceiling enclosing three sides. A floor mattress worked well when a woman needed to feel grounded. Lasondra said she looked incredibly empowered, eating grapes, hummus, and pita bread.

The laboring woman took a shower and washed her long, black hair. Then she sat on a birth stool while I soaked her feet with rose water. I gently placed argon oil in her hair and brushed it as she labored. I rubbed jasmine on her abdomen clockwise with a light effleurage (a stroking massage of the pregnant belly that causes contractions). I dried off her feet and used acupressure on the inside of her lower legs. Lasondra massaged clary sage into the soles of her feet.

Loving and pampering a woman increases her oxytocin levels. Because rose water and argon oil are used in the woman's culture, she felt at home. She longed for her mother and grandmother who were across the ocean. With the pampering complete, she returned to the floor mattress. Lavender was sprayed into the air, and she rested. Suddenly, she sat up and turned on Skype. She spoke in her language with her mother and grandmother. I don't know what was said, but I could understand the love being exchanged. She turned off the computer. Contractions became intense, and she labored on all fours. I provided counterpressure to her sacrum. The purple line showed she was ten centimeters. A cervical check confirmed she was completely dilated. She pushed in all fours. Descent was slow.

Instinctively, I knew this was going to be a complicated delivery. She pushed again. Progress was slow. She lifted one leg up into the runner's pose, and there was progress. She pushed again and crowned. I saw two fists presenting at either side of the baby's head.

"I need to lie down!" she exclaimed.

"Lie down flat on your back and pull your legs up to your chest," I said calmly.

Instinctively, I knew I could deliver this compound presentation in McRoberts position. The head was born with the eyes facing up (posterior position). Quickly, I maneuvered the arms out. With one more push, the body was born. The most remarkable thing was the woman did not have any tearing. Inwardly, I thanked God.

When the Moroccan woman and newborn were sleeping, I rocked on the front porch with Lasondra.

"What do you think of my traditional, wholistic midwifery practice?" I asked.

"I love that you bridge the gap between sage wisdom and modern medicine. I particularly admire that each aspect of your maternity practice is evidenced based. Women are clearly empowered under your care. Homebirth midwifery is night and day from hospital birth," Lasondra expressed.

Warrior Days

One late afternoon, Lasondra came with me to Amish country, where we labored a woman through dusk. Through the open window I heard the cows lowing and the call of a night bird. The yellow moon was rising in the clear night sky, when the baby came easily. Other than the bright moon, the only light that remained was the soft lamp light that glowed in the kitchen area and from the lamp lit in the bedroom. Lasondra and I sat in the kitchen in the comfortably padded Amish rockers. We charted the events of the birth in the dim light. I was very tired and had several women due to deliver. After we completed postpartum care on the Amish woman and newborn baby, we made the long drive home.

A few days later, a Mennonite woman called in labor in the middle of the night. Lasondra and I went to her farm for the birth, which was at the end of a long lane that had a creek flowing adjacent to it. The picturesque white farmhouse was built up on a knoll, and its lit windows stood out in the darkness. I opened the car door and noticed the bright stars, which reminded me of diamonds sparkling in the black velvet sky. The magnificence of nature was on full display. I grabbed my birth bags and walked up the wooden porch steps.

When we knocked on the screen door, an elderly Mennonite woman greeted us. She was wearing a white kapp, conservative dress with apron, and black nylon stockings and with black shoes. She introduced herself as grandmother to the laboring woman.

The master bedroom had beautifully carved oak furniture and patchwork quilts on racks. The labor was straightforward, and the birth was textbook. No stitches were needed and, there was minimal lochia (bleeding). The woman showered and put on a clean cotton nightgown. She rested in bed with pillows supporting her arms while she breastfed. The baby latched well and was alert.

I encouraged the mother to nurse every two to three hours to minimize engorgement of the breasts. I gave her a homemade rice pack that I had sewn from soft cotton fabric. The elderly Mennonite woman put the rice pack into the freezer next to some chilled cabbage leaves. Frozen rice packs and cold cabbage leaves relieve the engorgement pain and the hardness of engorged breasts. Cabbage leaves also are anti-inflammatory.

"Right now, you have colostrum. It is thick and yellow and rich in nutrients and antibodies. In three days, your transitional milk will come in. This thin white milk is a combination of colostrum and mature milk. It is high in fat, calories, protein, and vitamins. Around two weeks, there will be mature milk. It is mainly water with carbohydrates, proteins, fats, vitamins, minerals, and antibodies," I said.

"Remember to nurse your baby long enough each feed for the milk to change from foremilk to hindmilk. Foremilk is thinner and watery, while hindmilk is thick and creamy. Foremilk is mainly carbohydrates and protein, while hindmilk contains a lot of fat, vitamins, and calories. The high fat content of hindmilk is necessary for growth and development," I reminded her.

The woman had plenty of help from her family and church friends, who delivered casseroles, breads, and pies daily for weeks. I drove away from the farm house feeling content. Midwifery had some very beautiful moments.

By the time I got home, I was exhausted and fell into bed without eating breakfast. I had a few fitful hours of sleep, when my cellphone rang again.

A conservative Christian woman was in early labor. I asked her where she was most comfortable. She wanted to stay in her barn and brush her favorite horse. I told her to head to Hope House when her contractions were every five minutes.

The Christian couple drove two hours to cross the state line. She arrived to find Hope House ready for her. The lavender diffuser was on, the birth tub was filled with warm water, and the smell of a baking cake filled the room. I often baked a cake during a birth to celebrate the arrival of a baby earthside.

Dusk had fallen, and the cool breeze felt refreshing after the humid day. Lasondra, Neysa, and I sat quietly around the birth tub. I admired the familiar scene before me: a partially immersed pregnant abdomen, tussled hair, closed eyes, and perspiration on the forehead. She seemed to sleep.

"I feel pressure. The baby is coming," she said with eyes wide open.

"We are ready when you are ready," I said.

I watched as her perineum stretched to accommodate the baby's head. Slowly she stretched open with the water as a counterforce. I placed my hand on her perineum for support. Gently, the head was birthed into the water. I reduced the cord quickly off the neck during restitution (when the baby rotates its head). The laboring mother gave another small push, and the body was born into the water. I gave the baby to the smiling, relieved new mother. It was a beautiful birth.

The next day, I was driving with Lasondra and Lindsay, racing to another birth. Traffic was heavy on the highway, and the baby was trying to arrive before the midwife. We walked in to the bathroom just in time. The mom-to-be was on the floor panting. I quickly kneeled and delivered the baby. The baby cried spontaneously, which brought joyful cheering from her children in the adjacent room. That little bathroom was filled with boisterous laughter and euphoric conversation.

After delivering the placenta, the new mother had a shower. Tucked into her comfortable king-sized bed, she nursed the baby for thirty minutes. The baby nursed well with a good latch. I handed the baby off to the father because the mother needed stitches.

I positioned the mother's bottom at the edge of the bed. Sitting on a birth ball, I sutured the tear. A blend of comfrey, lavender, and plantain herbs steeped on the stove. After twenty minutes, the loose-leaf, dried herbs were strained. The warm herbal water was poured into a sitz bath basin, which was fit in the toilet seat. She audibly sighed as she sat down in the warm herbs. The aroma of lavender permeated the bathroom, creating a relaxing environment. An herbal sitz bath promotes healing of a sutured and swollen perineum. As she sat in the sitz bath, I filled a few peri-bottles with the remaining fresh herbal water. She could use these peri-bottles to spray off her bottom during her next trips to the toilet.

Lasondra was not just a nurse or an intern midwife; she was my friend. She watched me empower women even though my own heart was broken. She knew my mother had died recently, and my heart was on the ground. I was grieving so deeply, but I had to set feelings aside to do my job as a midwife. I had women due who needed me. After one birth, I cried privately. Lasondra and I sat on rocking chairs and talked as a gentle autumn breeze brushed by my face through the open porch window. I was mentally, physically, and emotionally exhausted. I found that watching the process unfold of a birthing woman becoming a new mother was overwhelming for me. I felt so lost without my mother. I would have walked twenty miles to have one more five-minute conversation with my mom.

Lasondra shared her viewpoint, having watched me attend births and give love and encouragement to laboring women, all while my grief was cutting me to the core.

"You are a warrior," she said. "You wake up in the middle of the night, even though you could have easily crawled into a hole. I've watched your strength as a woman during this difficult time. Your mom raised a warrior," she said.

"Thank you, Lasondra. I'm glad I made it through these births," I said tiredly. "I won't be booking any more women."

"I've decided to close Hope House," I shared mournfully. "It breaks my heart. But I cannot be on call seven days a week anymore. I need rest. I just cannot do this anymore."

Chapter 12: Turning Point

A nation is not conquered until the hearts of its women are on the ground. —*Lakota proverb*

In the middle of the night, I would wake in a state of terror. I had no memory of a dream or nightmare. I would sit up suddenly with my heart pounding out of my chest and a cold sweat drenching my body. My hands and feet were like ice. My heart would be beating so quickly that it hurt. I was exhibiting severe symptoms of PTSD.

I could not get a handle on it. It went on and on. I was fighting my own private battle. During the days, I kept busy, but the nights were filled with terror. I sucked it up and kept going.

I was invited to South Dakota to spend time in prayer with Lakota women. In preparation for my trip, I slept at a horse sanctuary in a tipi to fast and pray. I spent several days and nights in the tipi praying and fasting. I was surrounded by pasture and saw a creek in the distance. The sounds of nature were my only company.

The first night, a severe lightning storm brought torrential rain. I watched as the flashes of lightning lit up the stormy, night sky. The next night was clear and calm. In the quiet, I could clearly hear the buffalo snort and the mixed choir of crickets and frogs. Even though it was dark, I knew the horses were standing in the fenced pasture within twenty feet of me. I could see their silhouettes that the moon created. Other than the moon and stars, the only light I had was the soft light of the fire in the center of the tipi. During the day, I heard the horses gallop in the nearby field. The beautiful horses provided therapy for me. When I slept near the horses, I slept well.

One morning after praying, I walked into the pasture. The horses did not run from me. I believe they sensed my heart was on the ground. Standing among the herd, I talked to them, looking deep into their compassionate eyes.

What I did next was likely stupid, but in the moment, it seemed so right. I sat on the ground among the herd of horses. The horses took turns walking up to me and bending their heads down toward me. I felt they understood me, and we were having a conversation without words. I felt calm among them. I could have sat there forever. I felt safe.

When the horses walked off, I walked slowly to the pasture's fence and climbed over it. I went back to the tipi to continue to pray. Those moments seemed like a dream.

In South Dakota, I slept in the women's tipi. I would wake before dawn when I heard drumming. It seemed surreal that I was waking to drums in a tipi in South Dakota to the chilly morning air. The initial drumming was followed by quiet. I prayed outdoors in the dark under the last of the starlight.

When I rested from the scorching heat of the day in the tipi, I could see the bright blue sky where the poles met at the peak of the tipi. The dirt floor was underneath me. A breeze was occasionally heard when it blew against the canvas walls. During the night, the dark lit up the stars. The large fire burning outside was kept by fire keepers. When I went outside to look at the moon, I watched the sparks fly upward from the fire. It was beautiful. I slept well knowing wild horses were nearby in the river bottom.

I fasted and prayed for four nights and four days. I went to places inside my head I never wanted to go—but needed to go, to all the places I suppressed. The dark memories resurfaced one by one. In my mind, I saw images of myself on a bed performing chest compressions on dying soldiers. I saw their faces. I saw the distinctive boot print of my Army boots when I walked through blood covering the hospital floor. I saw myself placing a flower on my mother's coffin. As I went deep inside myself, silent tears streamed down my tanned face. My heart hurt, and it felt like I could not breathe, like I would never stop hurting. My chest was heavy with pain, sorrow, and sadness. The emotions were surfacing, and the years of repressing grief were over. The loss that came to the surface cut deep into my being. I wept.

Sweat lodge was held in the early morning hours. The second sweat was held in the evening. The inside of the dome-shaped sweat lodge was dark, and they are often compared to a woman's womb. A firepit outside heated the rocks. Seven large, hot rocks were brought in for each round of singing. The canvas door would shut, and the rocks would glow red in the center pit of the darkened sweat lodge.

Dried tobacco, cedar, sweetgrass, and sage were sprinkled onto the hot rocks, releasing comforting aromas. A gourd was filled with water from a bucket and poured over the hot rocks. The hot steam would permeate the air, which soaked our skin and sweat lodge dresses. In the dark sweat lodge, women sang songs while sitting on the cool dirt. I thought how appropriate it was that the sweat lodge brought together the elements of fire, air, earth, and water. When exiting the sweat lodge into the cool morning air, I felt refreshed.

The sun had risen higher in the sky while we were in the sweat lodge, but the heat of the day had not begun. In the morning, I prayed sitting on a large boulder that overlooked the beautiful Cheyene River. Parts of the river glistened from the sunlight. The beauty of South Dakota often made me speechless. It was humbling to be in the spectacular splendor of nature while praying. I saw a herd of wild horses running freely. The horses had a magnificent beauty and their untamed nature added to their majestic appearance. As I sat on the ridge overlooking the serene river that meandered through the valley, I was awestruck and overwhelmed at the scenic grandeur before me. I watched as the horses slowed to a walk, then stood quietly to graze.

Moments of solitude were balanced with learning from one another.

"When carrying a gourd filled with water, do not get distracted or the water will spill. In life, do not get distracted. Stay on the good path," said one Lakota woman.

"What works for labor and birth, works for life," said an indigenous midwife, which made perfect sense to me.

After four nights and four days, there was a closing flag ceremony. The heart-wrenching notes of "Taps" played. I stood at attention and saluted throughout the song. Tears streamed down my face, and I choked back a sob as anguish rose in my chest.

Several veterans participated in the folding of the flags, including me. The American flag belonged to Martha American Horse (Aunt to Loretta Afraid of Bear Cook). Standing in the breeze, another veteran and I folded the flag in half lengthwise, with the stars facing down. We folded it in half lengthwise again with the blue field on the outside. I made triangular folds from the fly end to the blue field. I tucked the loose end of the flag into the folds. Only the blue field and the stars were visible on both sides of the folded flag.

After the flag was folded, I was taken by surprise as Loretta Afraid of Bear Cook presented me with a shawl. This was monumental for me. Her love and her people's love wrapped around me like a warm blanket in a cold winter. My loneliness dissipated. I felt connected. Previously, I could be in a room filled with people, yet feel so alone. In that moment, my heart was lifted off the ground.

As my friend and I drove away from the ceremony site, she slammed on the brakes. A mountain lion had walked in front of us, stopped in the center of the road, and stood there staring at us. My first thought was, *Is that real?* Everything seemed surreal. After fasting four nights and four days, perhaps I was hallucinating.

The female mountain lion locked eyes with me. Time stopped for a moment. It was so intense it took my breath away. When I gazed into the mountain lion's piercing, golden eyes, I saw a kindred spirit. We were both fighters, both determined to survive. Abruptly, the lion finished crossing the road and went into the woods. As mysteriously as she had appeared, she was gone.

I asked, "Did you see what I saw?"

"Yes! A mountain lion!" my friend said, as astonished as I was.

As we drove, I pondered about the amazing creature God created. Her tawny-beige fur covered her muscular body. She had black markings on the tip of her ears and around her snout. Her large gold eyes were piercing. When I saw her, I was reminded of the beauty this world has to offer. It was time to stop mourning. It was time to see the beauty. I couldn't weaken now.

As we drove through the remote road in the Black Hills, I thought of what lie ahead. I had recently received a typed letter from the Office of the Governor conveying congratulatory remarks. The governor of Alabama had appointed me to a seat on the first Alabama State Board of Midwifery. I was confirmed by the Senate of Alabama. It took fourteen years of our grassroots effort to have the state legislature pass a statute granting licensure to Certified Professional Midwives. It seemed so long ago when I had driven to the state capitol and voiced my opinions from a podium to state legislators. Now, homebirth midwives could license and practice in Alabama. What an accomplishment. Serving a three-year term on the Alabama State Board of Midwifery would be a gratifying pinnacle of my career.

Hospital Work

After I closed Hope House, I worked labor and delivery as a Registered Nurse. I could start any given day in an operating room for a C-section, or I could be assigned a laboring patient who wanted an epidural. Sometimes, my shift started with a patient who was pushing. I also worked triage, managing the care of pregnant women who presented with a myriad of problems, such as preterm labor, urinary tract infections, and high blood pressure.

Women were attached to continuous fetal monitors, blood pressure cuffs, and intravenous lines for fluids. Most of the births occurred with the woman's legs up in stirrups.

My twelve-hour shifts were busy monitoring and charting fetal heart rates and contractions. Throughout the shifts, I hung bags of intravenous fluids, Pitocin, and antibiotics. Some days were complicated with magnesium drips, insulins drips, or blood transfusions.

At any moment, an emergency could come through the door, such as a placental abruption. Or a woman could walk in and have her baby in ten minutes.

It was night and day from homebirth midwifery, except for the baby in the end.

C-Sections

I educated and tried to alleviate fear for women who were going into the operating room for a C-section. I explained and communicated step by step. Kindness goes a long way. I worked hard to have their surgery be a special and positive birth experience.

When entering the operating room, the first sensation a patient notices is the cold air. All personnel are wearing masks. The woman is directed to sit on the edge of the operating room table with her back curled out like a cat. Cold antiseptic is felt on her back as the anesthetist prepares to place the spinal anesthesia. The prick of the needle is felt, and the legs and abdomen start to numb quickly. The woman is laid down and sees bright lights above her. Her arm is placed out to the side onto a specialized armboard. Warm intravenous fluids infuse into her arm. Her urethra is wiped with antiseptic, and a urinary catheter is inserted. Sequential compression devices are placed on both legs for prevention of blood clots. The curtain drape is placed across her body blocking her sight from her abdomen and pending surgery. She can hear the operating phone ringing, and she can sense the quick pace of the nurses who are preparing for surgery. She is about to become a mother, but these last moments are filled with a flurry of activity. She is having things done to her, while she is passive and can do nothing but wait. Cold liquid antiseptic is used to wash her entire abdomen to prevent infection. She hears a nurse loudly read the standard "time out" verifying right patient and right procedure. The operation begins. She feels the sensation of tugging as the baby, is brought out of her uterus. If a clear drape is used, she can see the obstetrician holding her baby up when it is first born. The nursery nurse warms and stimulates the baby, bringing the joyful noise of a loudly crying baby. After approximately ten minutes, the wrapped baby is shown to the waiting mother. With the hat on and swaddled in blankets, she can only see the eyes, nose, and mouth. The nursery nurse helps her hold the baby, while the operation continues.

Kindness before, during, and after the sterile surgical procedure shapes a beautiful positive birth memory.

Hope Suite

Prior to closing Hope House, I had a meeting with the CEO of a local hospital and with two nurse managers, Neysa Brown and Kendra Flanagan. I already knew these nurse managers were champions for birthing alternatives for women. As a direct result of our meeting, the CEO agreed to approve a natural birthing suite in labor and delivery with a labor tub—a wonderful step forward for birthing women in the hospital's surrounding area.

Neysa and Kendra designed the birthing suite with unmedicated labor in mind. There was a large water tub to soak in and an electric fireplace to use as a focal point. Other amenities included a squat bar, wooden birth stools, birth balls, peanut balls, and intermittent fetal monitoring. Women could achieve optimal fetal positioning through upright active labor. Soaking in warm tub water would provide pain relief and relaxation. This birthing suite would be wonderful for women who wanted to birth in hospital, but have similar choices and comforts as a home birth.

Neysa, Kendra, and I named the beautiful room "Hope Suite." I was so proud to be instrumental in bringing options to women in the hospital system.

Neysa arranged doula trainings for the nurses, which was beneficial for laboring both unmedicated and medicated women. The trainings, taught by April Howton, were very practical. One focus was optimal fetal positioning. By placing peanut balls between the legs while side-lying in bed, the pelvis maintains its widest opening, which aids labor progression. Sitting a woman in Queen's Throne, an upright position in bed, helps a baby's head descend. Relaxing the abdomen decreases the pain of labor. Relaxing the face by blowing raspberries helps dilation of the cervix. Moaning low opens the throat, which opens the cervix. Humming creates vibrations at the lips, throat, and cervix, all which help labor progress. If a woman used profanity, redirecting her is beneficial. Cussing creates a tight face and lips. Using vowel sounds loosens and opens the throat. Moooo, ahhh, oooohhh, uuuuhhh are the beautiful sounds of labor that work *with* the body. Nipple stimulation increases oxytocin production and creates strong effective contractions.

Melissa DeFoor, the subsequent nurse manager, wrote a VBAC policy and had it approved by hospital administration. *That* was a victory for all women who wanted a trial of labor after a Cesarean section birth.

Melissa was also instrumental in bringing wireless external monitoring to labor and delivery. Wireless monitoring meant a woman could walk around in labor and no longer be tethered to cords that plugged into an external fetal monitor. This promoted active upright labor.

She also brought clear drapes to the operating room, which allowed woman to see their babies as soon as they were born via Cesarean. Melissa encouraged nurses to take doula trainings, and she promoted breastfeeding.

Due to the hard work of Neysa, Kendra, and Melissa, these expanded birthing options were benefitting the local women. It was wonderful progress.

The Flood

During this season of my life, I was balancing the occasional homebirth while working my job at the hospital on labor delivery. One evening on the way home from a homebirth, I spoke on the phone with Peggy Bergeron, PhD, RN, CNE, an assistant professor teaching maternity courses at a local university. She was enthusiastic about midwifery and birth options. It was a long drive home, and I chatted with Peggy all the way. She was clearly a kindred spirit, and I liked her immediately.

She invited me to speak as a guest lecturer at the university. I accepted and spoke about natural birth and midwifery to nursing students during their maternity rotation.

After a few semesters of speaking as a guest lecturer, I applied to the university for an adjunct faculty position. I was hired as a clinical supervisor for third-level nursing students. The maternity clinicals consisted of rotations through labor, delivery, postpartum, nursery, and operating room for Cesarean section. Dr. Bergeron would be my direct supervisor.

While educating the nursing students with evidence-based information, I encouraged critical thinking. Respect for birthing women was the cornerstone of my clinicals. It felt good paying it forward to young, enthusiastic students.

I was a busy woman. Working shifts in hospital as a nurse, guest lecturing, and teaching university nursing students their maternity clinicals filled my time. I continued to serve on the

Alabama State Board of Midwifery and drove hours to the state capitol for board meetings. Even though Hope House was closed, I continued practicing as a midwife helping women in their own homes. I was a preceptor for midwifery interns because it was a priority for me to share the art of midwifery. It was a juggling act, but incredibly I received homebirth calls on my days off from my other jobs. The timing was by the grace of God.

Suddenly, Mother Nature sent a gut punch. Over the course of a week, our area received a historic twelve inches of rain, flooding my property. Almost every night, the rain pounded the roof. I laughed to myself cynically, thinking, *This must be how Noah felt!* With each weather forecast, more rain was predicted. My heart sank because I knew the floodwaters kept rising every day, and all I could do was watch as it surrounded my house like a moat. The driveway was impassable. My husband went to the breaker box and cut off the power to the hangar. Our HVAC unit was submerged in water and no longer worked. It was winter, and we had no central heat.

We could cook on the natural gas stove, and we had a natural gas fireplace. We huddled in the living room. I used to like hearing the rain fall softly on the roof, but that week of torrential rain caused anxiety and panic as the incessant pounding had us peering out the window watching the water rise. At one point in between storms, when the water partially receded, we watched a bobcat walk through our backyard. She was tired and clearly trying to escape the flood waters. I felt her pain.

Being a midwife is never easy. But this was beyond abnormal circumstances. My road was impassable. My cellphone rang, and the woman on the other end of the line was clearly in labor.

"I'm on my way," I told the laboring woman and hung up the phone.

"Where there is a will, there is a way," I muttered to myself.

I went to my husband's closet and found his waders. I pulled out my old Army rucksack and filled it with midwifery supplies. Neysa, my intern midwife, parked her car in the adjacent subdivision, which was located on higher ground. She would drive because it was impossible for my vehicle to exit the property. I walked through ice cold, mid-thigh-high water that had a slight current to it, so I was careful not to lose my footing. The first few steps were manageable, but the longer I waded the harder it became. My legs were tiring because I was pushing water with every step. I was getting cold and was grateful for my boots and waders. The rucksack added weight to my steps, which added to my fatigue. My cheeks were rosy cold because it was winter. The cold winter wind cut through my clothes. I was grateful to trudge up out of the flood waters. I took off my wet waders while standing outside Neysa's car. She put my wet clothes into a trash bag. It felt good to be in a warm car. I started shivering as I dressed in warm dry clothes. Neysa drove while I warmed up. Pesky floodwater was not going to interfere with our attendance at a homebirth. Thank God for Neysa.

When we arrived at the rural home, we found the woman in the living room in active labor, breathing with each contraction and going about her chores. The children were at school, but her husband was home. I palpated her abdomen and determined the baby was in LOA position. Knowing the position, I placed the doppler accordingly. Fetal heart tones sound like a trotting horse. The cloppity-clop sound of the fetal heart tone is different than the whooshing sound of the blooding flowing through the placenta. During labor, the position of the fetal heart tones descends as the baby drops in station.

Our exam revealed fetal heart tones were within the normal range. The baby had good variability, with several accelerations. The presence of accelerations is considered a reassuring sign of fetal well-being. Her blood pressure, pulse, and temperature were within normal limits.

When I palpated her abdomen, I estimated fetal weight to be over ten pounds. The woman had a proven pelvis with a history of large babies.

Her labor intensified, and she dropped to hands and knees on the floor.

The laboring woman started to grunt with contractions. She moved to a squat and held onto the birth rope, which was hanging from the ceiling by a large eyebolt. Neysa placed absorbent pads under her. With every push, the baby descended. The large head emerged and turtled. I told her to move into hands and knees position, which is known as the Gaskin maneuver. She did. I reached in and reduced the shoulder.

"Push!" I told her.

With a grand effort, she pushed and birthed her baby, who cried robustly while being dried off. The baby had rolls everywhere and weighed more than ten pounds. She nursed well and was content in her mother's arms.

Even though it was storming, the electricity was still on, and the house was warm and cozy. Neysa and I left with the mother and baby tucked into bed. I felt content. Being a midwife gave me a sense of satisfaction. As I packed up my equipment, I had a fleeting thought of midwives throughout history and wondered if they had this same sense of satisfaction. I smiled to myself as I thought of the Hebrew midwives, Shiprah and Puah. Someday I would have a good conversation with those midwives in heaven.

When Neysa and I walked outside, I was hit with reality. Contentment turned to dread when I remembered the cold floodwaters waiting and likely rising. I hardly remember the drive home. Neysa parked the car, and I exited the car into the frigid air. Dusk brought with it falling temperatures. I put on the waders and shouldered the old Army rucksack. When I arrived at the embankment, the dark water looked menacing. I noticed a visible current flowing through the water. The sun was setting, and I had no time to lose, so I took a deep breath and stepped into the icy water.

I was exhausted when I finally climbed up the steps to my front door. I dropped the waders on the doorstep and went inside and sat shaking in front of the gas fireplace to warm up.

I was chilled to the bone.

It turned out I made it home just in time. The rain started pounding on the roof again. I hoped that no one else would birth. I would never make it back through the water in the dark. The water rose higher the next day. I would not get out again until the flooding receded.

Chapter 13: India Births

Out beyond ideas of right and wrong doing, there is a field. I will meet you there. —Rumi

A culmination of events caused me to long for an escape. I wanted something different. I *needed* something different. The death of my father, my property flooding, and exhaustion caused a longing of my soul for something different. It was time for a bold change.

Visiting me from overseas was Donna, a midwife at a birth center in India. We had attended births together in America many years before. We had lunch together, and she shared how the birth center in India was a jewel. When she offered me the opportunity to return to India with her, I did not hesitate.

I walked into my house and told Jeff that I was taking an extended trip to India.

"Are you sure you want to do this?" he questioned.

"I need to go," I said.

"Alright, darling," Jeff said with a smile, recognizing the headstrong determination of his wife.

I would go to India with Donna and focus on healing my body, mind, and grieving spirit. I would relish the uniqueness of the birth center. Most importantly, I'd spend time with my friend Donna.

I went to India with the mindset of soaking in the culture—not the intention or assertion that Western ideas and medicine are better than theirs. I knew I would learn so much from observing antenatal appointments and births and simply listening.

It turned out that learning about the Indian herbs and midwifery practices would encourage my heart and soul. The Indian midwives were some of the most remarkable women I have ever met in my entire life. I spent seven weeks in India with Donna, and it changed my life.

Arriving in India, I was met with a sudden culture shock. The vehicles were driving on the opposite side of the road different than I was accustomed to in America. In cars, drivers were seated on the right. It reminded me of Great Britian. Cars, motorcycles, scooters, mopeds, and buses filled the roads. I was mesmerized as I saw rickshaws and men pulling carts sharing the busy roads. I heard many polite beeps from horns while the traffic hurriedly flowed in an organized, rhythmic chaos. Initially, I was on sensory overload as I watched the scooters deftly weave in and out of the heavy traffic. The world around me seemed to move so quickly. India had a vibrant energy. I found it exhilarating.

Donna drove a scooter, and I was her passenger. We both wore helmets. As she drove, I took in the surroundings. It was fascinating. Scooter drivers wore helmets, but their passengers often did not. It was not unusual to see two adults and two children on a scooter. Toddlers stood on mopeds behind their parent who drove. It seemed dangerous, but the children balanced themselves on the scooters like it was second nature. No one wore seatbelts in cars. In a few days, I was used to the constant beeping of horns in India.

Donna amazed me. She drove the scooter fearlessly through the roads of India with me as her passenger. Every day driving to the birth center, we would see goats, which seemed to be playing. It made me smile. One day, I saw a man bringing cows down the road, using a large stick to keep them moving. There are coconut trees everywhere, and the roadside stands sell coconuts and bananas. Clothing hung drying from every balcony, and the brightly colored clothing flapped with the wind. Suddenly, I would see a lone cow walking on a side road. Once I saw an elephant walking down an alley. Scooter rides were never boring.

One day while riding on the scooter, I saw a tall woman in a traditional sari and bangles on her arms and legs walking while balancing a jar on her head. It was like a scene from *Mowgli* without the jungle. I admired her for a moment—until the scooter lurched forward and we were on the move again, weaving in and out of traffic.

Donna advised me to avoid the cheap, but overcrowded public buses. The windows on the buses were down for ventilation, people were standing shoulder-to-shoulder, and locals said women get groped on the buses. I heeded her advice.

When using Uber, I noticed there were no women Uber drivers. Interestingly, Uber drivers always had religious items on their dashboard—Mary, Buddha, Ganesh statues, and occasionally Rosary beads.

I found the country of India to be energizing. Donna and I traveled to the port. The Arabian sea was breathtaking. The salty smell of the sea was refreshing. The light breeze coming in off the sea felt good because the hot weather was oppressive. We walked in an outdoor market where old cobblestones lined the streets. The fishermen weighed fish on scales and sold their fresh catches. Fishermen sitting on the shore repaired fishing nets near their dugout traditional canoes. Not too far from shore, the fishermen tossed their nets to fish from the canoes. It was as if I had stepped back in time.

A spice shop was a little slice of heaven as the aroma of dried teas and spices permeated the air. I have never seen so many spices, in such brilliant colors. Large burlap bags filled with spices were lined up in rows against the wall. The salty seaside air and the spice store with exotic aromas was nothing short of exhilarating to the senses.

While shopping, I saw Catholic nuns wearing white or blue habits. Married Hindu women had a bindi, a colorful bright dot, applied to the center of the forehead close to the eyebrows. Groups of Muslim women wore black burqa, which fully covered the body and face. Other Muslim women wore traditional Indian clothing with hijab (head covering).

Aside from the cultural shock, the hot, humid climate was a huge adjustment. I drank a great deal of bottled water and washed off in cool water daily. The bathroom was a wet room with no shower stall. I loved the bucket system of bathing because it felt good in the hot climate. In the morning, I filled two buckets. I poured water on myself and lathered up. Using the small bucket, I rinsed off the soap. It felt therapeutic, peaceful, soothing, and refreshing.

The water and electricity were unreliable, cutting off randomly. Both could stay off for hours. I learned the hard way to fill the bathing buckets first thing in the morning. One morning when I was bathing, the water suddenly stopped. I was lathered in soap, and just had to laugh. Somehow, I made due with the small amount of water in my bucket.

One afternoon, Donna and I were riding when suddenly her scooter got a flat tire. She called for roadside assistance, and a man showed up on a motorcycle with a variety of tires. I was mesmerized. It was incredulous, but I realized how practical and necessary this service was. He was prompt and professional, and we were one our way quickly. He ran an entire business while riding a motorcycle. Ingenious.

Monsoon season was upon us, and the rain poured down with such strength that it would sting. Donna and I rode her scooter wearing rain jackets. She amazed me with her talent driving her scooter during monsoon rains. The goal was to hop on the scooter in between the downpours. But inevitably the rain would catch us while riding on the scooter. I understood why everyone wore sandals. The water would splash upward and get our feet and lower legs wet. I never saw anyone wearing socks. During monsoon season, the weather constantly changed. It might be a light rain or a hard downpour. It could be sunny or cloudy.

What I found most remarkable about India was the distinct contrast between the old and new ways. Donna and I went to a restaurant inside of a hotel. We passed goats in the road on the way, but inside the hotel was exquisitely decorated with marble. I appreciated the goats as much as I enjoyed the restaurant. It took me a couple of weeks to adjust to the dichotomy.

The tourist hotels looked like palaces. I never slept in one. I chose not to be a tourist. I chose to be part of the everyday fabric of India

Chechi

In India, British influences remained because India was once colonized by England. "British Raj" refers to "British rule," which ended in 1947.

At the birth center, a Chechi would carry a tray and serve the best hot tea I ever tasted in lovely tea cups. The tea came from the local tea plantations. Tea cups were a reminder of the cultural complexity of India.

"Chechi" translates to "elder sister" from the Malayalam language. Most Chechi who worked at the birth center only spoke Malayalam. Malayalam means "people of the hills." The midwives spoke Malayalam, Hindi, and English.

In the mornings, the Chechi would say a group prayer and sing their prayer song while standing. One Chechi would light a small oil lamp and place it on the floor as part of the Hindu prayer tradition. I found the women to be humble and kind.

The Chechi worked at the birth center preparing traditional Indian foods for the staff and laboring women. I ate there daily and learned the different foods. I loved the rice and the mung beans (green gram).

The Chechi had a lot of duties, including drying and preparing medicinal herbs for the birth center. It was fascinating to watch them work.

I also watched the Chechi make coconut oil from coconuts. It was a multi-step process. The ladies cracked a hole into a coconut and drained the coconut water into a pot. The white coconut meat was manually squeezed and strained to separate the coconut milk from the pulp. The leftover pulp could be dehydrated and ground into coconut flour. The strained milk was placed into a large metal bowl over a fire that was started with coconut shells. Several Chechi sat in the shade around the outdoor fire, taking turns continuously stirring the coconut milk while it cooked over the open fire. Over time, the milk cooked down into coconut oil. It was fascinating watching them work. The Chechi cooked most of our food with the coconut oil. It was impressive.

One afternoon, I was surprised to see a Chechi carrying a very tiny cake.

"Happy birthday to you," she sang in English to another Chechi.

Others joined in, singing the song in English!

"Happy birthday to you, happy birthday to you," everyone sang.

What fun! I had no idea that custom had made its way to India. It was a moment of pure happiness and joy. The Chechi's face was radiant.

India was never dull.

Crawling on the Floor

Toileting in India necessitated another adjustment for me. Each toilet was equipped with a hand sprayer to wash. Rarely was toilet paper available.

After only a few days in India, I became very ill and weak. I had intestinal cramping and explosive diarrhea for four days. I must have drank bad water. Having limited toilet paper was unpleasant during that illness because I was used to Western toiletry. However, I used the sprayer and eventually adjusted to not having toilet paper. I prayed I would not need a hospital. After every bout of diarrhea, I became weaker. I prayed for no fever.

Thankfully, the Chechi made rice and hot tea for me. I bought bananas at the roadside stand. I drank bottled water and forced myself to eat the rice and bananas, but whenever I ate or drank, I had to hurry to a toilet. My appetite continued to decrease, and on the fourth day I had ten episodes of diarrhea. I was so weak that I crawled to the toilet. I decided that if I was not better when the sun came up, I would go to the local hospital.

Thank God, when the sun came up, the diarrhea ceased. I drank several cups of hot tea to start my recovery and ate a few small pieces of a banana for potassium. I was so grateful to get well.

Indian Food

I met incredible people in India. Reba was one of them. She worked at the birth center, and slept in the spare bedroom at Donna's apartment.

One morning, I watched Reba make rice cakes. She tried to teach me how to roll a flat cake with a rolling pin. I made one, but only with her help. It was harder than it looked to work with rice flour. Rice flat cakes are called *pathiri*. I loved them.

While in the kitchen, Reba also taught me how to make traditional golden milk. This hot drink contains tumeric with its active component curcumin, which are anti-inflammatory.

"Golden milk will help the pain and inflammation in your spine," Reba explained.

I watched her warm up coconut milk and add pepper.

"Curcumin needs to be activated with coconut milk, heat, and pepper to be absorbed by the stomach and small intestines," Reba said.

I drank it hot. It was delicious.

Tumeric is a common spice in India. Taking tumeric supplements and drinking golden milk is not encouraged during pregnancy according to the Indian midwives. However, turmeric used as a spice is fine.

Many Indian foods were new to me. I liked *aloo paratha*, which is a potato bread. I enjoyed *paneer butter*, which is a cottage cheese curry made with butter, tomatoes, cashews, and cream.

Donna and I traveled to the grocery store on the scooter, so we could only buy what we could reasonably carry back on the scooter. The grocery store was amazing with many fruits and vegetables that I did not recognize. Their colors, textures, and smells were foreign to me. It was overwhelming and yet exhilarating at the same time. Simply being in the grocery store was like Christmas. I bought bananas, water bottles, papaya, and carrot juice. I paid in rupees after Donna schooled me in Indian currency. I learned quickly because I had to pay for Ubers, rickshaws, and shopping. Every situation was new and exhilarating. India's vibrant energy renewed my spirit.

One thing I noticed in contrast to America was I did not see any obese people. Most Americans have poor health, poor eating habits, and seem to embrace obesity as a variation of normal. American society was sick and obese, and this was bleeding into poor outcomes of maternal and neonatal health.

While in India, I realized I needed to take charge of my health and eating habits. I needed to refrain from eating processed foods and high fructose corn syrup, which only fueled inflammation in the body.

Donna noticed I was detoxing from American processed foods and sugar. She was right. It was hard to go through the process. Even though I was not obese, I was addicted to the high fructose corn syrup in sodas and sweet tea. Coming to India, where I didn't have easy access to soda, broke that cycle because I could not cave the way I would have in America.

During all of the time I rode as a passenger on Donna's scooter, I never saw a fast-food restaurant. Junk food seemed nonexistent. Or at least it was not easily accessible.

I had arrived in India during Ramadan, when Muslims fast from dawn to sunset for thirty days. *Suhoor* is the meal eaten before dawn, and *Iftar* is the meal eaten to break the fast after sunset. Fasting during Ramadan is one of the five pillars of Islam. The first day off the fast after Ramadan is called EID—a celebration and the first daylight meal in a month. On EID, I went with several midwives to the Hyatt hotel restaurant, which had an EID buffet.

The hotel had very strict security. When we entered through the hotel gate, our vehicle was screened for bombs. A guard looked at the car's undercarriage with long mirrored poles. Armed guards searched the trunk.

Once through security, we entered the hotel. The architecture, ambiance, and décor were palatial. The buffet was in accordance with Islam. Muslims are forbidden to eat pork. The tables, silverware, and china were set in a similar manner as in Western culture because it was a tourist hotel. There was mutton and lamb. I ate salad, quinoa, pasta, and fresh fruit. It was a festive atmosphere. The hotel was magnificent, and I will always remember the carved wooden décor.

Donna and I were invited to eat a traditional breakfast at an Indian home. All the women were dressed in their finest traditional sari. I thought they were the most beautiful women I ever saw.

After that breakfast, we attended a Christian dedication of a new birth center. The foundation was being laid. It would take over a year to be built. The hope for the future was palpable in the air. It was touching to know so many babies would be born at that very spot for years to come.

One evening, the midwives and I went to a vegetarian Indian restaurant. My meal was served on a banana leaf! I ate bananas, rice, green gram, and eggs and drank water and hot tea. I enjoyed a delicious food called *idiyappam* "rice hopper," rice shaped like spaghetti. Foods were cooked with fresh spices, particularly turmeric. As I detoxed from sugar and incorporated Indian spices into my diet, I noticed my health improving.

The Birth Center

India was overwhelming, intriguing, and exhilarating all at the same time. Everything felt new. The only familiarity I had was midwifery, my grounding force, my constant. I felt at home in the birth rooms, listening to the sounds of labor.

The birth center was very beautiful and organized. No shoes were worn indoors; appointments and births were done barefoot. I never saw socks the entire time I was in India.

The birth center floors were kept spotless. The birth center was in a beautiful home with a gorgeous staircase that led upstairs to a birth room. Women would walk up and down the marble white steps during labor to encourage a good labor pattern and help the babies descend station. The solid wood railing on the staircase was magnificently carved. The birth center was built primarily from concrete with marble flooring due to the humidity and rain. Main doors were solid wood with exquisitely carved designs. Screen doors were at most doorways. The birth center had a warm, supportive environment.

The natural birth center perfectly blended the Western midwifery model, modern medicine, and Ayurveda. I believed the women who birthed there were more fortunate than any woman who was giving birth in America. Birth ropes attached to the ceiling were used for upright birthing positions. Birth stools, water labor, and stairclimbing were a routine part of labor. The birth center served first-time mothers, experienced birthers, and those seeking VBAC. Waterbirth was an option.

Women went into labor spontaneously from thirty-seven weeks to forty-two weeks. Ultimately, labor started when nature decided. If a midwife wanted to encourage labor, she would have women rub a combination of black pepper, clary sage, lavender, and rosemary oils in a base of almond oil on their abdomen, breasts, and back to help bring on contractions. If membranes were ruptured without contractions, there was not a rush to deliver. Days were given to go into labor. There was a calm and a patience regarding premature rupture of membranes.

On the first day that I observed antenatal appointments, I realized there was so much to learn. By the end of the day, my head was spinning with new information. Nutrition was the primary focus during antenatal appointments. Women were encouraged to eat high-protein pulses, such as beans and peas. Eating sweets were discouraged.

I learned that mosquitoes were currently causing an outbreak of fever, so women at the birth center were screened for malaria and Dengue fever. Malaria is caused by a parasite transmitted by mosquitoes. Dengue fever is a viral disease spread by Aedes mosquitoes.

That explained all the indoor screen doors in the birth center. Every bedroom at the birth center had a screen door at the doorway. Every room also had a ceiling fan, and I noticed while ceiling fans were in motion, mosquitoes were not present.

The women who came for appointments were as diverse as India itself. There were girls as young as thirteen and women almost forty. The Muslim women wore either a burqa or a hijab with traditional Indian clothing. Hindu women had a bindi if they were married. The Hindu women wore traditional Indian clothing. Some Christian women wore cross necklaces and traditional Indian clothing. It appeared that women ranged from poor to financially secure. The patients reflected the cultural diversity I noticed upon my arrival in India. I enjoyed meeting so many women from different backgrounds.

While in India, I soaked in their beautiful culture and birth practices. I admired the midwives and women very much. I was observing a childbirth class and noticed an Indian lady from Tamil was wearing beautiful bangles on her arms. I realized a lot of women wore bangles. I learned that bangles are worn in odd numbers. They are glass and break. According to the Indian midwives, the tradition of wearing bangles has health benefits. They provide acoustic stimulation, which reduces the stress of a pregnant woman. The vibrations of the bangles calm the pregnant woman and baby. Wearing multiple bangles on the wrists increases blood circulation. The clinking noises help the development of the baby's brain and help the fetus develop the ability to hear. Bangles are given to women at a baby shower ceremony or as gifts. I found the concept of bangles very fascinating.

One day while I was in India, I traveled with a lovely midwife named Bincy to a home for unwed pregnant teens. An older woman opened the door and welcomed us. She was the chaperone to the young girls. These impoverished girls, who were as young as thirteen, had suffered from traumatic abusive situations or had been manipulated by older men. Unwed pregnant teens in India face stigma and rejection by the family and the community. This home provided young pregnant girls a safe, nurturing place to live. The girls could access maternity care with midwives and birth in a nonjudgmental environment. This rare home run from donations empowered pregnant teens and gave them hope for a future. It was the only home of its kind in India.

All over the world young girls are manipulated, taken advantage of, drugged, trafficked, raped, or abused. Sometimes, they are simply naïve and manipulated by older men with the promise of a future marriage.

"When a thorn pokes a leaf, the leaf is ruined. The thorn is still the thorn and not hurt," Bincy said. She explained this was a customary saying to warn girls. There is truth to that in two ways. There is the obvious anatomical comparison. However, the deeper meaning is the man can walk away. The girl is left dealing with the pregnancy. Locals say that older men offer promises of marriage and gifts of vegetables to young, impoverished girls. The young naïve girls are manipulated into compromising situations. Some girls enter prostitution in exchange for food. In my heart, I knew how special this home was. It saved girls and gave them a second chance.

The midwife and I were welcomed into the house. The young girls all stood when we entered. The home was furnished modestly, but it was filled with hope.

The midwife and I went into the bedroom to start a postnatal exam on a young teen who recently had given birth. I observed the postnatal exam and took in the surroundings. The midwife treated her with compassion. Bincy was their breath of fresh air and ray of sunshine. This home might have been simple and plain, but it was a bright light for young girls.

Birth

In the middle of one night, Donna received a call to come to the birth center for a birth. She drove the scooter, and I rode on the back, arriving in a few minutes. Shoes were kicked off at the door when we entered the birth center. Donna was a seasoned midwife. She had provided clinical mentorship for the Indian midwives. She and the midwife staff worked well together.

During labors, the Chechi made hot tea for the midwives and cooked rice, eggs, green gram, and curry dishes. The midwives were well fed. If there was a long labor, the Chechi made the laboring woman green gram—a staple there for pregnant and lactating women.

Women were active, empowered participants in their labor. Women walked up and down the stairs during labor. They actively changed positions. For pain management, women soaked in a labor tub filled with water and found quiet tranquility. During most births, women would use the birth rope to push in a standing squat. During the last pushes, the baby would be delivered in a deep squat or in the hands and knees position.

I was enthralled watching the beautiful birth process unfold while the midwives spoke in either Hindi or Malayalam. The clothing, screen doors, ceiling fans, and aroma of herbs made the event seem surreal. Momentarily my mind was processing that I was in India participating in births. It was overwhelming, exhilarating, and beautiful.

After delivery, the new mother was tucked into bed. The perineum had been washed off with calendula oil in water. The baby nursed at the breast. Her husband rested on the far side of the double bed. It was a tender scene, heartwarming that a baby was not separated from its parents at birth.

After six hours, an Ayurvedic bucket bath was given to the mother in the wet room. The postpartum bucket baths were the most remarkable loving act provided for women. A woman is vulnerable after birth because her heart, body, and spirit has been opened wide for birth. A full body scrub bath with green gram, guava leaves, and neem leaves as a skin exfoliant was given to the woman by a loving Chechi postpartum provider. The woman was scrubbed and massaged while sitting naked on a birth stool. The room was hot and warm with steam. After bathing with guava leaves, she was rinsed in an herb water made of nalpamaradi, a bark used in Ayurvedic medicine. The bathing water was poured over her from the bucket.

I was amazed watching this process. It was the most beautiful thing I ever witnessed in caring for a postpartum woman. When the bath was over, the woman glowed with vitality. She had just given birth and looked like a queen. Every postpartum woman in America should have a massage and Ayurvedic bucket bath postpartum. Maybe American women would have less incidence of postpartum depression if they received Ayurvedic post-birth care.

Previously, I had watched several Chechi work together to prepare nalpamaradi, the bark used to prepare bathing water. The bark is chopped into pieces. Small amounts are put into small bags for future use. When a woman is in labor, it is boiled to make a red water. After removing the bark, the water is boiled again. It is now used as bathing water for the postpartum rinse. A lot of care goes into creating this postpartum bucket bath.

Indian women who need to increase breastmilk production use shatavari powder based on traditional Ayurvedic medicine. Shatavari powder is made from dried roots. It is taken orally and mixed with juice or milk. Interestingly, if shatavari is dried in the sun, it is light colored. If it is dried indoor under a fan during monsoon season, it is a redder color.

Postpartum abdominal binding called *veshtanam* is the practice where the new mother's belly is tightly wrapped with an old cotton sari. The binding prevents back pain and supports the abdominal muscles that were separated during pregnancy.

The postpartum women received excellent care.

I was enthralled by Ayurvedic medicine.

Volunteer Teaching

My volunteer contribution to the birth center was teaching the Indian midwives. Priyanka was the senior midwife and founder of the birth center. She was a beautiful woman with long black hair and of the Christian faith.

She had recently purchased the birth center's first electronic fetal monitor. Two soft elastic straps were wrapped around a woman's abdomen. The two sensors are held in place by the straps. One sensor tracks the fetal heart rate (cardiotocography), while the pressure sensor tracks uterine contractions. The sensors are plugged into a recording machine that shows the fetal heart rate and maternal contractions together on a screen, called external fetal monitoring. At the birth center, the monitor would be used for non-stress tests when warranted during prenatal care. It would not be used during labor.

I taught the midwives an electronic fetal monitoring class to interpret the results of the non-stress tests. The class focused on reading strips on the monitor. I taught baseline fetal heart rate, reassuring and non-reassuring strips, minimal and moderate variability, accelerations, and decelerations. The sub focus of the class was on identifying variable decelerations, early decelerations, and late decelerations.

While I was at the birth center, the midwives did many non-stress tests, and I reviewed their work. They were reading the strips perfectly.

During labor, the birth center used hand held dopplers for intermittent auscultation, which is quite effective and their preferred method of fetal heart monitoring during natural unmedicated labors.

The midwives were impressive. Their willingness to blend modern medicine, Ayurveda, and the midwivery model of care created a beautiful balance between human touch and technology.

Lasagna

Before I left India, I tried to bake homemade lasagna for the staff at the birth center. From the very beginning, it was an adventure. Donna and I had to travel on a bus to a larger grocery store. I looked for the ingredients to make my mother's recipe. There was no spinach, so I needed to use cheera. I found ricotta cheese, but it came from a sheep and not a cow. I found mozzarella, but it came from a buffalo. I wondered how this lasagna would turn out.

I realized I had not seen an oven since I'd been here. I found out the birth center had a small toaster oven that was in a box on a shelf in a closet. I learned that the average Indian does not own an oven! I realized that I had not seen any dishwashers or clothes dryers either.

Several Chechi helped me prepare the vegetables for the lasagna. We chopped zucchini and peppers. I enjoyed their company in the kitchen, and their enthusiasm was contagious. I put the lasagna into the toaster oven and waited. The Chechi was trying to tell me something was wrong, but we had a language barrier. She was using hand signals, but I thought she meant the food smelled good. Suddenly, I smelled something burning. After all that preparation, I BURNED IT. At first, I was embarrassed. I wanted to do something kind for all the women. My intentions were good.

Then I remembered that India had taught me to be kind to myself. As it turned out, the burned lasagna did not matter. While I had been cooking, the staff had arranged their own surprise.

I walked out of the kitchen into the dining area and saw the table filled with chicken! I was speechless and humbled by their gesture. *Their* food was good!

Chapter 14: Going Home

My flight out of India was late at night. I packed and went to the birth center to say goodbye. I ate lunch for the last time with people who had become dear to my heart. It was good Indian food. They gifted me beautiful ankle bracelets and earrings, which touched my heart and humbled me at their generosity.

The birth center arranged for a nice man named Bibbin to drive me to the airport. As we drove in the dark, I looked out the car window at the Indian homes, soaking in the scenery because I knew in a few hours I would be in Qatar.

I longed for my home, but I had grown to love what India had given me.

When Bibbin pulled up to the airport doors, I saw multiple guards. The airport's rules were strict: If you do not have a ticket, you cannot enter the airport. Bibbin carried my luggage, walked me to the door of the airport, and said goodbye.

In India, I had learned a lot about myself. My faith grew stronger, and my hope was restored. It was late at night when I boarded my flight. When the plane reached cruising altitude, I fell soundly asleep somewhere above the Indian Ocean enroute to Qatar.

I landed in Qatar. Wearing my headscarf and a long skirt, I made my way through the palatial airport. I was flying Qatar airlines which was clean and very professional.

When I landed in Philadelphia, I was shocked to see so many obese people. I didn't have time to mull over my observations because I had to catch my connecting flight to Alabama.

I was almost home! As the plane circled to land, I recognized the buildings of Birmingham, Alabama. I quickly put on makeup and brushed my hair. I made my way through the inside of the airport terminal. As I stepped onto the escalator taking me down, I saw Jeff, waiting with a big smile on his face.

My heart leapt with joy. We were together once again. The long hug at the bottom of the escalator completed my soul. I had traveled halfway around the world to go home to Jeff. But when I saw the bright light back in Jeff's eyes, I realized he had finally come home to *me*. The last time his heart was in his eyes was the day I watched him walk away, the last time I saw him walk without injury. It was good to be in his arms. *Finally, we were truly home.*

A Ukrainian Birth

When I returned from India, I resigned from the hospital. Within a few weeks of returning to America, I was attending a homebirth.

A Ukrainian woman called me. She was married to an American Army veteran who now worked in the civilian sector. She was in labor and had the master bedroom and bathroom readied for birth.

When Neysa and I arrived, her labor was going well. She was in contact with her mother and sister online during labor. She spoke English well, but her mother and sister did not. Throughout labor she spoke English with Neysa and me, but she spoke Ukrainian, an East Slavic language, with her overseas family.

Labor was becoming intense, so she said goodbye to her family. She never spoke another word of English. She was speaking only Ukrainian, so I had no idea what she was saying.

By watching the woman's body language, I knew the baby was coming. I delivered the baby with ease—no complications. As soon as she gave birth, she started speaking English again. I asked her about it. She had no idea she had stopped speaking English. Her primal mind took over in the most intense part of labor.

The new mother showered and put on a silk nightgown. Her hair was curled, and her make-up was flawless. We had bathed the baby at her request. She dressed the baby in a long white embroidered dress and white socks. She placed a silver cross necklace around the baby's neck.

"You may call my husband to come in," she said.

Her husband had been purposefully excluded from the birth room. Her birth plan stated that she would decide the time her husband could enter. She wanted the baby bathed and in exquisite clothing, presentable and beautiful, before her husband met her for the first time.

Her husband knocked and entered. She presented the baby daughter to her husband. They spent intimate moments together as a family. Her husband treated his wife as a queen. Birth is as unique as the woman who is experiencing it.

Black Women: A Fight Not to Be a Statistic
Listen.

Black women in the United States are at risk for poor maternal health outcomes. US maternal deaths in Black women are three times higher than in white women. Black women are at higher risk of pregnancy related complications than white women, including preeclampsia and postpartum hemorrhage. Additionally, Black women have a higher incidence of preterm birth.

Many Black women are deficient in Vitamin D. This deficiency can lead to preterm birth, increased risk of preeclampsia and maternal death. During prenatal appointments, I stressed the importance of vitamin D supplements. That one weekly pill and high vitamin D foods were essential for maternal health. I am convinced that the deficiency of this one vitamin has contributed to the maternal death rate of Black women.

One day, a pregnant Black woman knocked on my door. She was newly pregnant and wanted help. I listened to her story. She had a best friend from college who came dangerously close to dying in childbirth. Her friend had preeclampsia, HELLP (hemolysis, elevated liver enzymes, and low platelets), and DIC (disseminated intravascular coagulation). She sat in my prenatal office explaining her awareness that Black women are at higher risk for complications during pregnancy. She was willing to do everything possible to mitigate her risks.

I counseled that proper nutrition and maintaining a healthy weight were critical. I gave her advice, and she heeded it. She followed a 75 to 100 milligram per day protein diet to reduce the risk of preeclampsia. She drank three quarts of water per day. She did not eat any processed food and no fast food. She did not drink soda or diet soda. She did not smoke or drink alcohol. She cut out all high fructose corn syrup. She switched from vegetable oil to olive oil for oven-baked foods and salad dressing. She ate baked (without breading) chicken, salmon, eggs, quinoa, and lean cuts of steak. She ate a variety of colorful vegetables, which were oven-baked with olive oil. She ate papaya, kiwi, and spinach to support her blood platelets. She ate Greek yogurt with live cultures. She drank a small cup of prune juice daily for iron and intestinal health. She drank fresh organic red raspberry tea daily to support her uterus. She drank one cup of organic nettle tea once per week. Liquid Floradix was used twice daily for anemia prevention. (Anemia is dangerous because it reduces the amount of oxygen and iron available to the baby, leading to poor fetal growth, premature birth, and low birth weight.) She took a prescription vitamin D capsule once weekly. She soaked in Epsom salts until thirty-eight weeks gestation to maintain a normal blood pressure. She took one B12 sublingual tablet daily to support her blood platelets. She took probiotics for intestinal health. She ate approximately 2,200 calories per day because her pre-pregnancy weight was normal for her height. She walked outside daily and implemented optimal fetal positioning. (For women with obesity, my pregnancy food plan consisted of quality food not quantity. Daily calorie consumption of approximately 2,000 calories worked well for women with a high BMI to achieve a healthy pregnancy.)

I encouraged her to hire a doula because Black women who have doulas have fewer birth complications. She had already researched that Black women who receive care from a midwife are less likely to have a preterm birth and a C-section and are more likely to breastfeed. She decided to have a doula and midwife at her labor.

She and I had a wonderful conversation about Margaret Charles Smith (1906-2004), a Black midwife who attended more than 3,000 homebirth deliveries in the deep South for Black and white women. Her statistics were remarkable, yet she was forced out of practice when the public health department stopped issuing midwifery permits. The last permit given to Mrs. Margaret, as she was called, was in 1981. Cultural, traditional, and commonsense midwifery was in danger of dying when midwives were winnowed out.

Twenty years after Mrs. Margaret's death, there are Black midwives attending homebirths in Alabama once again.

I received a call from the woman in the middle of the night. I could tell by her voice that she was in labor. When I arrived at her home, her hair was wrapped in a deep-green turban headwrap, and she was wearing a black bikini top and colorful sarong.

When I checked her, the baby was OP (face-up). It was time to go to hands and knees. She labored on the floor and rocked her hips with each contraction. After two hours, I checked her again. The baby was OA (face-down).

She stood and I wrapped a rebozo around her waist to keep the baby in place. She sat on a birth ball and moved in the figure eight pattern.

Every time I listened with the doppler, the fetal heart tones were normal. Labor was going well. Because she was not anemic, she had more circulating oxygen in her blood due to a normal hemoglobin count in contrast to low hemoglobin in anemic women. Her baby was receiving plenty of oxygen.

After an hour, I heard a low moan. Labor was intensifying. After another hour, she was involuntarily pushing. Her body was directing her. She walked to the bed, stopping to squat with every contraction. When she made it to the bed, she laid on her left side with absorbent pads under her. She pulled one leg up toward her chest and pushed. The baby was born easily into my hands. I handed the baby to her and placed a warm receiving blanket over the baby. She cried and kissed her baby.

While nursing the baby, she pushed out the placenta. Her uterus clamped down nicely and remained firm with minimal bleeding. Her birth was beautiful.

She was amazed at the energy she had post birth. She was beaming.

Her husband thanked me profusely. He believed the whole foods they ate throughout the pregnancy improved both of their health. He was committed to maintaining whole foods as a permanent lifestyle change.

What a beautiful day.

A Filipino Birth

The phone rang the next day, and I found myself enroute to another birth. I arrived at a home carrying my three midwifery bags and oxygen tank. When I entered the living room, I smelled the wonderful aroma of roast pig and herbs. I put my bags on the floor. Three Filipino women welcomed me. I took off my shoes and placed them at the designated shoe area. I passed through the buffet area to wash my hands. I saw a large, whole pig that had been spit-roasted until perfectly done with an apple in its mouth. It was stuffed with lemongrass, garlic, bay leaves, and star anise. Pineapples and other sweet tropical fruits were used as garnishes on the pig's skin. My mouth started watering.

Pancit bihon, a Filipino noodle dish, was in a large bowl. It is stir-fried noodles with pork, cabbage, onions, carrots, and vegetables.

A pan was overflowing with lumpia, irresistible Filipino spring rolls with ground pork and vegetables.

Filipino BBQ pork skewers filled several pans. The pork was marinated in soy sauce, banana ketchup, lemon, garlic, brown sugar, salt, and pepper.

There were multiple bowls filled with fluffy white rice. I noticed a bottle of banana ketchup. I vowed to learn about banana ketchup when I had a chance. But not then because I heard a low moan coming from the other room.

I thoroughly washed my hands and headed to the labor room, where several Filipino women were helping the laboring woman. She was in a supported, standing squat with one woman on each side of her.

"I'm having pressure. The baby is coming soon," she said.

"Where do you want to have the baby?" I asked.

"Right here. I don't want to move," she said.

I smiled at her. "Whenever you are ready, I'm ready," I said.

She pushed, and I delivered the baby while she stayed in a standing squat. Because I delivered the baby while I was kneeling, I stood and handed her the baby. She and the women cried happily. I returned to a kneel, grabbed the bowl, and waited on the placenta. The cord lengthened, and a small gush of blood came. The placenta had released from the uterine wall. She pushed, and the placenta plopped into the bowl.

The family took care of the new mother and her baby. When I left the room, the baby was nursing well.

There was a huge celebration in the dining area. It was all women—aunts, cousins, sisters, mother, and grandmothers. They took turns taking plates to the new mother. When I left the house, I was full—from both food *and* love.

An Outdoor Birth by a Creek

Love bears all things, believes all things, hopes all things,
endures all things. Charity never fails.
— 1 Corinthians 13:7-8

Over the years as a midwife, I had witnessed the blend of fire, air, earth, water, *and* love.

Providing warmth keeps a woman nurtured and loved. Warm blankets, human touch, warm water, or a fire pit create the security and strength needed to shift the brain into a primal labor.

A woman needs to relax and breathe. Having fresh air, an open window, a fan, focused breathing, or standing under the stars allows her to labor well.

Being grounded gives a woman strength. Standing, walking, sitting on a birth stool, or squatting provides stability to a laboring woman and decreases fear.

Water is essential to refresh and hydrate. A shower, soaking in a tub, or wiping a forehead with a cold washcloth soothe a laboring woman.

In all cultures, I noticed when a woman has love, she labors better. Having love decreases her stress. Natural oxytocin increases endorphins, and the endorphins from love are equivalent to morphine. Love is nature's pain medication. The love hormone decreases pain and increases contractions. It is the beautiful dance of labor. I noticed women of faith labor very well. Faith immerses a woman in love.

In contrast, I notice if a woman is distressed, her pain increases. Labor is slowed and ineffective. Contractions decrease. Fear stops labor.

In some births, I see the symmetry and blend of all five elements, which is astonishing to watch unfold. Fire, air, earth, water, and love. Of course, love is the strongest.

I received a call on a warm spring afternoon to come to a farm in the rural back country. A short, beautiful woman with long, dark hair greeted me at the door. She and her husband were Native American. Her husband was serving in the Army and on a flight headed home. She had her husband's clean clothing on the kitchen table awaiting his arrival. She confidently stated, "He will arrive in time for the baby."

The birth of her baby would be outdoors near the creek. Her family had traveled to stay with her during the last month of her pregnancy. They created a camp on the high side of the creek. There were three sturdy, temporary shelters. Each had four poles in the ground, three sides and a sloping roof.

When the woman's contractions started, her brothers started preparing a bonfire. It was between the shelter for the female relatives and the shelter reserved for the birth. A circle of large stones created a firepit in which a fire was roaring and crackling. Soft bedding lined the ground inside the shelters. I could hear the creek's melody against the rocks nearby.

What a serene place to birth. Peace and tranquility permeated the atmosphere.

The woman's brothers built a large bonfire near the bank of the creek at their shelter. They would send prayers while she labored with the support of her mother and her sisters.

During the early stages of labor, the four women stood at the fence along the horse pasture. I could easily time contractions from a distance because she held onto the wooden fence rail and swayed with each contraction. The herd of horses made an amazing backdrop for labor. It was a beautiful spring afternoon with birds and butterflies adding to the tranquility. When the sun dropped in the sky, orange, yellow, and red hues painted the sky, setting it ablaze with the fire of the setting sun. The woman labored, standing by the fence until the warmth of the sun on her face faded.

The shelter was warm from the heat of the fire. I hung battery-powered lanterns on a rope that I tied between the wooden poles. The woman entered the shelter and labored reclining on her left side on the soft bedding.

On the edge of the creek, the woman's brothers were drumming and singing songs.

The drumming reduced the woman's stress and anxiety, allowing her to enter labor land, a deep mental state when labor is all consuming. Because she was experiencing an unmedicated labor, she moved deep within herself to cope with the pain and the rhythm of contractions.

The woman's mother and sister whispered words of encouragement to her. When the contractions intensified, her mother put handfuls of dried lavender into the fire. The sweet smell of lavender permeated the air, encouraging relaxation. By surrendering and letting go, contractions are less painful.

Suddenly the brothers' voices changed into a whooping. We heard the horses galloping in the fenced pasture near the shelter. After the contraction finished, the woman stood and walked out of the shelter with her mother and sisters following.

Her husband had arrived before the baby! He was tall with his black hair shaved short in a military style. He held his wife gently under the starlight. The night sky was clear, and the vast Milky Way held countless bright stars. There was a harmonious beauty to the patterns of constellations. The moon shined its soft light on us. She labored outdoors holding onto her husband. Her brothers sat in the shadows by the creek and drummed.

When the woman's contractions intensified and were every two minutes, she returned to the soft bedding and labored upright. Her husband held her. During a contraction, she moved into a standing squat with his strong, muscular arms supporting her.

The woman's mother and sister had boiled water in a pot, which was removed from the firepit and placed onto flat stones. Comfrey was added to the water to steep and would be strained from the herbal water after it cooled. Post-delivery, the herbal water will be used to bathe the woman's perineum.

Throughout labor, the woman's sisters served her strawberry water. She drank until she was satisfied.

"I need to push," she said.

She moved into a deep squat. I kneeled on the ground positioning myself to see her perineum. The head was crowning. I protected her labia and perineum from tearing with my gloved hands. With the next push, the head, shoulders, and body birthed easily. I held the baby momentarily as the woman shifted her body to lie back and recline onto her husband. I handed the baby girl to her mother. The baby cried loudly. The drumming stopped. When the baby let out another cry, the drummers whooped in response.

The cord continued pulsating, providing blood to the newborn. Interestingly, one-third of a baby's blood is in the placenta. In my practice, I did not hurry to cut a cord. After the umbilical cord stopped pulsating and became flaccid, a strong contraction came. The new mother pushed out the placenta while holding her baby girl. The flaccid umbilical cord remained attached to the baby and placenta.

Instead of clamping the cord and cutting it, the parents chose cord burning, a process that uses the flame of a candle to burn through and separate the umbilical cord. Her husband burned it, which took less than ten minutes.

The side of the umbilical cord that was still attached to the baby needed to be curled. I curled it around the belly button into a spiral, and there was no need of a clamp. Both mother and baby lay comfortably on the soft bedding. The pink baby nursed greedily.

The husband placed another log onto the fire. Sparks flew upward, and the fire crackled. He took the placenta and buried it at the base of a tree.

When the baby finished nursing, I examined her. She was nine pounds on my hanging sling scale. I swaddled her in blankets and handed her to her auntie.

Adjacent to the crackling fire, the tired woman sat on a wooden birth stool under the stars. Her mother used comfrey water to bathe her naked body. She washed her back and legs with a sponge. Comfrey water was poured multiple times over her perineum to promote healing of the tissue. A quilt was wrapped around her, and she walked to the shelter.

Both mother and baby drifted to sleep on the warm bedding with a quilt covering them. The only sounds were the crickets and an occasional owl. It was a beautiful night. As I washed my hands using lavender water, I noticed the wrinkles on my hands. They were no longer the hands of my youth, but of a much older, seasoned woman.

Chapter 15: Darkness

The world breaks everyone, and afterward many are
strong at the broken places. —Ernest Hemingway

On a cold December day, Jeff started having trouble walking due to intense pain in his stump. I handed him his crutches. In the past when his stump caused him pain, he would rest in his recliner, and time healed the stump.

This time was different. When Jeff wore the prosthetic, he had fifteen minutes before he rushed to sit down and take it off. His pain was agonizing. Every time he walked, the pain returned. When upright, he started standing on one leg, leaning on a wall or counter. The pain when he walked never went away. The life he knew as an amputee changed.

After months of many doctors' visits and tests, we had zero answers. My feelings of powerlessness grew over time. I did not recognize what was happening to me. It was a gradual undoing of my mental health.

One rainy day, one of our daughters called after being stranded on the side of the road. Her tire blew, and her first call was to her dad, who had always helped his daughters in the past. After changing the tire in the rain, he returned home. He barely made it to the recliner. He was in excruciating pain. He was angry at his inability to walk.

"The kids are on their own now," he said with bitterness and frustration in his voice.

I felt his impotence. Years ago, he said his hope was to walk with a prosthetic until his daughters were raised to adulthood. He had accomplished that. It was devastating for me to see him capitulate. His admission hit me like a steamroller. He knew his leg was not going to improve. This was his new reality.

Jeff looked defeated. I remembered this life. It felt long ago. I recognized the pain, anger, frustration, and hardship.

Please, God, let him walk again without pain! I silently pleaded.

Memories swirled around me. I had lived this nightmare before, with his outbursts of anger when he didn't have a prosthetic. I had watched him suffer from post-traumatic stress disorder. I supported him as he navigated the stages of grief, anger and depression being the hardest. I had weathered this long, tumultuous storm before, and I couldn't do it again. I was drained.

I felt overwhelmed. I watched Jeff's face quickly change from anger to sadness as he silently resigned himself to sitting in the recliner. He looked so sad.

Jeff's sadness was compounded by the recent death of his faithful dog. Years earlier, he had flown to Kentucky to purchase the pure bred golden retriever puppy, and she flew home with him. He named her Aero, short for aerodynamics. She followed Jeff everywhere. Even after she was graying, old, and infirmed, she remained his faithful dog and best friend. She disliked the vet, so Jeff wanted her to spend her last moments outdoors. He sat with her in the grass, petting her while she chewed a bone. He put her down in the sunshine with the smell of grass around her. He wept. She had been faithful and had helped him cope with PTSD. She had done more for him than any doctor ever did. He dug her grave and laid her to rest. He shoveled the dirt over her into her grave.

Jeff cried for four days after that. In twenty-five years of marriage, I had never seen him cry. Aero had penetrated his armor. She had comforted him in a way no human could. She was not an official service animal, but she filled that role. She was his companion and friend.

Now Jeff's stump was failing him. He sat in his recliner without his dog and unable to walk without crutches.

I felt tears spilling onto my cheek as I looked at Jeff.

I walked outside and stood under the oak tree.

"Why, God? Why again? Haven't we suffered enough?" I asked aloud.

Suddenly, nausea hit me, and my heart sunk in my chest. I took a deep breath. I felt my body go ice cold. I was covered in a cold sweat. I grabbed the old wooden fence rail to steady myself.

That night, it stormed. As I fell asleep, the rain fell hard on the roof. Boom! I woke up hearing thunder. I saw flashes of lightning through the curtains. I heard the rain pounding on the roof. I felt fear consuming me. I could not shake it. Would the house flood? That was an unreasonable fear. We had recently moved to a home above the flood plain. What was wrong with me? Panic gripped me. With a blanket wrapped around me, I paced the floor. When I fell asleep, I woke up in terror. My heart raced, and I was drenched in cold sweat. I found myself sitting in bed, rocking back and forth.

As the days wore on, I could not stop the cycle of panic. I was sleep deprived with as little as one hour sleep per night. I didn't understand why I couldn't get a handle on this. My body was out of control.

For several weeks, I tried to cope with my anxiety and fear on my own. In desperation, I sought medical care. Even after one office appointment with a doctor and two emergency room visits, my body continued spiraling out of control. My body was in fight-or-flight mode, sending adrenaline coursing through my veins. The panic attacks would not stop. I was having chest pain due to a high heart rate. My blood pressure was high. I vomited from the anxiety. I could not go on like this.

Jeff drove me to the Veteran's Administration (VA). That morning, I must have had angels watching over me because I received the right help. Jeff drove me home and watched as I collapsed into our bed, the medication taking effect. I knew Jeff would be watching over me. I slept more than twelve hours.

The cycle was broken, and I was sleeping again. My body was exhausted. I had experienced panic attacks before, but never like this. I had been blindsided by a new level of anxiety. I was relieved to have the crippling cycle broken.

The Rabbit Hole

Hope deferred makes the heart sick: But when hope comes, it is a tree of life.—Proverbs 13:12

In the days that followed, I felt detached and vacant. I stared into the distance. I was processing all the trauma, grief, and anxiety that I had never acknowledged. I had swept the impact of Jeff's amputation and the subsequent emotional trauma under the carpet. Loss and the deep visceral pain that accompanies it were sitting there with me. They sat next to me and wouldn't leave this time. I couldn't hide. Depression and darkness pressed around me. I felt like a failure on many levels. I felt myself being pulled downward. Hopelessness and despair surrounded me. Loneliness filled my soul. I felt like I was hanging on the edge of a cliff, with my fingers slipping. The depression and the deep dark pit made it impossible to remember if there was anyone left to lean on. Feelings of loss were intensified by the death of my precious mother-in-law six months earlier.

When despair overwhelmed my hope, there was intense sadness. Weeks and months went by, and I barely functioned. As I battled the depression, I randomly thought of my middle name, Hope. I thought of my mother. She held me as a baby and named me Tori Hope. Suddenly, I missed my mom. Her death years earlier had shattered me. I had become lost in my grief after her funeral, but I had managed to press forward. My mom was one of the few people who routinely called me Hope instead of Tori.

I thought about the past decade since her death. I did not walk with God the way I should have. I had tried desperately to stay faithful to God. But the overwhelming struggles of anxiety and PTSD had taken their toll. The feelings of unworthiness and despair had hampered my ability to walk with God. I was beaten down. It became more depressing to attend church than stay home. I gave up and stopped attending services. This spiral caused me to make a habit of only going to God when I needed a favor. I believed the chasm between me and God was so wide that I had no redemption. Dark, blinding despair would not let me see that Jesus stood on the far side of the chasm with his arms wide open to me.

As I reminisced about my mother, it was hard to believe she had been dead almost ten years. I had been healthy and fit ten years ago. Time had taken its toll on me. I was no longer the young fit woman who stubbornly pushed forward. My body was tired, and I struggled from chronic nerve pain that radiated into my legs and contributed to my depression. My anxiety escalated when I saw Jeff unable to walk well. I had no idea how we would manage now that my health declined. Two back surgeries did not give me the miracle I had hoped for to eliminate my pain and allow me to be the physically strong woman I was before.

During the dark bouts of depression, many thoughts raced in my head. *Does God still love me? Am I redeemable? Can I forgive myself?* Inevitably, I condemned myself. I often felt hopeless and alone. I would alternate between anger and despair. I would sob while sitting alone in my car. I had spiraled so low. I had lost my faith. I found myself struggling for the will to go on. Pain and depression fed off one another and consumed me.

During one extremely desperate night when I found myself going down the dark rabbit hole, I thought of my mom singing to me when I was a little girl. Her soprano voice echoed in my head.

"Have faith, hope, and charity," she sang as she washed dishes in the white cast-iron double basin sink.

In that moment, I chose hope. I had no answers. But I did not need answers. I chose faith. I surrendered all myself and my control to God. My broken heart thanked Jesus for his grace and mercy. I felt a deep peace and knew God was with me. No matter what the future brings, I knew I would not give up. I would confront pain and hardship with redemption and hope.

The memory of my mother's voice of Hope directed me to my Savior and saved my life.

As the peace washed over me, I was too tired to move. I sat in silence on the floor in the closet. My thoughts went to the tattoo on my back. Years ago during my Army days, I had an anchor tattooed on my back, which was symbolic of my name, Hope. Anchors resist the forces of wind and currents, holding a ship steady.

I picked up my Bible and held it to my chest.

"Hope anchors the soul," I quoted from the Bible.

I thought of the strong anchors that ships rely on. Then I thought of the God of hope. Hope was an anchor for my soul. But it was more than that. My hope is an unbreakable anchor that tied my soul to God. No matter what life storm raged around me, I had God's gift of hope tethering me to Him. I was grounded and secure in the knowledge that nothing can separate me from the love of God.

My Last Birth

For this child I prayed; and the Lord hath given me my petition which I asked of him.—Samuel 1:27

This true birth story is included with permission of Jennifer W.

I received a call from an old friend. She was pregnant with her seventh baby. I would need to tailor my midwifery advice because she was over forty years old.

I had met her twenty years earlier when she was in labor with her second baby. I worked at the birth center as a nurse and arrived when she was in transition. I remember the midwife only had time to put one glove on, so I helped catch the baby in a towel. He was a healthy, strong baby boy.

We both lived in rural Tennessee and became good friends. She asked me to be at her third labor and birth. When she was in early labor, we walked outdoors at her rural Tennessee home waiting for labor to pick up. Her delivery at the birth center went well, and it was a joyful day welcoming a baby girl.

Her family moved to Indiana, but she and I remained friends. When she was pregnant with her fourth baby, a wonderful midwife who had privileges at a hospital provided her quality care. When she was pregnant with her fifth baby, she and I anticipated the same outcome. During her second trimester at twenty-two weeks, a routine prenatal appointment turned into heartache. Her little boy no longer had a heartbeat. She birthed her still baby at the hospital into the hands of her compassionate midwife.

She petitioned the Lord for a healthy strong baby if it was his will. When the next pregnancy was a miscarriage, she continued to seek the Lord's blessing on her life. She continued to petition the Lord for a baby if it was his will. It was her heart's desire to birth a baby and not have empty arms. It was during this difficult time in her life that her faith shined.

She was no stranger to hardship. Her father had died of cancer when she was nine years old. After her father died, she often felt panicky and unsettled during church altar calls. She had prayed with her father as a small child, knew the gospel, and had a strong faith in God, but didn't accept the Lord Jesus as her Savior until the age of fifteen at church camp. The potter and clay was the message preached. (Jeremiah 18:4) A challenge was given to be moldable in the hands of the potter, which symbolizes the Lord and Savior Jesus Christ molding lives.

The preacher continued his challenge, "If you have not surrendered to the Lord, seek his will for your lives."

Jennifer was convicted to give her life to God. Her mind was flooded with repentance for uncontrollable anger. She had tried to in her own strength to control her anger, but it was impossible. She'd have outbursts of anger. After surrendering to the Lord, He gave her victory in that area. She wept and confessed her sins to the Lord, surrendering her heart to Him at the altar. She made a profession of faith and repented of sins, recognizing Jesus Christ was the only way to have victory in her life.

Over the course of her life, she had unwavering faith and a deep commitment to share God's love, even after suffering a stillborn.

Through the nine months of Jennifer's seventh pregnancy, I advised her on pregnancy nutrition, herbs, and teas. Most importantly, I was her friend. She was receiving prenatal care from wonderful midwives at a beautiful birth center in Indiana. It would be a lovely place to birth.

Her baby turned breech in the ninth month. I advised her to place a warm compress at her lower abdomen and a cold ice pack at the top. She slept on her left side in the hammock position. By morning, her baby was head down. What a relief!

The day of Jennifer's labor, I met her and her husband at the birth center. I rubbed clary sage essential oil on her feet and jasmine essential oil on her abdomen. I noticed my wrinkled hands, which were now aged and arthritic and matched my graying hair. It had been more than twenty years since I had caught Jennifer's second baby in a towel.

This labor was progressing quickly. Jennifer's midwife surprised me and graciously permitted me to deliver the baby. She recognized the magnitude of the moment—my last birth after a long career. The birth went perfectly. God blessed them with a healthy baby boy. There wasn't a dry eye in the room. They prayed for a baby, and God heard them. Fittingly, they named him Samuel. (1 Samuel 1:27)

Chapter 16: Generations

It's not what you gather, but what you scatter that tells you what kind of life you have lived.—Helen Walton

For years, I had been a guest lecturer at a university. I started the lecture with a song that I learned from a beautiful Lakota woman. I sang it with all my heart while beating a drum.

The focus of the lecture was on natural childbirth options, homebirths, and cultural aspects of childbirth. The subject matter would revolve around midwifery, along with pearls of wisdom from my career as a nurse. I spoke about my time as an Army Nurse.

I lectured of my openness as a health care provider to learn and study herbs, roots, and bark. I believe in blending Western medicine with herbal wisdom from many cultures. My midwifery practice had tried to bridge the gap between modern medicine and traditional midwifery.

When I started the lecture, I had flashbacks of places I had been. I remembered the painted horses that seemed to dance on the tipi's canvas wall as the light of the fire cast shadows on them.

I remembered India and the Chechi dressed in traditional Indian clothing lovingly bathing, massaging, and scrubbing a new mother with an herbal bucket bath. All women deserve that love.

I remembered the Mexican women clinging to their Rosary, saying prayers in labor with colorful rebozos tied around their abdomens. Their love of faith and family was of great importance.

I remembered the Amish women smiling when I arrived on their front porches. Riding in a black buggy watching the horse playfully shake its head made me feel like I had stepped back in time.

Suddenly, I thought of a cherished memory: sitting on lawn chairs with my grandparents at their humble country home, watching the American flag blow in the breeze.

The memories stirred a deep passion in me. That emotion spilled out of my heart as I lectured.

After discussing natural childbirth, herbs, homebirth, and cultural aspects to childbirth, I asked a shocking question.

"Do you poop in bed," I asked.

There was surprise, laughter, and inquisitive looks.

"Would you lie down flat on your back in bed? And put your feet in the air? With a bright light shining on your anus? Would you poop under those circumstances with people watching?"

"No!" the students responded.

"Why should a woman birth a baby on her back with her feet in stirrups?" I asked.

The growing comprehension showed on their faces. The light bulb moment happened. Not one student in my lectures ever said it was preferable to defecate lying in bed.

Since antiquity, women birthed upright. In America, birthing in a bed in Lithotomy position has become normalized. I told the students how the lousy Lithotomy position started.

French King Louis XIV liked to watch women giving birth. If a woman was upright or sitting on a birth stool, his view was obstructed. A reclining woman gave him a good view. King Louis XIV changed the next 200 years of birthing—and not for the better. The fact is that the pelvic outlet is wider when a woman is squatting, in hands and knees, and kneeling. When the pelvic outlet is wider, it shortens labor time. Reclining prolongs labor and makes the pelvic outlet smaller.

In addition to the French king, French doctor Francois Mariceau influenced reclining childbirth because it was a more accessible position for the doctor.

During a break in the lecture, I spoke to the students. Several students were entering the military to serve as Army Nurses. Other students were interested in midwifery. I saw the light in their eyes. They were young, energetic, and passionate about their careers. I experienced a deep sense of satisfaction knowing the students were motivated and wanting to be the best of the best. It was refreshing to share moments with people who are going to move and shake the world. They are destined for greatness. I felt it.

At the conclusion of the lecture, I drummed and sang a Cherokee song the way I was taught by Cherokee women. When I set down my drum, there was thunderous applause. Tears filled my eyes. Those students healed my heart more than they could ever know. It was not because of accolades. It was because they heard my voice. I had passed the torch forward. My heart was filled to the brim with Hope.

My voice had been belittled as a child. During that lecture, it was bold, passionate, and heartfelt. It was not lost on me the woman I had become.

The Cemetery

Because our Lord Jesus lives, we know that death is defeated, and we have unbreakable hope in Him.

Memorial Day was coming, and I decided it was time. As I drove to a military cemetery, I was lost in my thoughts. When I arrived, I felt the tranquility of the cemetery. It was a beautiful place to be laid to rest. The grass was mowed meticulously, and the graves were lined up in rows with order and precision. I placed a single coin on the grave. The last time I had seen him, he had been whisked away in a military hospital's elevator. I needed to say goodbye. I needed to say I cared. I needed to let go.

Suddenly, I was overcome with emotion. I dropped to my knees and bent forward. I wept. I wailed. In time, my sobs subsided. I sat up, and through my tears I saw a man looking in my direction. His face was kind, and his eyes were full of sympathy. When I stood, he approached me.

"I felt your pain as you cried," he said.

I didn't know what to say. I was exhausted from the release of such deep grief. It was cathartic for me, but tiring.

"Was he family?" he asked softly.

"No. I was his nurse," I said with renewed tears silently streaming down my face.

"I spent time in Iraq and Afghanistan, and I'm alive today because of a nurse," he said. "I don't even know her name. Know that you mattered. I did my job. You did your job. It's that simple."

"Thank you," I said choking back a sob. "I'll never forget."

"Neither will I," he said resolutely.

As the man walked away, I read the back of his T-shirt, which said, "In the darkest hour, when the demons come, call on me, brother. We will fight them together."

The Anchor

*We have hope, an unbreakable anchor holding our souls
to God.*

Near our thirtieth wedding anniversary, Jeff and I stayed at a condominium on a beach. I love the beach. The sound of the waves and the smell of the salt air has always been soothing to my soul.

Jeff had not walked on the beach with me in twenty-five years. Jeff disliked walking on the sand with his prosthetic. He had tried it shortly after receiving his prosthetic when the children were young. It was the only time he was on the beach with the children and me. *Once.*

It was difficult and painful for Jeff to walk on uneven sand with a prosthesis. For him, sand was not fun. It found every crevice of his prosthetic leg, which then had to be cleaned.

Years ago, I had accepted the reality that Jeff would rather not sit on the beach with me. I would take our daughters to the beach myself. I dragged the cooler filled with drinks and sandwiches, while the girls carried Barbie dolls, sand buckets, shovels, lotion, and beach towels.

We built sand castles and swam in the waves. I alone had the task and responsibility of keeping a watchful eye on the three girls. I repeatedly lathered them up with sunscreen and did all the duties of a mom and dad.

I admit, my heart was filled with jealousy when I saw husbands setting up tents and umbrellas. The pit of my stomach hurt in the evenings when I saw couples holding hands walking where the waves crashed. I shook off the thoughts, even though inwardly it hurt. It was simply my reality. It was just another thing that was stolen from me the day Jeff was permanently injured. It was just another loss added to the many I faced over the years. I prayed the girls didn't feel the emptiness of not having their father on the beach. I joyfully tried to fill the void left by his absence.

On this trip, after thirty years of marriage, Jeff and I sat on the balcony overlooking the ocean. We drank our morning coffee and took in the serenity.

Later that day, one of my adult daughters and I were lying on beach towels when I saw *him*. I was astounded. My eyes swelled with happy tears of joy. Jeff was walking in the sand toward me. He still walked with the pride of a soldier. I had a fleeting memory of him walking away from me the day he left for that fateful training with the Golden Knights. This time, he was walking toward me giving me a gift. The gift was not tangible. He was answering a deep need in my heart. He was doing this for me. It was a gift of one shared moment on the beach. This moment was worth more than diamonds, rubies, and pearls. I knew the effort it took for Jeff to give me this moment. Every painful step with the prosthetic was torturous.

I didn't notice the other people on the beach. I only saw Jeff. The world around me was momentarily shut out as he hugged me on the beach. We had lived an entire lifetime of insurmountable odds. But we were still standing. As my tears spilled onto his shirt, my whole soul felt our shared bond of Unbreakable Hope.

Epilogue

Anna

Anna, my sixth grandmother, found herself in the center of the American Revolution. Her farm was in Pennsylvania, a colony that saw bloody military battles. The battles of Germantown, Paoli, and Brandywine, in addition to the starving, freezing winter camp at Valley Forge, made the Revolutionary War a backyard reality, not a distant fight. Anna was an herbalist, which benefitted her family because the doctors were away at war, and antibiotics did not yet exist.

Anna married Johan Hepler in 1772, two years after the Boston Massacre and one year before the Boston Tea Party. She had two toddlers when the representatives of the colonies signed their Declaration of Independence in Philadelphia in 1776. She birthed three more children by the war's end in 1783. What is remarkable is she birthed a total of thirteen children.

Anna's use of plants, herbs, roots, and bark carried her family through the American Revolution with outstanding statistics. Her husband, Johan, and his two brothers, George and Christopher, survived the war and did not die from infection or illnesses that swept the military camps. While the Hepler men are remembered on their graves for their role in war, Anna was behind the scenes as their herbalist.

In the combined households of Johan, George, and Christopher, only one child out of twenty-six did not survive into adulthood. Anna and her two sisters-in-law, Elisabethe and Catarina, did not die from childbed fever or postpartum hemorrhage. Anna, Elisabethe, and Catarina, kept their families well without modern pharmaceutical pills or treatments. In fact, Elisabethe safely delivered twins in 1790.

Anna gathered herbs during the American Revolution 250 years ago. She did not know she would have a direct descendent who would serve as an Army Nurse and then be a rural midwife. Similarly, I do not know what my descendants will do.

God provided the plants, herbs, roots, and bark for our use. They will be in the ground growing and waiting for that future woman herbalist. Wherever my descendants' journeys take them, I know they will bring Hope to many.

Appendix A: Infertility and Preconception

- Chart menstrual cycle on fertility apps or paper charts.
- Exercise.
- Maintain or achieve optimal BMI.
- Eat whole foods. Avoid processed foods. Don't eat junk food.
- Instead of vegetable oils, use olive oil, coconut oil, or avocado oil.
- Don't drink soda. Minimize sugar intake. Don't eat anything containing high fructose corn syrup.
- Vitex (chasteberry) tincture improves fertility.
- Chlorophyll through whole foods (dark leafy greens) promotes healthy ovulation.
- Myo inositol with D-Chiro-inositol capsules for ovaries (40:1 natural ratio) and eat foods high in D-chiro-inositol.
- Take folic acid and B vitamins to prevent birth defects.
- Take refrigerated probiotic capsules orally for intestinal health.
- Use pre-seed lubricant to aid carrying of sperm.
- Avoid tampons because they are a conduit for Group B Strep.
- Wear a silver toe ring on your second toe to increase fertility.
- For low progesterone, eat more avocado, eggs, salmon, banana, spinach, and kale and take B vitamins, vitamin C, and zinc.

Appendix B: Pregnancy

o Take B12 to alleviate morning sickness.
o Eat more protein to minimize morning sickness.
o Drink three quarts of water per day.
o Drink prune juice daily to reduce constipation and increase iron.
o Do not wipe from anus to vagina. Wipe front to back. Wiping improperly leads to bladder infections and colonization of GBS at the vagina.
o Take probiotics capsules for healthy colon (use probiotics which are specific to eradicating GBS).
o Shower after sex
o Take a *whole food* multivitamin.
o Don't eat anything containing high fructose corn syrup.
o Eat whole foods, especially colorful vegetables, not junk food.
o Avoid ibuprofen
o Don't take Tylenol or aspirin.
o Don't drink soda, not even diet soda.
o Minimize cane sugar intake
o Don't smoke, vape, drink alcohol, or do drugs.
o Eat **75 mg protein minimum daily**
o Eat chicken and lean meats.
o Eat complete proteins - quinoa, buckwheat
o Combine foods to make complete protein- rice and beans
o Adequate protein intake decreases the risk of preeclampsia
o Eat 2200 calories per day. Do not over eat. Eat quality food. Count calories.
o If starting pregnancy with obesity, eat 2000 calories per day. Focus on quality food.

- Eat grains-oatmeal
- Eat fresh blueberries, strawberries, apples, grapes
- Drink organic milk, Greek yogurt with acidophilus, and quality cheese (do not eat processed cheese)
- Walk daily
- Soak in Epsom salts for optimal blood pressure
- Eat high iron foods
- Drink liquid iron (Floradix) to prevent anemia
- Chelated iron tablets (if unable to drink Floradix)
- Chlorophyll through whole foods: dark leafy greens, spinach, kale, kiwi, broccoli
- Vit D3 capsule
- Eat eggs from pasture-raised chickens (provides higher quality Vit D)
- Starting at 20 weeks, sleep on left side to promote optimal fetal positioning
- Start red raspberry leaf tea at 20 weeks to tone and strengthen the uterus. Red raspberry shortens labor.
- Sit on a birth ball in third trimester
- If a baby remains breech at 35 weeks, see a chiropractor for Webster technique
- Warm compress to lower abdomen, cold pack to upper abdomen to turn a breech baby
- External version to turn breech baby
- Acupuncture to ripen cervix and improve Bishop score
- Starting at 35 weeks, take 500 mg evening primrose oil daily to aid in cervical ripening and improve the Bishop score. EPO has a rich composition of gamma-linolenic acid which softens the cervix and allows for dilation. Capsules of EPO are taken orally. Additionally, the oil can be placed on the sterile glove of a midwife when checking the cervix.
- Starting at 35 weeks, eat 6 dates per day to ripen cervix, and improve the Bishop score

- ○ Starting at 35 weeks, start Gentle Birth Formula liquid herbal extract to support birth and have a better Bishop score. (Blessed thistle herb, red raspberry leaf, false unicorn root, partridge berry herb, blue cohosh root, ginger root, skullcap herb, motherwort herb, wild yam root, and bayberry bark.)
- ○ Fear or trauma: journal fears and burn the paper
- ○ Fear or trauma: birth art to release fear

Appendix C: Labor

o   Jasmine essential oil rubbed on abdomen clockwise to encourage contractions
o   Clary sage essential oil rubbed onto the feet to encourage contractions
o   Lavender essential oil in a room spray or diffuser to aid in relaxation
o   Nipple stimulation encourages contractions
o   Tens unit on lower back for pain control
o   Water labor or water birth (pool from Waterbirth International)
o   Rice pack –for counter pressure, warm pain relief
o   Sit on birth ball- releases prostaglandins at cervix

Appendix D: Post Birth

- o Floradix liquid to prevent anemia
- o Sitz bath herbal blend of lavender, plantain, and comfrey
- o Witch hazel (Tuck's pads) decreases pain at hemorrhoids
- o Drink three quarts of water daily
- o Oat milk, oatmeal, and barley soup increase milk supply
- o Small amounts of alfalfa sprouts provide vit K and increase milk supply
- o Lactation tea blend of fennel, fenugreek, red raspberry leaf, oat straw, nettle leaf, blessed thistle, and anise seed increase milk supply
- o Lactation tea blend from Mothering Herbs
- o Goat's Rue tincture to increase milk supply
- o Sunflower lecithin capsules orally to prevent clogged ducts
- o Lavender essential oil spray- decrease stress to prevent postpartum depression

Disclaimer: This book is not a substitute for healthcare and not intended as professional medical or midwifery advice, diagnosis, or treatment.

Resources

Midwife:
Stacie Hunt, CPM
88 W Edan Rd., Ethridge, TN 38456
931-629-5043

Herbalist:
Mothering Herbs
Summer McCreless, M.S. (History), B.S. (Biology)
bluitmcc@aol.com
www.motheringherbs.link
Pregnancy tea (Herbal tea blend)
Lactation tea (Herbal tea blend)
Postpartum sitz bath (Herbal blend)
Lavender spray (essential oil)

Acknowledgments

My deepest gratitude to Lindsay Crowson and Karaline Dennis for supporting this endeavor.

My heartfelt appreciation to Neysa Brown for attending homebirths with me. From Amish farms to Hope House, you were always by my side.

My thankfulness to Uncle Jack Clemmer, a Navy Veteran, for loving me.

About the Author

Tori Hope Dennis grew up in Pennsylvania. She is a graduate of the Ivy League University of Pennsylvania. She graduated Magna Cum Laude with a Bachelor's of Science in Nursing. She is a Registered Nurse and served as a commissioned officer in the United States Army Nurse Corps, serving at the rank of Captain.

In the Army, Tori worked the ortho-surgical floor, recovery room, and the surgical intensive care unit. While stationed at Fort Bragg, North Carolina, she nursed soldiers assigned to the 82nd Airborne Division and U.S. Army Special Forces.

After the Army, Tori managed her large farm for several years. She worked more than 1,500 clinical hours as an intern midwife and became a Certified Professional Midwife. Certified Labor Doula, Certified Childbirth Educator, and Certified Lactation Educator were additional credentials. She received specialized training in waterbirth by Waterbirth International.

Tori's unique career included NICU nurse, birth center staff nurse, labor delivery nurse, and C-section circulator nurse. As a Certified Professional Midwife, she delivered babies in home settings, including Mennonite and Amish farms. She was immersed in a multitude of cultures within the realm of childbirth, including overseas in India. Her broad experience in birth settings includes hospitals, birth centers, homes, outdoor births, and out-of-country births. She opened her beloved home, Hope House, to birthing women who needed a safe, loving birth space.

For years, Tori generously served as a preceptor to intern midwives. She worked as adjunct faculty at the University of North Alabama serving as a clinical supervisor for nursing students in maternity rotations. She was appointed by the Alabama Governor and confirmed by the Alabama State Senate to serve on the first Alabama State Board of Midwifery. She has been a guest lecturer at the University of North Alabama, speaking about natural childbirth, midwifery, herbs, and cultural aspects of birth.

Tori is a Christian, Army veteran, wife of thirty years, mother, and grandmother.

www.ingramcontent.com/pod-product-compliance
Lightning Source LLC
Chambersburg PA
CBHW071138130626
46553CB00004B/1425